# Chicago*Maritime*

# Chicago *Maritime*

## An Illustrated History

*David M. Young*

NORTHERN ILLINOIS UNIVERSITY PRESS / DeKalb

© 2001 by Northern Illinois University Press

Published by the Northern Illinois University Press, DeKalb, Illinois   60115

Manufactured in the United States using acid-free paper

All Rights Reserved

Design by Julia Fauci

Library of Congress Cataloging-in-Publication Data

Young, David, 1940 Sept. 22 –

    Chicago maritime : an illustrated history / David M. Young.

      p.   cm.

    Includes bibliographical references (p.) and index.

    ISBN 0-87580-282-6 (acid-free paper)

      1. Harbors—Illinois—Chicago—History. 2.

Harbors—Illinois—Chicago—History—Pictoral works. I. Title.

HE554.C5 Y68 2001

386'.8'0977311—dc21    2001037011

# Contents

# Maps

# Tables

# Preface

• My interest in the sea began more than half a century ago when my father went away to it and the war. It was an exciting time to be growing up; I was too young to understand the calamity that had engulfed the world and just old enough to remember some of the events that occurred far from the hostilities. There were the air raid drills in school, when we hid under our desks and had to be quiet so the German bomber crews overhead couldn't hear us, and the crash landing of a *B-17* at the local airport, an event witnessed by everyone in town. There was the wild, spontaneous celebration on V-J Day when all the kids got free ice cream cones and candy from the local merchants and everyone danced in the streets to the peal of church bells and the wail of sirens.

But the most indelible memory was the visit to my father's ship on one of its rare visits to the States. It was a great warship, larger than anything I had ever seen, with bristling cannons and imposing machinery on its decks and the nomenclature RB5 painted on its bow. I was given a grand, one-child tour by a group of very nice sailors. The insides of the turrets were impressive, as was the engine room deep in the bowels of the ship, but I was most curious about a scar of mangled metal amidships. That, the sailors told me, was where the engine of a kamikaze plane hit the ship after disintegrating under antiaircraft fire, its bomb falling harmlessly into the sea.

It took me years to figure out that not everyone got such a grand tour. I was the captain's son. It also took a while to deduce that RB5 was not a battleship but the *Midas,* a repair ship. RB stood for "repair battle damage." The scrapbooks my father brought home told more of a story about the sea than Captain Robert A. Young ever did. I spent hours looking at pictures of the *Midas* crew partying with headhunters in New Guinea (at least it looked like a party). There were photographs of the *Midas* beside a smoldering Australian cruiser, a couple of exotic tropical islands and their natives, divers getting ready to descend to remove bodies from a holed hulk before they welded plates in place to keep it afloat, a kamikaze screaming overhead, and crewmen chipping ice off the deck on a Murmansk run.

Some years later I also discovered among the family's papers an unused ticket for Saturday, July 24, 1915, on the *Eastland,* the excursion ship that on that day capsized on the Chicago River with a terrible loss of life. My grandfather, a Hawthorne Works employee, and my father were running late that day and arrived after the ship was wallowing on the river bottom.

I never did run away to sea, but in my career as a reporter and transportation writer for the *Chicago Tribune* I managed to cover every story I could about it—shipping on the Great Lakes, the canals, and the river system. I also read everything on hand about the lore and history of the inland seas and rivers and paddled my canoe on Lake Michigan, Wisconsin and Illinois Rivers, and the Hennepin and I & M Canals. Finally, after my writing books about early local aviation and Chicago's mass transit system, my editor suggested a maritime history—a topic that, although it has hardly been ignored by historians, has tended to be focused on the Great Lakes.

What follows is a maritime survey that attempts to deal with the rivers and canals as well as the lakes. As the twentieth century closed, more traffic flowed to and from Chicago on its rivers and canals than on Lake Michigan. The Sanitary and Ship

Canal in Lemont, though not as glamorous, is a far busier place than either the Chicago River, now largely a recreational waterway, or the Calumet River, where the big ships now dock. Squat towboats churn back and forth, moving barges laden with coal, petrochemicals, and sand, with far greater frequency than the occasional salties that tie up at Iroquois Landing at the mouth of the Calumet.

The iron horses, motor trucks, automobiles, pipelines, and airplanes of the twentieth century have diminished the role of the maritime industry, but it is still an important, if ignored, segment of the local economy. Chicago in 1994 was the twenty-first busiest port in the United States in tonnage and the second busiest on the Great Lakes behind Duluth-Superior. Traffic on the Great Lakes diminished considerably during the second half of the century but has been augmented by a substantial increase in river and canal traffic.

For that reason, the scope of the book has been broadened extensively to include what happened not only at the port of Chicago but on the western rivers far from Chicago—the Ohio, Mississippi, and Illinois—as well as such now obscure canals as the Hennepin. The effect of the railroads on the near demise and rise of western river traffic is also covered, as is the massive federal effort to rebuild the rivers after the railroads became choked with traffic in World War I. Both events were important to the city's economy. The emergence of Chicago as the largest city of the American interior, eclipsing Pittsburgh, Cincinnati, and Saint Louis, is an effect of the commercial patterns made possible by the canals, Great Lakes, and railroads.

## A Note on Maritime Terminology

The language of the sea evolved over centuries and can be confusing to landlubbers, myself included. For example, a "gallows" on a ship is not a device built to hang mutineers but a similar-looking frame amidships used to store spars, oars,

and boats. To "scandalize" at sea is to leave a sail partially set. Sailing-ship terminology is particularly arcane, made even more so by the fact that it has changed over the years: a brigantine was once a square-rigged ship lacking a main-course sail, but later came to describe a two-masted ship with a square-rigged foremast and a fore-and-aft rigged mainmast. Schooners, a supposedly fore-and-aft rigged ship popular on the Great Lakes, came in a variety of sail configurations, including square sails on the foremast, similar to a brigantine.

On the oceans, a ship is a large vessel, but on the Great Lakes everything is a boat, even a 1,000-foot ore boat larger than a battleship. Because this book deals with canal and river craft, also universally called boats, to avoid confusion between such things as river steamboats and lake steamboats, I am ignoring the purists and referring to large vessels on the lakes as ships. However, the book adheres to convention in that the speed of river and lake craft is given in miles per hour, not knots, or nautical miles per hour, as is the practice on the oceans.

Especially difficult to fathom are the standards used to measure ships. The beam, for example, is the width of the ship, and the draft is the depth to which the ship sits in the water—a critical measurement that changes with the load and is necessary to determine whether vessels are in danger of running aground.

Another critical measurement is tonnage, which has varied considerably over the years and which maritime historians have not always made clear, so a schooner described in 1871 as a 200-tonner may not have the same capacity as a 200-ton scow in 1999. Confusing things even more is the practice of identifying ships by their gross registered tonnage, which is not a measurement of weight but the volume (or cube, in contemporary transportation terminology) of the interior of the hull. One ton equals 100 cubic feet, which means a ship carrying 200 "tons" of styrofoam isn't going to weigh nearly as much as one carrying 200 "tons" of lead. Such nomenclature dates back at least to fifteenth-century Portugal, where a *tun* was a wine vessel.[1]

Other measurements of ships are deadweight capacity, or how many long tons of 2,240 pounds (2,204 pounds for a metric ton) a vessel can lift in salt water to its summer freeboard marks. Displacement is the weight of the water displaced by the ship's hull. At present, most lakes maritime carriers rate their ships' cargo capacity by burden, or burthen—essentially a measurement of the difference between light (unloaded) and loaded displacements. Burden, in fact, is the cargo capacity of the ship in tons, and its use is a practice that makes it easier for shippers, not to mention casual readers of maritime books. Where possible, I have attempted to identify ships by their burden, which was no mean task in view of the fact that early nineteenth-century accounts often gave capacities in terms of bushels of corn or coal, or bales of cotton.

The arbiter of all terms nautical was my trusty and well-thumbed copy of the 1948 edition of Rene de Kerchove's *International Maritime Dictionary*. For contemporary vessel identification, I used the bible of the Great Lakes—John O. Greenwood's *Greenwood's Guide to Great Lakes Shipping*, 1997 edition. Greenwood, who has a formidable technical library on Great Lakes vessels, also was helpful in providing some arcane data on vessels.

## Acknowledgments

M. J. Grandinetti, editor of the transportation section of the *Chicago Tribune*, not only published some of my articles about unusual aspects of maritime Chicago that were later expanded in this book but encouraged me to write more. Owen Youngman, another *Tribune* editor, was supportive in getting published in the paper's business section a rather lengthy series on the contemporary maritime industry the research for which became the nucleus for the third part of this work.

Robert Rockafield, a longtime newspaper editor, now retired, edited the manuscript and provided some helpful comments.

David O. Solzman, the urban geographer of the University of Illinois in Chicago who conducts tours of Chicago's rivers and canals, was helpful in translating geography into transportation under the Polybian admonition, somewhat paraphrased, that you cannot write a history of the battle until you have seen the field on which it was fought. Others who helped me mollify Polybius were officials of the Sioux City and New Orleans barge line, who taught me the river on a 1980 trip by towboat from Lemont to Grafton, and Audrie Inc., who let me roam from forepeak to fantail over their tug barge *Integrity* on a trip down the lake a few years ago. The late Charles Conrad let me climb all over his coal-fire steamship *Badger* from bridge to engine room on a cross-lake trip in 1992. The Wisconsin Lake Schooner Education Association let me crawl around the skeleton of a schooner they were building in Milwaukee and talk to their shipwrights about how it was done in the days before laminates had been developed. Jeff Covinsky, president of Hannah Marine Corporation, provided me the history of his company and information on the contemporary Great Lakes towing industry, and William Arnold, head of Garvey Marine Inc., allowed me to tour his towboat and barge terminal on the Sanitary and Ship Canal at Lemont.

Ted Karamanski, the Loyola University historian who probably knows more about Chicago's maritime heritage than anyone alive, was generous in allowing me to pick his brain, as was George Hilton, the author of a number of works on the Great Lakes, who was kind enough to share his manuscript, now in press, on the Lake Michigan packet companies. Ralph Frese was willing to talk canoes anytime I called. Paul Connors and Clay Skinner provided me with copies of their dissertations dealing with Lake Michigan piracy and the great canoe route, respectively, and chatted freely about some of the unpublished observations they got from their research. John Lamb of Lewis University over the years provided considerable information on the Illinois and Michigan Canal, a subject on which he is *the* expert, provided some photographs, and read an early draft of the manuscript on canals.

Alan D. Harn, archaeologist at the Dickson Mounds Museum, very kindly got up from his sickbed to show me a dugout canoe in the museum's collection, furnish literature and photographs of it, and discuss its probable origins. Floyd Mansberger of Fever River Research generously shared his report and photographs on canal boat archaeology done for the Illinois Department of Natural Resources. Charles Balesi, Carl Ekberg, and Joseph Peyser patiently walked me through French colonial history, and Brendon Baillod, who maintains a large web site on Great Lakes shipwreck research, was never too busy to dig out some needed data.

The staffs of the Great Lakes Historical Society in Vermillion, Ohio; the Historical Collections of Great Lakes at nearby Bowling Green; the Milwaukee Public Library;

and the Wisconsin Maritime Museum in Manitowoc were always helpful in digging out some arcane fact or document. Officials of the Illinois Waterway Visitor Center in Utica, the Illinois and Michigan Canal Museum in Lockport, and Judi Jacksohn of the Hennepin Canal Parkway State Park were especially helpful in sharing information and photos.

Deane Tank of the Chicago Maritime Society allowed me to rummage through the society's large photo collection and look for illustrations for this book, and the architectural photographer David Phillips generously made copies of some of his fine collection. Randy Sweitzer, a fine cartographer and calligrapher, prepared most of the maps. Mike Brown not only chauffeured me along the shore of Lake Erie to look for maritime sites, including Cleveland's Hulett loaders and the Johnson Island Civil War prison camp site, but shot some pictures as well. Bill Chapman of the Beaver Island Historical Society showed me around Saint James and took me to a recently discovered shipwreck site on a beach just outside of town.

# Chicago *Maritime*

# Introduction

• Its waters and the boats that sailed them built Chicago, not the iron horse or horseless carriage. By reputation the city is the nation's railroad capital, the site of two of the world's busiest airports, and home to some of the most congested express highways on earth. But the city owes its existence to its waters—the two sluggish rivers that empty into Lake Michigan and a third that wanders off to the southwest.

As the twenty-first century dawns, a Loop commuter plodding home over the Dearborn Street bridge can glance down upon the cool green waters of the Chicago River dotted with nothing but small pleasure craft, and a commuting autoist dodging trucks in heavy traffic on the Tri-State Tollway will only occasionally see a barge on the placid Sanitary and Ship Canal. The Chicago River, now a canyon lined by skyscrapers, was once one of the busiest ports on earth, and the forest of masts of the ships that choked its waters formed the city's skyline. The "San," or rather its predecessor, was the last great waterway dug during America's now largely forgotten canal age: an abandoned fort and moribund trading post on the shore of Lake Michigan were platted as a city to serve as the proposed canal's eastern terminus.

Long before the first steam locomotive puffed down a track anywhere in the world, Portage Checagou, as it was known to the French *voyageurs,* was a canoe portage in a remote corner of the Great Lakes. Long-distance transportation before the middle of the nineteenth century was invariably by water—canoes and rafts on the rivers and sailing ships on the lakes and oceans. Where there we no natural navigable waterways, civilized countries dug canals. The mails, not passenger traffic, sustained the stagecoach system in most countries, but overland transportation was too slow, arduous, and expensive for large-scale commerce. *Le roi* might travel between Versailles and Chambord by coach, but his goods moved by canal boat.

France and Britain had little interest in developing the interior of the North American continent except to harvest beaver furs; however, the new American republic was another matter. It was the manifest destiny of speculators, assorted commercial enterprises in the cities of the East, and pioneers to harvest and transform the vast wilderness from coast to coast, and to do that they needed a transportation system somewhat more advanced than the canoe. The steam engine and the schooner made the rivers and Great Lakes navigable, and where there were gaps in the waterways, Americans dug canals to connect them.

The first European to visit the site suggested in the seventeenth century to dig a relatively short canal at Chicago to connect the two great watersheds of the North American continent, the Saint Lawrence River system, which drains the Great Lakes basin into the Atlantic Ocean 1,800 miles northeast of Chicago, and the Mississippi River system, which flows into the Gulf of Mexico more than 1,500 miles to the south. That canal, when it was finally dug a century and a half later, effectively extended the navigable Mississippi River system 97 miles to the east to meet the Saint Lawrence; so Chicago became the fulcrum of the major east-west and north-south transportation axes serving the interior of the continent. The fulcrum enabled Chicago to survive the changes in trade patterns over the next century and a half at the expense of its not similarly endowed municipal rivals on the lakes and rivers.

When the railroads came along after 1850, they repeated the pattern of the waterways and extended the city's commercial reach across the Great Plains to the Rocky Mountains, where no steamboat could go. All railroads stopped in Chicago, and eventually all of them—even those in the South and Canada—found they had to get a line to Chicago to interchange traffic.

The skyscraper has been cruel to archaeology, obliterating whatever traces remained of earlier settlements. But when the French ruled the Midwest, they established in the late seventeenth century an outpost on the site of Chicago at the western edge of a long, east-west canoe route for the fur trade. That settlement was abandoned early in the eighteenth century after France established its Louisiana colony and trade from Illinois shifted to a north-south route on the Mississippi.

The Erie Canal in the nineteenth century reestablished the east-west route, but through New York City, not Montreal. The railroads late in the century put the big packet steamboats out of business, establishing the east-west axis through Chicago as the nation's principal interior trade route. In the twentieth century the rivers, with a massive federal investment in locks, dams, and barge lines, made a comeback, and traffic once again began to move north and south on the Mississippi, though not with the dominance it had in the era of Mark Twain. The railroads also got competition from such new transportation systems as motor trucks, airplanes, and pipelines.

As the twenty-first century dawned, traffic was moving in all directions to and from Chicago, and in a variety of modes. Each system seemed to have found a niche: airplanes carried passengers and light express freight; pipelines handled petroleum and natural gas; motor trucks had the package freight business; and railroads hauled coal, heavy manufactures, and shipping containers. That left the waterways of the interior with a niche in heavy bulk commodities too expensive for the competition—such things as ores, coal, cement, stone, fuel, chemicals, and grain.

Despite all that new competition, the inland waterways survived because none of the newcomers could match them on price. A company in Chicago wanting to place an order with a counterpart in London 170 years ago would have done so by letter, a process taking something like 80 days in transit. Today the order would likely be placed by e-mail in seconds. The same company, wanting to ship an important legal document to the United Kingdom, would use one of the air courier services, but if the commodity was a load of stainless-steel bolts, it would probably go by shipping container by a combination of rail and ocean freighter. Ten thousand tons of corn would be quite another matter: they would certainly go by barge down the Mississippi to New Orleans and from there by ship. Today, as in the past, Chicago remains one of North America's premier rail, road, and maritime hubs.

# Part One

## From Canoes to Schooners

Mississippian Indian Settlements
A.D. 900~1100

Aztalan

Illinois
Valley

Cahokia

# *Chapter One* The Canoe Routes

It is unlikely that an Illiniwek warrior standing on the beach and looking inland at the inhospitable marshland cut by sluggish, meandering rivers along the southwestern shore of Lake Michigan could envision a great city someday arising on the site. Ancient man invariably chose to live along watercourses, and, at least before the coming of the Europeans, the rivers and trails were more important to them than the inland seas known to us today as the Great Lakes. Long before Chicago was a Hog Butcher, Tool Maker, Stacker of Wheat, Player with Railroads, and Freight Handler to the Nation, it was an occasional portage for Illiniwek canoes and a meeting place of Wea and Potawatomi trails. It was a place the nomadic pre-Columbian inhabitants passed through but rarely stopped at for more than a few days at a time.[1]

Even after the arrival of Europeans in the Midwest in the second half of the seventeenth century, Lake Michigan's importance to Chicago was mainly as a barrier to transportation, a factor that to some extent persists into the third millennium, as any motorist trapped in a traffic jam on Interstate Highway 80 just south of the lake can attest.

The Wisconsin glacier ten thousand years earlier had carved a canyon roughly three hundred miles long, a hundred miles wide, and nine hundred feet deep in the center of the continent and filled it with water as the Wisconsin ice sheet melted. Lake Michigan as it is now known became a natural barrier to the migrations of game and humans, so their trails inevitably skirted the southern shore, crossing at a place the natives began to call Checagou.

Frozen for three months of each year and whipped by violent storms in the spring and autumn, the lake was a formidable obstacle to the frail watercraft available to the Indians. Just such a storm in

Although sailing ships made occasional visits to the settlement and trading post around Fort Dearborn, the principal transportation vehicle in Chicago as late as 1830 was still the canoe. (*Chicago in Early Days*, from a lithograph in the collection of Historic Urban Plans, Ithaca, N.Y.)

prehistoric times had claimed the lives of several hundred Winnebago warriors when their flotilla of canoes capsized.[2]

The canoe was one of the two principal methods of transportation of cargo in the North American interior until the beginning of the nineteenth century. The other was walking. Beasts of burden were unknown and unnecessary to the pre-Columbian Woodland Indian cultures, who subsisted on hunting, gathering, and primitive farming with minimal commerce. The locals did much of their traveling on foot, and the sandy beaches at the south end of Lake Michigan where metropolitan Chicago was to rise made for easy walking. A network of footpaths snaked from the beaches to the interior. The straight road was a European invention; Indian trails followed the path of least resistance, meandering around marshes, hills, and dense forests.[3]

Whenever possible the Illiniwek, Miami, and Potawatomi tribes who successively but sporadically occupied the southwestern shore of Lake Michigan traveled by canoe, and by 1500 the Indian canoe was a well-developed watercraft. Dugouts made from hollowed logs were used by the Illiniwek and Miami, whose ancestral homelands were southeast and southwest of the lake, respectively, where birch was relatively rare. To the north, where birch forests were common, the better-known birchbark canoe—a wooden frame covered with a skin of bark—was more popular, although barks from other types of trees were sometimes used. Indian canoes were family vessels rarely exceeding 16 feet in length; there was no commercial need for anything larger.[4]

However, the very geography and topography that was an annoyance to the pre-Columbian inhabitants with their Neolithic technology was Chicago's destiny: it was the place where the two great inland river systems that drained the interior of the North American continent converged, or at least came closest. The Mississippi River by its tributary Illinois and Des Plaines Rivers meandered within five miles of a tributary of the Chicago River, which via the Great Lakes and Saint Lawrence River ultimately emptied its water into the Atlantic Ocean.

Between the two was a slough appropriately named Mud Lake that during a rainy spring in an average year was deep enough for canoes to navigate after a portage of only a few hundred yards and in times of extreme high water allowed the Chicago River to reverse itself and flow into the Des Plaines. The proximity of those two river systems was of no particular consequence to the Indians except as a shortcut but immediately attracted the attention of the first European explorer to see the place: Louis Jolliet noted that Chicago was an excellent site for a canal to replace the portage.[5]

**Pre-Columbian Commerce**

Surprisingly, commerce may have been more common in the Midwest five centuries before the Europeans arrived and encountered the Woodland Indians. Archaeological evidence from the more sophisticated mound-building cultures along the river valleys of the Midwest as far back as 1400 B.C. suggests the rivers may have a carried a healthy trade to and from the cities the ancient societies built. The Adena culture, which appeared at that time, as well as the subsequent Hopewell and Mississippian cultures, all seem to have been concentrated along major rivers, mainly the Ohio and Mississippi. However, the extent and glory of the Mississippians remained something of a mystery until the second half of the twentieth century when archaeologists began to dig their sites in earnest.[6]

The fortified city at Cahokia, Illinois, on the American Bottoms flood plain near the site of modern Saint Louis flourished and conducted extensive trade between about a.d. 900 and 1300. The city at its height occupied four thousand acres and had a population estimated at between fifteen thousand and forty thousand. By way of contrast, Chicago did not reach forty thousand inhabitants until after 1850. Cahokia

at one point was fortified with a stockade and was dominated by a giant, ten-story earthen pyramid that probably served as a temple and possibly as the residence of its priest kings. The existence of at least one wood henge north of the central mound indicates to some archaeologists that the Cahokians had developed a primitive form of astronomy to predict the seasons, a requisite for large-scale agriculture.

Excavations at Cahokia have uncovered sharks' teeth from species known to inhabit the Gulf of Mexico, copper from the Lake Superior area, mica from the Great Smoky mountains, flint from Wisconsin and Oklahoma, and pottery designs from the southern and southeastern United States. There may also have been a trade in maize with Mississippian settlements in south central Wisconsin and central Illinois. There is no evidence the Mississippians got any closer than that to Chicago.[7]

There is enough circumstantial evidence to suggest that Cahokia and its environs may have been the gateway to a river trading network between Mississippian settlements in the South as well as the Midwest. In that respect, Cahokia may have filled in a primitive river-based society in a.d. 1000 the role Chicago assumed in the industrial world after 1850. Smaller Missis-

sippian communities have been identified near Savannah in the Apple River valley area roughly 340 miles north (by river) from Cahokia, strung out along the Illinois River south of Peoria about 80 to 180 miles northeast of Cahokia, and along the middle fork of the Vermilion River about 165 miles east of Cahokia. The farthest outpost, Aztalan, Wisconsin, is approximately 380 miles north by modern highway but more than 530 miles by the Mississippi and Wisconsin Rivers.[8]

Although the archaeological record is silent, the fact that the Mississippians invariably located their settlements in river valleys and conducted an extensive trade between communities implies that they used those rivers as transportation arteries. There is little doubt that the river valleys provided fertile soil for growing crops, a major part of their subsistence. The Illiniwek, who succeeded them, also did some farming in the same river valleys and were proficient in carving dugout canoes with Stone Age tools.[9]

It is a mystery why the Mississippians disappeared and Cahokia was abandoned long before the arrival of Europeans in the New World. Theories about the demise of Cahokia range from a cyclic cooling of the climate, which made growing maize

Although there is no archaeological evidence to confirm it, the extensive trade carried on at Cahokia's market suggests the Mississippians used dugout canoes. (Painting by Michael Hampshire in the Cahokia Mounds Historic Site Collection)

The extensive river system of the Midwest even before Europeans arrived was a factor in the development by A.D. 1150 of cities like Cahokia, Illinois, by the Upper Mississippian culture. Monk's Mound is in the background on the far side of the plaza. (Painting by Lloyd K. Townsend in the Cahokia Mounds Historic Site Collection)

difficult, to the possibility that the population exhausted the natural resources of the area. Whatever the reasons for its disappearance, Cahokia was barely a memory among local Indians when Europeans founded the outpost of Saint Louis on the opposite bank of the Mississippi in 1764, and it was more than a century and a half later that the first serious archaeological expedition was mounted to the Cahokian mounds.[10]

### Portage Checagou

The French in the second half of the seventeenth century came to the Midwest looking for a water route across North America to the Pacific Ocean and Cathay, and, when they discovered it didn't exist, they stayed to trade for furs that were shipped through Canada to Europe in what became the first commercial transportation system to touch Chicago. However, the Saint Lawrence River was frozen during much of the long winters in the north, making commerce between Canada and Europe difficult, so the French began searching for an all-weather port and in 1699 established a colony in Louisiana at the mouth of the Mississippi. That event resulted in the beginning of a maritime tug of war for trade on the continent's two great inland waterways that was to last for three centuries and persists to the present day.

The Cahokians' trade axis had a north-south orientation along the Mississippi and its tributaries, but in the second half of the seventeenth century the French established east-west trade along the Great Lakes and Saint Lawrence River. Half a century later the French Louisiana colony revived the Mississippi River as an avenue of commerce to the interior, and it grew in importance until after New York built the Erie Canal in 1825 as a trade route to the Great Lakes. By then, the big ships that began appearing on the lakes had driven the canoe to extinction as a vessel of commerce.

Throughout the more than a century and a half that the canoe was the dominant form of transportation in the interior of North America (1650–1820), Chicago remained little more than a backwater portage, but one that held a lot of promise. The French attempted to establish a settlement there in the late 1600s—a mission, fur warehouse, and perhaps a small fort dangling at the end of a 1,000-mile canoe trail to Montreal—but abandoned it in favor of settlements in Illinois along the Mississippi River roughly the same distance from its mouth. Chicago was about 1,500 miles by river from the point where the Mississippi flows into the Gulf and 1,800 miles from the mouth of the Saint Lawrence.[11]

*Voyageurs* could reach the Chicago portage by crossing the bar and paddling four or five miles down the south branch of the river of the same name to a prairie atop a slight elevation that today would be identified as Thirty-first Street between Leavitt Street and Kedzie Avenue. At that point they could portage a few hundred yards to Mud Lake, which, depending upon water levels, carried them to a small creek that fed into the Des Plaines River at what is now Forty-ninth Street and Harlem Avenue near the suburb of Forest View. The Des Plaines about thirty miles to the southwest joined the Kankakee River to form the Illinois River, which ultimately emptied into the Mississippi at Grafton, Illinois, just north of Saint Louis. However, during periods of drought when the water level in Mud Lake was low, canoists were forced to carry their craft as many as ten miles around the quagmire to reach the Des Plaines. Pierre de Liette complained of low water and the difficulty of paddling in his 1687 passage of the Chicago portage.[12]

The first two Europeans known to have used the Chicago portage were Louis Jolliet and Jacques Marquette, who probably learned of its existence from the Illiniwek in 1673 while they were attempting to return—Marquette to Michilimackinac and Jolliet to Montreal—after exploring the Mississippi River as far south as Arkansas. They had used the longer portage between the Fox and Wisconsin Rivers for their trip downstream. Jolliet noted after returning to Montreal that a canal could be cut through "half a league"—roughly four to

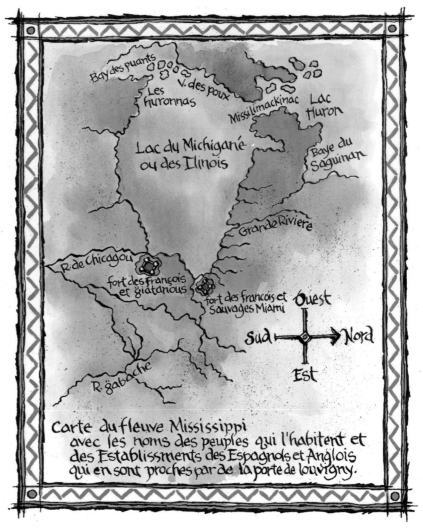

One of the earliest maps of the American interior was by Louis de La Porte de Louvigny in 1697. The primitive map, a portion of which is redrawn here, has the directions wrong but clearly identifies a French settlement labeled a "fort" and an "Ouiatanon" (Wea tribe of Miamis) settlement near the mouth of R. de Chicagou.

**Above:** A statue depicting the discovery of the Chicago canoe portage by Jolliet and Marquette now stands in a forest preserve at Harlem Avenue and Forty-fifth Street near the suburb of Forest View where in 1673 they found a small creek leading from the Des Plaines River to Mud Lake.

**Right:** The portage now identified by the Jolliet-Marquette statue in a Cook County Forest Preserve in west suburban Forest View was easily navigable by canoe only a few months of each year, but it put Chicago on the map.

five miles—of prairie to make it possible to sail from Lake Erie to the Mississippi.[13]

Jolliet, a fur trader native to Quebec, was one of two Frenchmen to have designs on colonizing Illinois; the other was Robert Cavelier, better known by his title, sieur de la Salle, a member of the French bourgeois class who sought his fortune in the New World. Jolliet's status as a colonial may explain why he did not have as much success as La Salle in convincing the court of Louis XIV, especially the king's powerful finance minister, Jean-Baptiste Colbert, of the merit of his proposals for ventures in the *Pays d'en haut,* or "upper country," as the Great Lakes were known to the French. Colbert and the king feared that colonization of the interior would dilute the strength of the sparsely populated French colony of only 6,500 inhabitants; however, they were interested in finding a water route across North America to the Pacific as well as a warm-water port to serve New France.[14]

La Salle not only had access to Colbert but to his family's money and private investors in France, and he ingratiated himself to Canadian Governor Louis Baude, better known as Count Frontenac, who wanted to develop trade in the interior to rebuild his personal fortune. The problem was that the colony could not afford an expedition and someone had to be found to finance it. Jean Talon, Louis XIV's intendant, or representative, in New France, gave Jolliet a trading license to help defray the cost. He owned one canoe and borrowed another from his sister-in-law.[15]

Talon soon thereafter gave the then nearly penniless La Salle nothing more than a letter authorizing his first western expedition. La Salle was forced to finance it by selling some land he had acquired near Lachine Rapids, and with the resulting 2,800 livres he bought four canoes, hired fourteen men, and outfitted an expedition. The paths of Jolliet and La Salle crossed several times during the next few years as they went their own ways in the western wilderness. They both discovered the remote Chicago portage, and they

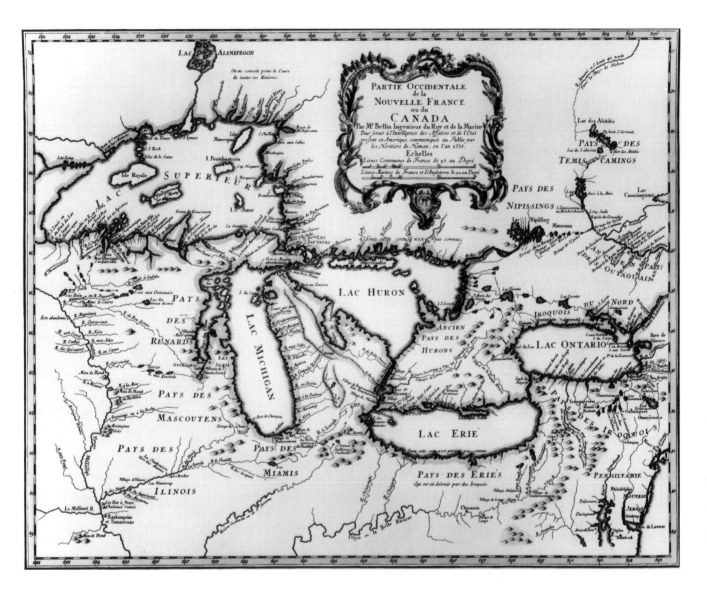

both independently concluded a place called Illinois would be an excellent site for a colony.[16]

## Chicago's First Fort

Jolliet in 1674 after his return to Montreal asked Colbert for twenty men to establish a trading station in Illinois but was turned down. However, La Salle a year later convinced the king to let him explore and build forts there. La Salle had even better luck with Frontenac, who simply ignored Colbert's wishes and let La Salle establish trading posts.[17]

His interest in the area was not so much in the site of Chicago but the great Illiniwek villages farther to the southwest along the Illinois River near present-day Peoria and Starved Rock, which the French knew as Le Rocher and from where his subalterns could trade for furs and he could build a ship and sail to the mouth of the Mississippi. Chicago was simply a place where his assistant, Henri de Tonty, built a fort or warehouse to store furs for shipment east. In the nearly two decades of the French presence in central and northern Illinois (ca. 1681–1700) La Salle and his successors built their principal forts at a distance of a hundred or more miles from Chicago at Peoria and Le Rocher to serve and protect their trading enterprise.[18]

From 1683 until just after 1700, Chicago apparently was used by Tonty as a location for a warehouse, although the

This reproduction of a 1755 French engraving shows the Chicago portage, although it was uninhabited, as well as Miami, Potawatomi, and llinois villages and the long-abandoned French fort at Le Rocher (Starved Rock). At the bottom left the "Chaleaux Ruines," apparently the surviving mounds from the pre-Columbian city of Cahokia, can be seen, although the cartographer placed them too far to the north. (Historic Urban Plans, Ithaca, N.Y.)

extent of the French settlement there is not certain. The Jesuits in the spring of 1683 underwrote construction of a post there, the first attempt to build a permanent settlement on the future site of Chicago, to steer trade away from La Salle's fort at Le Rocher. Louvigny's 1697 map identified the Chicago post as a "fort."[19]

The Chicago settlement may have been little more than a fortified warehouse with an adjacent religious mission. French forts in the *Pays d'en haut* typically were little more than a few log cabins surrounded by a wooden palisade and occupied by no more than twenty soldiers and assorted traders. There may have been as many as six hundred French traders in all of Illinois in 1683, about sixty of them living there on a permanent basis.[20]

After Frontenac's death in 1697 and the founding in 1699 of the Louisiana colony, Tonty headed down the Mississippi to cast his lot with Pierre Lemoyne, sieur d'Iberville, the new governor of that enterprise. La Salle had been assassinated in 1687 on the south branch of the Trinity River in Texas by disenchanted members of his misguided expedition to found a Louisiana colony, and Tonty's interest in Louisiana more than a decade later may have been to preserve an outlet for his Illinois fur trade. The renewed Indian wars that made commerce between Montreal and the *Pays d'en haut* difficult, the glutted fur market in Montreal and France, and the ability of the English to offer the Indians better deals on trade goods made Tonty's Illinois River enterprise—at best a marginal operation financially—less tenable. Tonty, who died in 1704 in Louisiana, abandoned the fort atop Starved Rock, but Pierre de Liette, his nephew, may have maintained the Chicago post for a few more years.[21]

De Liette mentioned in his memoirs that he lived four consecutive years at Chicago (1698–1702), but had little to say about the place except that he found there a "considerable" village of Ouiatanon, a Miami tribe now known as Wea. Although he discussed the portage in some detail, he made no mention of any French fort or warehouse at Chicago when he first passed through in 1687 on his way to Starved Rock. His memoirs deal primarily with the Illiniwek and their customs.[22]

By 1700, the French communication with Illinois was increasingly becoming focused on the Mississippi River, and the Chicago portage was abandoned and forgotten except as an occasional staging ground for expeditions against the hostile Fox Indians. Rival Catholic orders quickly established missions on the Mississippi at Kaskaskia, Illinois, in 1699—the same year Iberville founded the French colony of Louisiana—and Cahokia, Illinois, in ca. 1700. New Orleans was founded in 1718, and the French built two forts along the Mississippi in Illinois to protect that route, Fort Saint Chartres in 1720 and Saint Philippe in 1726.[23]

The French fur trade continued long after Chicago's abandonment, and for a time before the French expulsion from North America in 1763 at the end of the French and Indian War, a rivalry developed between New Orleans and Montreal over it. The British took over the trade after the war, often using French *voyageurs* to man the canoes, and the Americans at the dawn of the nineteenth century built a trading post and government factory at Chicago. A few *voyageurs* still worked around the Chicago docks in the 1830s, ferrying passengers and cargo from ships in their birch-bark "Mackinaw boats" over the bar that blocked the mouth of the Chicago River.[24]

The fur trade between the Indians of North America and Europeans had begun long before any colonies were established. The French interest in beaver furs, which were used in Europe for making hats, began about 1500 when fishermen visiting the Gulf of Saint Lawrence and Labrador began trading for them with the local Indians. The trade had become important enough that by 1608 a group of Rouen merchants obtained a monopoly from the crown and sent Samuel Champlain to build a fortified factory on the site of Quebec to process furs. For the first half of the century, groups of Algonquins, Ottawa, Huron, and Menominee brought their own pelts and those acquired from other tribes east for sale to the French, first at Quebec and later Montreal.[25]

As early as 1623, 60 canoes of Huron and Algonquins arrived in Canada via the Ottawa River, and by 1633 the number of canoes in the fur trade had swelled to 150. A rival trade soon sprang up between the Iroquois in New York, bitter rivals of the Huron, and the Dutch in New Amsterdam. By 1629 the so-called Beaver Wars, which lasted most of the rest of the century, between the Iroquois and the tribes allied with the French had broken out and soon spread westward into the Great Lakes basin as demand for the pelts increased, exhausting supplies farther east. The Seneca (Iroquois) attack on the Illiniwek between Utica and Peoria witnessed by Tonty in 1680 was a part of that war.[26]

What developed was an unusual transportation route—a 6,000-mile system of waterways that served as canoe trails over which convoys of birchbark canoes were paddled each spring and autumn between Montreal and remote outposts like Chicago. The poor condition of Indian trails and the danger of ambush during the Beaver Wars made overland transport difficult. A man might be able to carry on his back a pack of half his own weight, but in a canoe he might be able to move as much as half a ton.

## The Great Canoe Route

The French canoe route across Ontario was not particularly efficient, less so than the Mississippi River, but it served its purpose for more than a century. The French originally used Indian canoes, *canots du nord* (canoes of the north), but built successively larger vessels until some paddled by as many as eight men were capable of carrying 5 tons of goods, the upper limit of what crews could carry on portages around the numerous rapids. The *voyageurs* stuck to the rivers and small lakes wherever possible because the Great Lakes, although they offered unobstructed paddling, were often too stormy for the small craft and the hostile Iroquois controlled the Niagara portage between Lakes Erie and Ontario. Only in the western Great Lakes region, where there were few alternative routes by river, did the voyageurs brave those Inland Seas.

*Voyageurs* leaving Montreal each spring put their canoes into water in the Saint Lawrence River just above the dangerous Lachine Rapids upstream from Montreal where Jolliet had almost lost his life trying to shoot them. They then paddled up the Ottawa and Mattawa Rivers, across Lake Nipissing, and down the French River, which emptied into Georgian Bay on Lake Huron. From there they paddled across Lake Huron to Michilimackinac and fanned out over routes to the interior. Some *voyageurs* ascended the Saint Marys River onto Lake Superior, others paddled down Green Bay to reach the Fox-Wisconsin Rivers portage, or along the eastern shore of Lake Michigan to the Saint Joseph River, which led to the Saint Joseph–Kankakee Rivers portage at Niles, Michigan. The route down the western shore of Lake Michigan led to the Chicago portage and the Illinois River valley. Despite the fact that the Ontario river route had as many as thirty-three portages and the Great Lakes route only one, the river route was more direct and cut 300 to 400 miles off the journey to Chicago.[27]

Life on the canoe route was hard, and the average *voyageur,* if he wasn't drowned in an accident or killed by injury or Indians, survived in the trade only to age thirty-five. He worked twelve- to fourteen-hour days, rising before dawn to load the canoes and paddling until 8 A.M. when he and his comrades stopped for a breakfast of leached corn and fat boiled the night before. Dried peas, twice-baked bread—biscuits known as hardtack to the English—and salted pork were the other staples of their diet. Every few hours they took a break and smoked pipes, a trick learned from the Huron to suppress appetite. Lunch consisted of the leftovers from breakfast.[28]

The crews usually pulled to shore before

Fur traders before 1800 used a river route to the West to avoid traversing the circuitous and dangerous Great Lakes route between Chicago and Montreal. The risks were from storms and the Iroquois tribes that controlled the Erie-Ontario portage.

dusk, when there was still enough light to be able to see submerged rocks that might poke a hole in the fragile bark skin of the canoe. The *voyageurs* then patched the canoes, cooked dinner, and went to sleep under the overturned craft. Paddling by night was common to make up for lost time and to avoid the high winds that often occurred during daylight hours.

To move in strong currents, the crews put their paddles aside and poled their craft, or pulled them with ropes. On the Great Lakes where waves were high the stern paddler steered a zigzag course, putting bow into the crest at a forty-five-degree angle, then turning the canoe par-allel to the wave to make as much distance as possible before the arrival of the next crest. Even though the canoes favored by the French had high bows and sterns adopted from the Hurons to negotiate waves and rapids, storms on the Great Lakes often forced *voyageurs* ashore for days at a time. Jean-Francois Buisson de Saint-Cosme spent fifteen of the forty-six days of his 1698 voyage from Michilimack-inac to Chicago on shore, waiting for favorable weather.[29]

The dangers at river rapids were so great that Montreal traders prohibited their crews from shooting them and required laborious portages instead. The portages often required each crewman to make as many as four trips on foot around the rapids—one with the canoe and two or three with the cargo. Rapids often became known by the names of the *voyageurs* who had lost their lives there.

But it was the relative ease in carrying the lightweight birchbark canoe at portages that made it a favorite in the fur trade. The sturdier dugout canoe, or *pirogue* as it was known by the French, was easier to build and could take more punishment than the birchbark but was heavier and rode lower in the water, making it vulnerable to swamping in high waves or rapids. The *pirogue* was popular among tribes south of Chicago, where birch trees were scarce and the rivers were not as wild. In fact, cargoes were often transferred between birchbark canoes and *pirogues* at Great Lakes portages such as Chicago.[30]

Although some such dugouts in the Deep South were 50 feet in length, a dugout discovered along the LaMoine River near Brooklyn in west central Illinois in 1994 is somewhat more typical of what was used in the fur trade. The excellently preserved black-walnut canoe now in the Dickson Mounds Museum near Lewistown, Illinois, is slightly more than 18 feet long, but only 15 1/2 inches wide, and weighs nearly 57 pounds, although it was certainly considerably heavier before its wood dried. The canoe probably was carved by Europeans between 1670 and 1830, because marks indicate that metal tools were used and local Indians generally hollowed out their dugouts by burning.[31]

The French also favored the bateau, a double-ended, planked rowboat that could be powered by oar, pole, or sail on relatively calm rivers like the Saint Lawrence and Mississippi, but it was too heavy for portages. Sailing ships, primarily square-rigged barques, for the most part proved to be too expensive to build and too dangerous to operate on the Great Lakes for the fur trade during the French colonial period, although a few were used. Sailing ships came into popularity among the big English trading companies toward the end of the eighteenth century when fore-and-aft rigged sloops and schooners were developed, but even then canoes continued to be used in the fur trade on rivers and lakes inaccessible to the ships.[32]

The French first adopted the 13- to 16-foot Huron and Algonquin canoes, then as the fur trade grew built successively larger craft. The *canot du nord* was 24 to 28 feet long and could carry up to six paddlers and a ton and a half of cargo. The birchbark canoe culminated after 1720 in the *canot du maître*, a 33- to 36-foot, eight-place vessel capable of carrying up to 5 tons of cargo and named after Louis LeMaître, the owner of a yard in Trois-Rivieres, which built them. An intermediate-size craft was

The birchbark canoe shown in this three-hundredth anniversary of the Jolliet-Marquette voyage of discovery was favored by the Huron and French alike because its light weight made portaging easier and its high bow and stern made it less vulnerable to swamping in swift rivers and on the Great Lakes. (*Chicago Tribune*)

**Above:** The fact that the interior of this dugout canoe now on display at the Dickson Mounds Museum near Lewistown, Illinois, was hewn with metal tools and not burned out indicates it was probably made by Europeans, not local tribes. (Dickson Mounds Museum)

**Right:** Only three dugout canoes, the most popular method of travel south of the Great Lakes before European settlement and for some time thereafter, have been unearthed in Illinois. This excellently preserved pirogue made of black walnut and found along the LaMoine River in the west-central part of the state was carved using metal tools sometime between 1765 and 1830. (Dickson Mounds Museum)

called the *bâtard* (bastard).[33]

Attempts by the Canadian government to regulate the highly individualistic traders were never very successful, and illicit trade flourished. Individual *coureurs de bois*, or illicit traders, began taking canoes west even before the voyages of exploration of Jolliet and La Salle in the 1670s, and by the end of that century scores of canoes, only a handful of them operated by licensed traders—the *voyageurs*—were making the trip each year. By the middle of the next century it is likely that hundreds of canoes, singly and in convoys, were making the trip, although the government never handed out more than seventy-eight licenses in any one year.[34]

Frontenac probably sold *coureurs de bois* licenses in defiance of orders from Paris, and the commanders of many posts in the interior were paid subsistence wages and became dependent upon revenue from the fur trade to support themselves and their families. Between 1722 and 1734, as many as 36 percent of the fur-trading companies had post commanders as partners and an additional 10 percent had other colonial officers as partners. In fact, the only French settlements in the interior that relied more on farming than the fur trade were the villages along the Mississippi River (Cahokia, Chartres, and Kaskaskia), which became the breadbasket for the Louisiana colony and New Orleans.[35]

Between 1675 and 1685, French imports of Canadian beaver increased from 61,000 livres (45,750 pounds) to 137,568 livres (103,176 pounds), worth on average over that span something in the vicinity of 400,000 livres per season.[36] Typically a single canoe of trade goods would produce two canoes full of pelts. In the 1680s two pelts would buy from Montreal merchants a blanket, four shirts, or six pairs of stockings. A gun cost five pelts, eight pounds of powder four pelts, and forty pounds of lead three pelts. However, trade goods cost considerably more by the time they were hauled to the interior, and the ability of the English to offer better prices was a continual source of disenchantment to the Indian allies of France.[37]

The canoe proved to be an expensive way to haul goods. By the time the cost of taxes (25%), licensing, provisions, and crew were deducted, an outfitter made only 1,500 livres or 20 to 25 percent return on his investment. Paddlers worked for 200 livres a season, plus permission to trade some goods on their own, but experienced steersmen and the commander of the expedition got more. It was possible for a *voyageur* to earn a fairly good living; experienced paddlers used in the bow and stern got a wage of 250 livres in 1754, which had increased to between 300 and 400 livres by 1780. They were also expected to do some trading on their own to augment their income. It was possible for a good native hunter to trap fifty or sixty beavers a season, although that rate of attrition resulted in a decline of the animal population.[38]

## The American Trading Post at Chicago

The abandoned French post at Chicago was revived a century later when the U.S. government in 1803 built Fort Dearborn and shortly thereafter an adjacent "factory," as the government trading post was called. The fort was to assert U.S. hegemony after years of British control of the Great Lakes following the Revolutionary War; the task of the factor of the trading post was to break the British monopoly on trade by providing the Indians goods at lower prices than the British did. Ebenezer Belknap, the factor who opened post in 1805, was paid $1,000 plus $365 in lieu of subsistence.

Fur remained the main currency used by the Indians and continued to move in some volume over the Chicago portage until the 1820s. John Kinzie, a merchant who arrived the year before the government factory opened, traded with the Indi-

ans as well as local settlers and *voyageurs* using the portage. Antoine Ouilmette, a French Canadian, for a time ran a business hauling goods over the portage by both boat and wagon. The government posts were supplied by sailing ship, although fur traders continued for a time to use canoes between Chicago and Michilimackinac.[39]

The fort's garrison notwithstanding, the American trading community at Chicago on the eve of the War of 1812 probably did not much exceed in population or commerce the French settlement of a century earlier. The fort, a rude stockade at the mouth of the Chicago River, was manned by a detachment of fifty-five soldiers; the adjacent community had no more than forty residents. Enumeration of the victims of the August 15, 1812, Fort Dearborn Massacre by the Potawatomi as the settlement was being evacuated to Detroit indicates a civilian population of twelve men, nine women, and eighteen children.[40]

The fort was rebuilt in 1816 after the end of the War of 1812, and settlers once again drifted into the area. Although the government reestablished the trading factory, its volume was never large and declined further after 1817 primarily because the government was unable to compete with private traders, who could offer the Indians liquor and credit. By 1822, the government gave up and closed the factory, and the following year the military detachment was withdrawn. Private fur trading also declined as the Potawatomi and Illiniwek ceded lands for settlement.[41]

The last trader of note was Gurdon S. Hubbard, a native of Vermont, who gravitated into the Montreal fur trade with the American Fur Company and wound up in the 1820s as its Illinois River superintendent, based on Mackinac Island, which had replaced Michilimackinac as the nexus of the great canoe route. It was Hubbard who finally abandoned the Chicago–Mud Lake–Des Plaines canoe portage and substituted pack trains of as many as fifty horses to get his furs to Chicago for shipment on the lake. By then the portage route across Ontario had been largely abandoned; furs

The towboat *Ed Renshaw* in 2000 passes through the Illinois River locks near Utica, Illinois, where in 1682, 318 years earlier, La Salle built Fort Saint Louis atop Starved Rock (in the background) across the river.

The Army Corps of Engineers operates a lock and dam on the Illinois River at the natural fortification the colonial French three centuries earlier called Le Rocher, now known as Starved Rock (background at extreme right).

vessels with up to sixty-four paddlers.

Individual traders in French colonial times couldn't afford sailing ships, which could cost 6,000 to 8,000 livres ($60,000 to $80,000) to build. The loss of the *Griffon* almost bankrupted La Salle. But when trading companies came into existence in the second half of the eighteenth century and merged into larger firms, they had the capital to build ships and found them cheaper to operate than flotillas of canoes. By 1793 the Northwest Company of Benjamin and Joseph Frobisher had schooners on Lakes Huron and Superior. The death knell for the canoe, except on small streams, came after the 1821 merger of the Northwest and Hudson Bay companies; over the next four years the combined company cut its payroll by 58 percent.[44]

Fur trading and the military had been Chicago's only industries in the first two decades of its existence, and their loss was devastating to the struggling settlement. The village in 1829 was a backwater as sluggish as the river that flowed through it and could sustain a population that numbered only thirty-five voters, surrounded by an Potawatomi population many times that size.

There was a boom occurring in the American interior, but it was along the great rivers, the Ohio and Mississippi, along which pioneers settled after crossing the mountains from the east. Steamboats were carrying increasing commerce on the rivers, and towns like Pittsburgh, Cincinnati, and Saint Louis were being transformed into cities.

Chicago's only ray of hope was that in 1825 the state of New York had opened the Erie Canal, linking New York City with the Upper Great Lakes via the Hudson River. The canal, in effect, made Chicago the potential western terminus of a transportation artery connecting New York, the nation's largest and fastest growing port, with the vast wilderness of the interior. Illinois for its part was organizing to build a canal that would connect the Great Lakes with all that steamboat traffic on the Mississippi River.

were stockpiled in warehouses and sent by sailing ship via the Great Lakes.[42]

By 1832 the fur trade had declined to the point that Hubbard turned his downstate Danville, Illinois, warehouse into a store selling retail merchandise to white settlers. The following year he moved to Chicago.[43]

The canoe age was coming to an end. The decline began rather abruptly in 1820s as sailing ships came into wider use. A relatively small sailing ship in La Salle's time could carry 40 tons of cargo with a crew of only five or six, but to haul the same cargo in canoes would require eight

# Chapter Two  The Riverboat Era

• La Salle, when he first gazed on the Mississippi in 1680, saw opportunity—the great avenue of Middle America that could link the distant settlements of Illinois with the ocean and Mother France. Land transport of the time was difficult, slow, and expensive, especially in a wilderness like North America. The vast Mississippi and its tributaries became the interstate highway system of its day, at least before the railroads came along. Pioneers colonized its banks, settlements grew up along it, and it carried the mail, immigrants, and their harvests.

Historical geographers called it a potamic system, after the Greek word (potamos) for river. After the French lost their colonies in North America, Ameri-can pioneers who moved west over the mountains and into the interior planted their farms on the riverbanks. Their flat-boats, laden with the harvest each autumn, drifted south on the Mississippi to New Orleans, as the French *bateau* had done earlier.[1]

The development of steamboats in the early nineteenth century resulted in a boom of river traffic, and the boatsman's cry "Mark twain!" became part of American lore. Chicago remained a backwater until a canal was finally dug connecting it to the Father of Waters. Then some antebellum southern planters and their families used the new river-canal route to escape the summer heat of Dixie for the cooler climate on the Great Lakes, and

The *City of Metropolis,* built in 1888 in its namesake town and destroyed by fire in 1901 in Quincy, Illinois, was typical of the packets in the waning years of the steamboat era—a small stern-wheel steamer designed to handle local traffic between towns with marginal or no railroad service. (U.S. Army Corps of Engineers, Illinois Waterway Visitor Center)

others sent sugar over it to northern markets. But the Civil War and the railroads put an end to the river's golden age: the war choked off the river to commerce for several years, and some time afterward the railroads took away what remained of the traffic for more than half a century.

La Salle, after his 1677 trip to France to seek the financial backing and support of Versailles for a scheme to develop the interior of North America, returned to Canada with the nautical equipment necessary to build two small square-rigged ships for inland service. The ill-fated *Griffon* was built to sail the Upper Great Lakes, and an uncompleted sister ship built on the Illinois River near modern Peoria was intended to sail the Mississsippi River. Although Louis XIV had rejected La Salle's proposal to colonize the interior, he had granted him the authority to develop a fur trade there.[2]

The *Griffon* was completed near the mouth of the Niagara River at the eastern end of Lake Erie in early 1679 and was sailed west with La Salle, his men, and anchors and equipment for the second ship. At the present site of Green Bay, Wisconsin, a pile of furs his agents had assembled was loaded, and on September 18 the *Griffon,* because of the lateness of the season, was dispatched back to Niagara. La Salle and the rest of his men went south by canoe to start construction of the second ship on the Illinois. The second, partially constructed vessel was doomed in its stocks when the *Griffon* mysteriously was lost on its voyage east with the equipment for its sister ship still aboard—the first of a long list of ship disappearances on the lakes. La Salle then made his trip down the Mississippi to its mouth by canoe.

Trying to maintain a colony dangling in the middle of a 2,700-mile canoe trail from Montreal through Chicago to New Orleans was not a particularly sound idea, so La Salle decided to approach the problem from the other direction. He returned to Paris in 1684 and talked his financial backers into paying for a four-ship expedition to the mouth of the Mississippi. Un-

fortunately the expedition was plagued with difficulties from the start and overshot the mouth of the Mississippi, landing instead at Matagorda Bay in what is today Texas about 480 miles west of its intended destination and with only two of its ships surviving. La Salle was assassinated by some disgruntled expedition members on March 19, 1687, near the Trinity River while trying to lead them overland to find the Mississippi.[3]

Twelve years later, because of concern that either the British or Spanish would get control of the mouth of the river, Versailles sent two warships under Le Moyne d'Iberville to build forts there. After struggling for several years, the Louisiana colony was finally able to extend its influence up the Mississippi to Illinois country. Cahokia, founded in 1699 as a mission and trading post, and Kaskaskia, founded four years later as a trading post, quickly replaced Tonty's settlements at Peoria and Chicago as the French presence in Illinois. In 1717 they were transferred from control of the Canadian colony to Louisiana, although the by then abandoned Chicago remained part of Canada.[4]

Gradually in the first two decades of the seventeenth century Cahokia and Kaskaskia evolved into agricultural communities. They had sent a flour shipment to Louisiana as early as 1713, five years before New Orleans was founded, and by the 1730s were regularly sending flour, salted pork and beef, cured hams, bear oil, and tallow. In the spring convoy of 1732 alone Illinois sent 200,000 livres (a French measure of weight, as well as coinage, equal to 1.08 English pounds), or about 108 tons, of flour in twenty-five to thirty *pirogues.* Although some fur moved south, the French continued to prefer the great canoe route to Montreal over New Orleans for the fur trade because extreme heat spoiled beaver pelts.[5]

*Pirogues,* or dugout canoes, generally used by the Indians and many French on the Mississippi, were limited by the size of the trees from which they could be carved—most frequently cypress or

The steamboats on the marginally navigable Illinois River were considerably smaller than the big steamers of the Mark Twain era on the Mississippi River. This stern-wheeler, *Dove,* had its main deck stacked with freight and carried only a few local passengers. (Illinois Department of Natural Resources)

cottonwood—but often were as much as 40 to 50 feet long and 6 feet wide. *Pirogues* from Illinois country seemed to be somewhat smaller, with a cargo capacity, or burden, of 3,000 to 5,000 livres (roughly 1.5 to 2.5 tons), although a few such vessels with a burden of 17,000 livres (about 9 tons) were built at Kaskaskia. The larger of these vessels were equipped with decks and sails, although rowing, poling, and towing were the most common methods of power.[6]

## Bateaux

As commerce increased, the French began experimenting with larger vessels. The solution was a double-ended rowboat made with planks and simply called *bateau* (boat)—the evolutionary predecessor to a series of river craft that would ply the Mississippi for more than a century. Mariners and historians in the eighteenth and early nineteenth century were not always fussy about terminology, dimensions, and cargo capacity: bateaux were referred to as "batoes" by anglophones but have also been called galleys. Their distinction between bateaux, barges, and keelboats also was a little fuzzy.

For a time bateaux were the largest vessels on the rivers and managed to survive the competition until the 1820s, by which time Americans were building them under an assortment of names. When Pierre Dugue, sieur de Boisbriant, was sent in 1718 with a company of marines to take command in Illinois and build Ft. de Chartres, he traveled upriver in a convoy of bateaux. For commercial purposes, the standard eighteenth-century Louisiana bateau was approximately 40 feet long and 9 feet wide and carried 12 to 15 tons of cargo. Versions built in Illinois apparently conformed to those dimensions.[7]

Travel by *bateau* was little better than by canoe. The trip downriver from Kaskaskia to New Orleans took three to four weeks, but the return trip took four months of backbreaking labor, not to mention the hazards of snags (tree stumps), bars, and hostile Indians. The long round trip meant that the Illinois colony communicated with New Orleans once or twice a year by convoy. The typical vessel required eighteen rowers, but as many as twenty-four, some of them slaves, were used on trips upriver against the current. Bateaux also came equipped with sails.[8]

The idea of powering river vessels with sails seems absurd in the twentieth century, but until the development of the steam engine it was tried with marginal success for nearly a century and a half after La Salle's unfinished 1679 vessel. Schooners, one as large as 250 tons, were built on the Ohio River as far north as Pittsburgh in the early nineteenth century, although they were intended for ocean service after being floated downriver to New Orleans. It was not uncommon to equip early river barges with sails: later in the nineteenth century barges were pushed by towboats, but the early ones were more closely related to bateaux in that they were propelled by a combination of sails, oars, and poles.[9]

Given the American capacity for finding the cheapest and easiest way of getting around, it wasn't long before some competitors appeared to challenge the *bateau*. Barges were one of a number of craft adopted by the American pioneers as they poured over the mountains after the French and Indian War and began settling the Ohio River valley. Perhaps the most common, if not the vessel most romantically linked to the Daniel Boone era, was the flatboat. It was a raft anywhere from 20 to 60 feet long, sometimes with a shack or tent for shelter mounted on the deck, on which the early settlers piled their worldly belongings for the trip downriver to their new homestead. They were inexpensive to buy and operate because they drifted with the current and family members could steer, using fore-and-aft sweeps or long oars. Upon reaching the new homestead, the flatboat was frequently dismantled and its wood used to build a house. A somewhat more expensive version of the flatboat was the ark, which had two V-shaped ends.[10]

As trade on the river developed, flatboats became an inexpensive, if slow, way to get the harvest to market in New Orleans. A farmer could leave the Ohio River valley after the autumn harvest and return in time for spring planting. Owners often

sold their flatboats for the lumber in New Orleans and walked home or, somewhat later, booked deck passage (steerage) on steamboats. Because they were relatively cheap—$60 to $75 for a vessel capable of carrying 25 to 100 tons of cargo—flatboats survived on the rivers long after steamboats had driven the oar-powered craft from the market.

Flatboat arrivals in New Orleans, many of them from Cincinnati, the center of the flatboat trade in the Midwest, increased steadily from 598 in 1814 to a peak of 2,792 between 1846 and 1847 before declining to 541 between 1856 and 1857. Probably because the Upper Mississippi and Illinois Rivers were narrower and harder to negotiate and their banks were settled after the steamboat appeared, the flatboat was never much of a factor on them. The Upper Illinois and Des Plaines Rivers were simply too shallow for anything larger than a canoe, and not even that during droughts. An average of only fifty-three flatboats a year reached New Orleans from the Upper-Mississippi-River states of Missouri, Iowa, and Illinois in the twelve-year period ending between 1856 and 1857, forty-two of them from Illinois.[11]

Barges and their close relatives, the keelboats, so named because they had a four-by-four timber keel to give the craft strength in the event of a collision with another vessel, sawyer, snag, or bar, came into vogue in the late 1700s. The principal advantage of the barge, besides its low cost ($4 to $5 per foot to build in 1808, compared to $1 to $3 for canoes) was its substantial increase in cargo capacity over the *bateau*. Some barges had a burden of 170 tons, although the average was more like 40 tons. They also required large crews of fifteen to fifty men and sometimes had a forecastle to house them.[12]

Keelboats for the most part had shallower drafts—as little as 2 feet when fully loaded—and could be used on tributaries too small for barges. They were built as large as 80 feet long and 10 feet wide and typically could carry up to 40 tons of

Canal boats built for mule power were interchangeable as barges on the rivers and sometimes on the Great Lakes. The Hennepin Canal barge *Peerless,* loaded with barrels of Morton salt, is being maneuvered by the towboat *Redwing* on the Mississippi just below the government bridge at Rock Island. (Judi Jacksohn Collection)

cargo. As a practical matter, barges were used in the deeper channels, and their cargoes were transferred to keelboats at rapids or tributaries.

Barges, which may have numbered as many as three hundred on the Mississippi in the years between 1810 and 1817, were an early victim of the steamboat, which was considerably faster and could carry more cargo. Although early steamboats had difficulty competing with the lower freight rates of barges, for the most part they had driven those craft from the rivers in the 1820s, even though a few continued to be used for hauling coal on the Ohio River. Keelboats survived for another half century on the small tributaries, which were unsuitable for steam navigation, or in coal service on the Ohio. On the major rivers they became a forerunner of the modern barge, lashed to the sides of steamboats and towed to their destinations. There were 108 keelboat arrivals

noted in Saint Louis in 1841, and as late as 1847 as many as 55 were still in use on the Upper Mississippi above Saint Louis.[13]

The danger from rapids on the Upper Mississippi between Saint Louis and the Fever River in northern Illinois led to the practice of using keelboats, known as "safety barges," lashed to the sides of steamboats to carry a portion of the cargo, thereby lightening the load and reducing the draft to clear the rocks. By 1839, tows of as many as three such safety barges were common on that stretch of the river and in 1843 the 112-ton steamboat *Iowa* towed ten of them between Galena and Saint Louis. The vessel made twenty-three trips that season, clearing $10,000 on freight and $8,000 on passengers.[14]

## Steamboats

Steam propulsion revolutionized transportation in the nineteenth century, and its effect was felt the fastest on the western rivers with the introduction of the steamboat. Within twenty years of its introduction on the Ohio River in 1811, and despite a seven-year legal battle over the Fulton-Livingston monopoly, which retarded development somewhat, the steamboat was the dominant form of transportation in the North American interior. Cities with steamboat service, like Saint Louis and Louisville, thrived; places without it, like Chicago, languished as backwaters.

Robert Fulton is popularly credited with developing the steamboat in 1807, but in reality a number of inventors produced working vessels before him. As early as 1790 John Fitch had a steamboat operating in commercial service for a time between Philadelphia and Trenton. Oliver Evans, the advocate of the high-pressure engine that ultimately proved successful on the western rivers, built a steamboat in New Orleans in 1802, but it was beached in a flood the next year before being put into service. Fulton and his partner, Robert Livingston, were successful in obtaining from New York an exclusive franchise to operate their *Steam Boat* (also known as *North River Steamboat of Clermont* or, simply, *Clermont*) on the Hudson River. Livingston, whose brother, Edward, was a lawyer in New Orleans, later obtained a similar exclusive franchise from Louisiana but was unable to convince the other western states and territories to grant similar monopolies.[15]

Almost all of the steamboat pioneers realized from the beginning the potential of the western rivers. Within two weeks of the maiden voyage of his vessel, Fulton was writing to obtain information on Mississippi River navigation, including data on currents and traffic. Evans began building a steamboat named for him in 1812 in Pittsburgh, but his financial troubles delayed completion. The Fulton and Livingston group also used Pittsburgh to build their 371-ton steamboat *New Orleans* in 1811. She left on her 2,000-mile maiden voyage to New Orleans on October and

took nearly three months to get downstream. The group then built three more steamboats over the next four years.

By then another Pittsburgh group, headed by the barge operator Henry M. Shreve, was building steamboats to challenge the Fulton-Livingston monopoly. Shreve's group built four steamboats from 1814 to 1816 and immediately became embroiled in litigation with the eastern monopoly. The dispute wasn't resolved until 1818, when the heirs of Fulton and Livingston, apparently discouraged by the amount of competition and difficulty of prosecuting their case, dropped the matter. Six years later they also lost their Hudson River monopoly when the U.S. Supreme Court ruled against them in the famous *Gibbons* v. *Ogden* case.[16]

With the legal impediments resolved, there was a virtual explosion of steamboat building in the West. Only seventeen steamboats were operating in 1817, but by the end of 1820 a total of sixty-nine were in service. Although historians have traditionally associated the steamboat boom with the end of the monopoly, Louis C. Hunter in his monumental work, *Steamboats on the Western Rivers*, said that it was the dramatic increase in upstream speeds at about the same time that captured the public's imagination. The best known was the voyage of Shreve's steamboat *Washington* upstream from New Orleans to Louisville in a record twenty-five days.[17]

Within a decade, the steamboat industry was booming and vessels were chugging up tributaries to within a hundred miles of the Chicago trading post. By 1835 scheduled stagecoaches provided a connection between the steamboat dock at La Salle and Chicago around the upper sections of the Illinois and Des Plaines Rivers that were not navigable, although by then Illinois was already planning a canal to close the gap.

By 1850 there were 740 steamboats with a combined capacity of more than 141,000 tons plying the western rivers. Although steamboats had a limited freight capacity because their shallow drafts meant they lacked holds and all freight had to be stacked on deck, builders were able to dramatically increase capacity by the simple expediency of building longer vessels. Early steamboats were 150 feet long, 20 to 30 feet wide, and had a burden of 150 tons. By 1860, steamboats were 240 to 270 feet long, 40 feet wide, and could carry 1,200 tons.[18]

The 1850s are generally considered to be the golden age of the steamboat with an average of 3,629 of the vessels annually docking at Cincinnati and 3,100 at Saint Louis early in the decade. The populations of most states in the interior were concentrated along the rivers, and no off-river community without access to steamboats could expect to amount to much. In 1835, just before the state capital was shifted from Vandalia to Springfield, Abraham Lincoln supported a bill in the Illinois General Assembly incorporating a com-

pany to build a canal from Beardstown on the Illinois River to Sangamon County, of which Springfield was the seat, although the canal was never built.[19]

However, despite the domination of the packet steamboat in antebellum times, competition was arising that would render it obsolete before the end of the century. The Great Lakes with their new canals connecting to the western rivers in Ohio, Indiana, and Illinois were beginning to emerge as competitors, as were the railroads. The Civil War, which was to prove disastrous to river trade, loomed. The rivers also were nearing their capacities without a substantial investment to improve their navigability. According to an 1840s topographical engineering report, the Mississippi River and its tributaries were navigable by steamboats for 16,674 miles, but in fact only a fraction of those—less than 2,500 miles—had a six-foot-deep channel, which was necessary for any sort of meaningful river commerce.[20]

Sternwheel steamboats like this one pulling away from shore under a full head of steam were common from the 1830s until the early twentieth century, as they were designed especially for the shallow rivers and creeks of the Mississippi, Missouri, and Ohio river systems. (University of Chicago Library, Department of Special Collections, AEP-OHS2)

Problems with navigating the northern sections of the Mississippi by both steamboats and keelboats was a major, if little understood, factor in Chicago's eventual ascendancy over the river cities as the transportation center of the Midwest. Low water often halted commerce in summer, as did ice in the winter, even on the Ohio. The Illinois was navigable by small or medium-sized steamboats only six to seven months a year to its head of navigation at Peru, Illinois, 225 miles northeast of its confluence with the Mississippi at Grafton, Illinois, and about 97 miles southwest of any navigable stretch of the Chicago River. Steamboat service started on the Illinois as far as Peru in 1828, and in 1832, when the area was still sparsely populated and the Black Hawk uprising was threatening, only three steamboats made it there. However, by 1841, when Peru and its sister city of La Salle were connected to Chicago by daily stagecoach service, a daily packet steamboat operated to Peoria when water levels permitted. Peoria that year reported 143 arrivals from

Peru and 259 from Saint Louis.[21]

The steamboat season was half as long at Lafayette, Indiana, the practical head of navigation on the Wabash River 370 miles north of the Ohio River and 102 miles south of Chicago, although in 1852 a total of ninety-nine steamboats visited the city. Lafayette's link to Chicago at the time was the old Vincennes Trace, an Indian trail, which after 1829 became a major route for Hoosier wagons hauling farm products to the Chicago port for shipment to New York instead of downriver to New Orleans.[22]

The Upper Mississippi Valley, an area that became a battleground in an economic rivalry between Saint Louis and Chicago by midcentury, turned out to be a lost cause for the steamboat industry although Saint Louis was 200 miles closer by water to Rock Island than was Chicago even after the Illinois and Michigan Canal was completed. Rapids at the mouth of the Des Moines River 200 miles north of Saint Louis and at Rock Island another 150 miles upriver proved to be an obstacle to river traffic despite various attempts to blast a

Low water and ice have always been a problem for navigation on the rivers. In more recent years, after the Illinois River was deepened with a system of dams, two towboats were sometimes required to smash through the ice, as was the case on January 25, 1948, at the Bull's Island cut on the Illinois Waterway at mile 240.6 near Joliet. (U.S. Army Corps of Engineers, Illinois Waterway Visitor Center)

deeper channel. The biggest source of commercial traffic in the early 1800s was the lead-mining town of Galena on the Fever River in the northwest corner of Illinois. It had first attracted the attention of the French and their bateaux in the eighteenth century and by the first half of the nineteenth century was one of the largest cities in Illinois.

Galena was at the western end of a 143-mile road that made shipping of its principal commodity to Chicago by wagon a very expensive proposition and enabled the steamboats to keep a 95 percent share of the lead market. Chicago's canal never got more than a trickle, and not even the railroads were able to dent the steamboat monopoly on lead traffic. The first wagonload of 3,000 pounds of lead was shipped to Chicago as early as 1829 and some of the overland traffic continued until the railroads put the teamsters out of

business. It was no coincidence that Chicago's first two chartered railroads—Galena and Chicago Union and Illinois Central—both had Galena as their intended destination, although the original plans of the Illinois Central did not include a line to Chicago and the Galena (later Chicago & North Western Railway) never made it to its namesake.[23]

The lead traffic became the first impetus to conquer the Upper Mississippi. As early as 1807, Shreve took a 35-ton barge with a cargo of lead from Galena to Saint Louis. Three years later he netted $11,000 when he took a barge to Galena and returned with a load of lead. The first steamboat made it over both the Des Moines and Rock Island rapids in 1823, and on March 4, 1828, the steamboat *Missouri* was able to run the rapids with a safety barge lashed to its side to carry a portion of its 200-ton cargo and run light in only twenty-two inches of water. Later the same year a steamboat was able to tow two keelboats with a 40-ton burden each from the Fever River to Saint Louis. That was the beginning of the end for independent keelboats in the lead trade, except when used as barges. A keelboat required a month to travel the 400 miles upstream from Saint Louis to Galena; a steamboat made the round trip in eight days.[24]

The potential passenger market to Galena also had attracted the attention of steamboat operators. By 1827 steamboats advertised regular service from Saint Louis to the Fever River, even during low water, by transferring passengers to keelboats for the last leg of the trip from the lower rapids to the mining region. Within twenty years passenger traffic replaced lead as the principal commodity hauled on the Upper Mississippi. That trade could be lucrative; in a single year (1857) the *Ocean Wave*, which had cost $19,500 to build, earned $26,451.63 on passenger fares and $9.373.44 on freight. However, by that time the lead mines were in decline, and no less than four railroads based in Chicago had reached or crossed the Upper

Mississippi, making the journey by rail via Chicago to New York considerably faster than the old steamboat route through Saint Louis and Pittsburgh and via Pennsylvania's Main Line Canal over the mountains to Philadelphia.[25]

## The Hazards of River Travel

Between 1807 and 1853, when the Steamboat Inspection Act went into effect, the federal government on the basis of imprecise records that often were little more than local newspaper accounts estimated that more than 7,000 persons were killed in steamboat accidents, and between 1811 and 1849, 520 steamboats were destroyed in accidents. Although many of the fatalities resulted from fires or explosions, a significant number can be attributed to the general term "hazards to navigation," everything from grounding due to unmarked channels to collisions in fog. In the 1860–1869 decade, 393 of the 726 steamboat accidents reported in the United States were attributable to collisions, snaggings (hitting submerged tree trunks and stumps), striking sawyers (floating trees), or wrecks. The loss of life numbered 1,765.[26]

The accident toll on the rivers even by nineteenth-century standards was serious enough to cause the federal government as early as 1852 to establish the Steamboat Inspection Service, a forerunner of the U.S. Coast Guard. Tighter safety standards and inspections in the 1860s reduced the accident rate for fires and explosions; although there were 265 fires and explosions with a death toll of 3,208, a single accident accounted for nearly half those fatalities. A boiler explosion on the overloaded steamboat *Sultana* on the Mississippi above Memphis on April 27, 1865, killed more than 1,500 repatriated Union soldiers on the way home from prison camps in the worst maritime disaster in U.S. history.[27]

Such explosions captured the headlines, but most accidents were more mundane and didn't involve any loss of life. Probably more typical of the hazards of river travel was the loss on the rapids of two lead-laden keelboats being towed by the steamboat *New Brazil* or the sinking at the mouth of the Fever River of the steamboat *Fortune* and its attached keelboat laden

Although canal boats were of considerably heavier construction than the birchbark canoes, pirogues, and bateaux used on Chicago-area waterways earlier, none survived the end of the twentieth century. The bow (p. 30) and stern (p. 31) of these I & M Canal boats, found at Morris after the canal was desiccated when a dam broke in a storm in 1996, were subjects of considerable interest to archaeologists. The boats were probably abandoned just before or after 1900 and allowed to rot at their moorings. (Fever River Research and Illinois Department of Natural Resources)

Through most of the steamboat era, packets on the Mississippi River were typically
side-wheelers with space for
cargo on the main deck and
passengers consigned to the
"between-deck" above it.
The Upper Mississippi
steamboat *Quincy,* pictured
at Davenport, Iowa, had a
third, or "texas," deck with
cabins for passengers and
crew. (American Environ-
mental Photographs Collection [AEP-IAS3], Department
of Special Collections, University of Chicago Library)

with lead. Mark Twain's *Life on the Mississippi,* written in 1883, is a recollection of
his days as a cub riverboat pilot, and in it
he explains the hazards of snags, keelboats, bars, soundings in low water, and
bluff reefs—things that a steamboat pilot
had to keep in his head because there
were no navigation markers or manuals in
antebellum times:

> . . . but piloting becomes another matter
> when you apply it to vast streams like the
> Mississippi and the Missouri, whose allu-
> vial banks cave and change constantly,
> whose snags are always hunting up new
> quarters, whose sand bars are never at
> rest, whose channels are forever dodging
> and shirking, and whose obstructions
> must be confronted in all nights and all
> weathers without the aid of a single light-
> house or a single buoy; for there is nei-
> ther light nor buoy to be found anywhere
> in all this three or four thousand miles of
> villainous river.

When I had learned the name and position of every visible feature of the river,
when I had so mastered its shape that I
could shut my eyes and trace it from St.
Louis to New Orleans; when I had learned
to read the face of the water as one would
cull the news from the morning paper; and
finally, when I had trained my dull memory to treasure up an endless array of
soundings and crossing-marks, and to keep
fast hold of them, I judged that my education was complete; so I got to tilting my
cap to the side of my head, and wearing a
toothpick in my mouth at the wheel.[28]

Twain worked on the river between 1857
and the Civil War, and when he returned
(by train) twenty-one years later for a nos-
talgic trip on the Father of Waters he was
America's best-known author. He immediately noticed after arrival at his Saint Louis
hotel that there were no river men loung-
ing in the billiard room: "But the change of
changes was on the 'levee.' Half a dozen

sound-asleep steamboats where I used to see a solid mile of wide awake ones. This was melancholy, this was woeful. The absence of the pervading and jocund steamboatman from the billiard saloon was explained. He is absent because he is no more. His occupation is gone. . . . The towboat and railroad had done their work."[29]

The river industry and its proponents had not done theirs, however. When the steamboat arrived, the rivers were open and free. Anyone with access to $10,000 dollars in 1849 could buy a steamboat and hire a crew to run it. Annual operating expenses at the time were estimated at more than $26,000; the rivers were free. With luck, the owner could make back his investment and a handsome profit during the four-year life expectancy of the vessel. Steamboat owners for the most part were groups of local merchants, freight forwarders, and boat captains in river towns. Unlike the railroads, steamboating was a fragmented industry, small-scale operations with one or two boats that started their trips only when they had decks full of cargo.[30]

The problem was that the vessel owners in this highly fragmented industry did not have the wherewithal to finance expensive programs to upgrade and extend the rivers. The young western states were in the same boat, and federal assistance was slow to materialize. Congress in 1820 authorized a survey by army engineers of the Mississippi and Ohio Rivers: their recommendation a year later was to build a canal around the falls of Louisville and do some dredging and snag removal on the Ohio. But President James Monroe had doubts about the constitutionality of spending federal money on local improvements, so the project languished for several years until Congress appropriated $75,000 to get it under way. The problem of snags was attacked first, and crews, using a snag boat designed by Shreve, had greatly reduced that hazard on that river by 1830, the same year the Louisville canal was finished.[31]

Progress elsewhere was slow. Between 1787 and 1850, by which time the federal

government had taken prime responsibility for waterway improvements, Washington had spent only about $13 million in river and harbor work for the entire nation. In 1846 President James K. Polk vetoed the Harbors and Rivers Bill on fiscal grounds, and for the next twenty years there were no major appropriations for river work except for the Rivers and Harbors Act of 1852, which included $30,000 in appropriations for improvements to the Illinois River. The veto caused a furor in the western states, which had held a River Improvement Convention in Memphis in 1845, and they met with northeastern maritime states to organize a River and Harbor Convention for 1847. The place they selected was not on the Mighty Miss or the East Coast but the new Lake Michigan port called Chicago, and the July 5, 1847, convention was its first.[32]

Hotel space was insufficient for the expected crowd of twenty thousand delegates, so Chicago requisitioned private homes and ships in the harbor to handle the overflow. Chicago didn't have a building large enough to handle that kind of a crowd, so the meeting was ultimately staged in a big tent in a park. As expected, the delegates overwhelmingly adopted a resolution disagreeing with Polk's veto of a bill providing federal aid to rivers and ports. The resolution claimed that federal expenditures were disproportionately directed to ocean ports engaged in foreign trade at the expense of the inland rivers and lakes of the interior that fed traffic to those ports.[33]

A year later U.S. Representative Abraham Lincoln, who had attended the convention, arose on the floor of Congress and addressed the constitutional issue of interstate commerce and federal responsibility for the waterways. Referring to a load of sugar from New Orleans, which had passed through the new Illinois and Michigan Canal and Chicago earlier in the year, Lincoln told his colleagues: "The sugar took this route, doubtless because it was cheaper than the old route. Supposing the benefit of the reduction in the cost of carriage to be shared between seller and buyer, the result is, that the New Orleans merchant sold his sugar a little dearer; and the people of Buffalo sweetened their coffee a little cheaper than before—a benefit resulting from the canal, not to Illinois where it is, but to Louisiana and New York where it is not."[34]

The Chicago meeting was not the last waterway convention held in the United States because it took until the third decade of the twentieth century to get a comprehensive federal program rolling. The states over the years attempted projects on a piecemeal and parochial basis, often opposing projects that would benefit their rival states. Illinois spent its limited resources attempting to upgrade the Illinois River to make it an economic tributary of Chicago, not to improve the Mississippi River to benefit Saint Louis. The state built dams at Henry and Copperas Creek before the federal government got into the program and in 1889 completed a lock on the Illinois River at downstate LaGrange, and the second one in 1892 in Kampsville. Their combined cost was $1,145,886.

The federal government, which since 1836 had been sporadically blasting away at the limestone mass at the Des Moines Rapids before digging between 1866 and 1877 a 7.6-mile canal around the obstruc-tion, began what was supposed to be a substantial program to improve the western rivers after the Civil War; however, progress was glacial. In 1879 Congress authorized at Davis Island south of Pittsburgh, the first of fifty planned dams across the Ohio River between the Steel City and Cairo, but the entire project was not completed until 1929.[35]

Congress created the Mississippi River Commission also in 1879 to put together a plan for that waterway. The enormous scope of the project and declining traffic on the river caused the commission late in the century to rethink its position. After 1896, flood control, not navigation, became its major concern. Some of the money was squandered on pork-barrel projects like the virtually useless Hennepin Canal, built as a shortcut across northern Illinois between the Mississippi River at Rock Island and the Illinois River at Bureau.[36]

Meanwhile, Illinois continued to struggle with trying to finance projects to improve the navigability of the Illinois River and rapidly obsolescing Illinois and Michigan Canal to Chicago. The canal had put Chicago on the map and was its lifeline to the Mississippi River. But by the time the federal government decided to proceed with the Hennepin Canal, the I & M was already in decline.

# *Chapter Three* The Age of Canals

• It is a popular myth that the covered wagon and iron horse were the vehicles that settled America. That may be true for the trans-Mississippi West, but in the Midwest it was boats that hauled the settlers and their belongings into the wilderness—flatboats, schooners, and canal boats. The canals, a now largely forgotten transportation system, were the waterways built where the rivers and Great Lakes didn't run. They were the carriers of immigrants, harvests, and tools during the early Industrial Revolution before the railroads drove them out of business. A canal put Chicago on the map.

Fragments of the canal system that once exceeded 4,000 miles in length and stretched from the Atlantic Ocean to the Mississippi River still exist as linear parks along the Potomac River and in northern Illinois. A few of their descendents, much enlarged and modernized, remain as functioning waterways: the New York Barge Canal succeeded the Erie Canal, and the much-enlarged Sanitary and Ship Canal replaced the Illinois and Michigan Canal.

Canals in Europe initially were built for irrigation or drainage but were quickly enlarged to handle commerce. Some were built as shortcuts between navigable rivers or as feeders to the rivers to cheaply carry ores or fuel from mines to factories; others hauled grain from farm to market. In wilderness America, at least in the first half of the nineteenth century, they were built primarily as aquatic highways to encourage

Side-wheeled steamers were not used on the canals because of potential damage to the paddles and banks. A few stern-wheelers were used, but screw-propeller-powered steamers like the *Nashotan*, shown loading while the crew poses for a photograph, were common. (Lewis University, Canal and Regional History Collection)

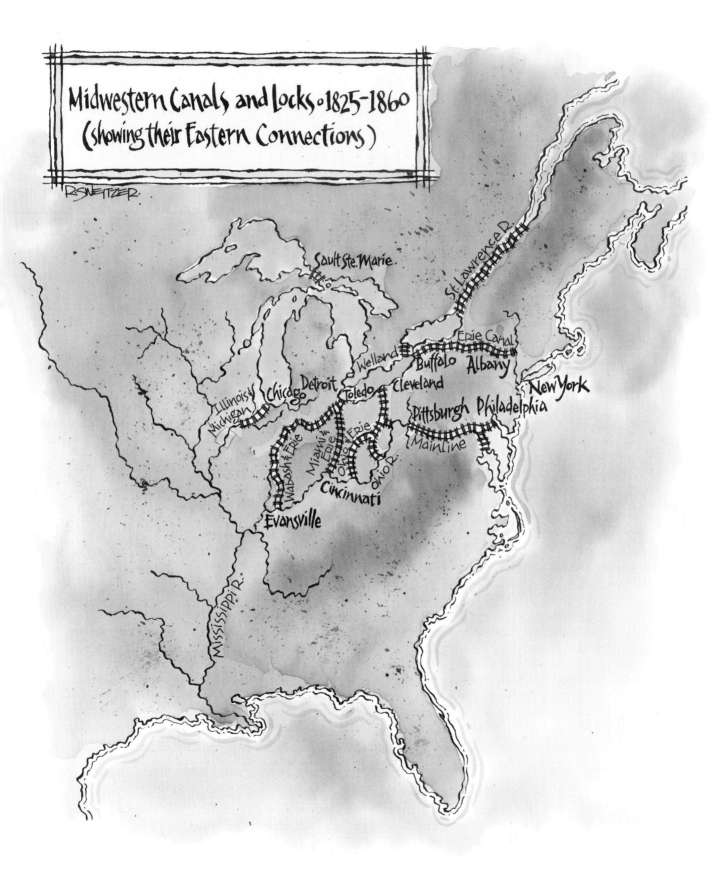

Midwestern Canals and Locks • 1825-1860
(showing their Eastern Connections)

development or to extend the economic reach of cities more than the 25 to 30 miles that drays could operate with any sort of efficiency. Canals were one of the major public works programs used by rival cities and states to compete for economic domination.[1]

America's canal age was brief, lasting only a few decades after the opening of the Erie Canal in 1825, but its influence was substantial. The Chicago municipality was the result of the building of that canal, and the announced intention to build another 900 miles west in Illinois to connect the Great Lakes with the Mississippi River system. Collectively the canals of the Midwest had the effect of realigning the transportation axis in North America from the north-south route along the Mississippi River that favored New Orleans and Saint Louis to an east-west route over the Great Lakes that favored New York, Buffalo, and Chicago. Although not a particularly rapid method of transportation when contrasted to steamboats on the rivers and lakes, canals permitted cheaper and faster east-west travel than was possible on the primitive roads of the day or by means of the long ocean-river route via New Orleans.[2]

By the time the United States emerged as an independent nation in the late eighteenth century, canal technology, which dates from ancient Egypt and was refined and adapted to uneven topography during the Renaissance, was well established in industrializing Europe. The United States was still largely agrarian, however, and the earliest canal schemes proposed in the new nation were less intended to sustain industrialization than to encourage the development of the vast wilderness in the interior. The great distances involved, the Appalachian mountain chain that separated the coastal plain from the interior, and the lack of capital were the biggest obstacles to canalization of the United States.[3]

The national government in the first quarter century of its existence was too poor and preoccupied with other matters to worry much about transportation schemes. The Louisiana Purchase, which in 1803 added a huge territory to the western part of the new nation, suddenly made the development of east-west transportation routes more important than they had been. By 1807, Congress could turn its attention to that problem and commissioned a study of potential federal projects.[4]

The report that Treasury Secretary Albert Gallatin submitted in 1808 is the seminal document in U.S. transportation, although few of its recommended roads and canals came to pass as federal projects. A number of the proposed transportation corridors ultimately were developed as state or private ventures. Major portions of the report dealt with canals that could be cut as aids to coastal navigation—then an important issue—and as a connection between New York's Hudson River and the Great Lakes.

The section of Gallatin's report that ultimately proved to be most important dealt with four corridors that could be built to connect the Atlantic Seaboard with the river systems west of the Appalachian range. He suggested a northern outlet for the Hudson River by means of a canal between the Mohawk River, a Hudson tributary, and Lake Ontario. It quickly occurred to New York officials that a better destination than Lake Ontario, a lake isolated by the Saint Lawrence rapids to the east and Niagara Falls to the west, would be Lake Erie, which connected with the other Upper Great Lakes and would extend the state's commercial reach more than 1,000 miles inland to the head of Lake Superior and the old Chicago portage at the foot of Lake Michigan. That is exactly what New York State did nearly a decade later by building the Erie Canal.[5]

As it turned out, the national government, except for providing financing for the ill-fated Chesapeake and Ohio Canal intended to link the Potomac and Ohio Rivers and building the National Road west from Baltimore over approximately the same route, was a relatively minor

Barges and towboats on many canals were quite small. The barge *Rambler,* pushed by an unidentified boat, visited Tampico, Illinois, on November 18, 1907, on the Hennepin Feeder Canal, built to supply the main Hennepin Canal with water from the Rock River. The future president Ronald Reagan was born in Tampico three years and three months after this photograph was taken. (Illinois Department of Natural Resources)

factor in most transportation projects until after the Civil War. After Gallatin's report, reservations by successive administrations over the constitutionality of what was viewed as essentially intrastate transportation projects left canal building in the hands of the individual states. What ensued was a race by various eastern states to reach and tap the riches of the interior. Virginia was the first state to enter the race by attempting to build a canal west from the Potomac River, but New York was the first state to complete one.

### The Race Inland

George Washington, who like many of the nation's fathers dabbled in speculative land ventures in the interior, had realized even before the French and Indian War the importance of linking the colonies with the wilderness west of the mountains. In 1784, he suggested canal links to the Ohio River and Lake Erie, and the following year he became president of a newly established company to build the link to the Ohio. Ultimately, the firm cut locks around several falls to extend navigation as far as 200 miles inland from the tidewater, but the project stopped far short of the Ohio and never proved satisfactory for large-scale commerce.[6]

That was followed in 1815 by a joint venture between the states of Virginia and Maryland and the federal government to build a canal over the mountains connecting the Potomac and Ohio Rivers. Progress on the Chesapeake and Ohio Canal was slow because of the difficult terrain, and since Congress did not appropriate any money for the project until 1828, construction on the first 60 miles from Georgetown to Harper's Ferry, Virginia, was not completed until 1834. By then both New York and Pennsylvania already had canals in operation.

The Chesapeake and Ohio Canal didn't reach its midpoint at Cumberland, Maryland, until 1850, and by then was clearly running out of steam. Although the 184.5-mile canal was an impressive work of engineering, climbing 609 feet above the tidewater at Georgetown by means of seventy-four locks, crossing streams and rivers on eleven aqueducts, and boring 3,118 feet through a mountain in a tunnel, it was doomed by slow progress, high costs, a depression in the late 1830s, and competition from the other canals and the Baltimore & Ohio Railroad.[7]

Pennsylvania's earliest canals were intended to interdict Baltimore's spreading commercial influence along the Susquehanna River in the central part of that state and later to counteract New York's growing maritime supremacy. By 1823, when the Erie Canal was nearing completion in New York, both Pittsburgh and Philadelphia felt sufficiently threatened to agitate for countermeasures to protect the western trade. The problem of crossing the Allegheny Mountains was solved with a system of five inclined railways to haul canal boats over the ridges. The 178-mile Pennsylvania Main Line (or Main Line of Public Works), as the project became known, was completed in 1834 but operated for only twenty years before high maintenance costs and competition from the railroads put it out of business. The canal had cost the state $1,826,000 to build and $2,143,000 to maintain during its twenty years of existence.[8]

Topographically and geographically, New York State was in the best position to build a canal inland because it was the site of a natural cut in the Appalachian mountain range formed by the Hudson River and its tributary, the Mohawk River. The Dutch, who originally settled New York, contemplated a canal as early as the seventeenth century, but the political consensus to proceed was not reached until after the War of 1812, which ended British control of the Great Lakes. Concern in New York that the British in Canada would dig a canal around Niagara Falls on their side of the border to control traffic to and from the Upper Great Lakes was a major factor in New York's decision to proceed.[9]

The election of De Witt Clinton, an ardent backer of the project, as governor in 1816 gave the project the impetus it needed. Construction of what was to become the nation's most successful domestic canal, and certainly its most influential, began on July 4, 1817, three days after he took the oath of office, and it was completed in 1825. At first the new canal drew primarily eastbound traffic only from western New York State, but within a decade the Great Lakes basin was becoming the state's economic hegemony and Buffalo was one of the busiest ports in the world.

Prior to 1830, traffic from beyond Buffalo at the western terminal of the canal was negligible, and New Orleans remained the dominant port serving the Midwest. Some Ohio grain began to show up at Buffalo by 1830, and Michigan wheat began to move on the canal to export markets by 1835, followed by wheat from Chicago in 1838 and from Wisconsin in 1841. By 1842, the tonnage on the Erie Canal from the Midwestern states equaled local traffic from New York and by 1847 exceeded it.[10]

Even after the railroads were built parallel to it, beginning in the 1830s, and took away most of its passenger traffic, the canal remained the favored route for freight. Traffic at the Buffalo terminal reached 900,000 tons in 1835, about 22,000 tons of which originated in the Midwestern states, and continued to increase, equaling that on the Mississippi River before the Civil War. Its traffic peaked at 6.7 million tons in 1872 before the long decline began.[11]

## The Inland Canals

The immediate success of the Erie Canal seems to have caused a canal-building binge for the next quarter of a century, despite the appearance of a formidable competitor in the form of the railroad. The sparsely settled Great Lakes states particularly caught the canal craze and drove themselves to the verge of bankruptcy digging waterways to extend to the Mississippi River system the Great Lakes route opened by the Erie Canal. It was an unequal race: topography favored Illinois, as it had New York before it. Nevertheless, three Great Lakes states launched public works programs as ambitious as anything in the East, among them Louis Jolliet's long-dormant proposal for a canal at the Chicago portage. By 1830, more than 1,200 miles of canals were in operation in the United States, and by the Civil War that mileage had nearly quadrupled, although 350 miles of canals had already been abandoned (table 3.1).

**Table 3.1** U.S. Canal and Railroad Mileage

| Year | Canals | Railroads |
|------|--------|-----------|
| 1830 | 1,277 | 73 |
| 1840 | 3,326 | 3,328 |
| 1850 | 3,698 | 8,879 |
| 1860 | 4,254* | 30,636 |

\* Excludes 350 miles of canals that were by then closed.

*Source:* Hadfield, *World Canals,* 335.

Stern-wheelers proved superior to side-wheelers in pushing strings of barges and typically had flat bows to fit against the rear of the barge. The government-owned, stern-wheeled towboat *Marion,* shown here in 1895, twelve years later became the first vessel to use the Hennepin Canal across northwestern Illinois. (Illinois Department of Natural Resources)

Many of the canals built during the spree were the result of overly ambitious capital programs or political compromises, like Ohio's insistence on two long canals linking the Ohio River with the Great Lakes. Cincinnati got a canal to Toledo, so Cleveland had to have one to the Ohio River. Perhaps the biggest folly was the Wabash and Erie Canal, which wandered the length and breadth of Indiana for 468 miles from the Maumee River near Fort Wayne to Evansville on the Ohio, but bypassed the unpopulated northwestern cor-

ner of the state that touched on Lake Michigan. Construction began in 1832 and lasted until 1855, but the southern 111 miles were virtually abandoned within five years of their completion.[12]

The effect of such an expensive public works program on the rather meager public treasuries was disastrous and nearly bankrupted several states after the panic of 1837. None of the western canals matched the success of the Erie, few were as successful as transportation ventures, and only a handful were able to recover their construction costs in reasonable time. Despite their cost to the treasury, the canals were successful in one respect: they were a catalyst for development of the wilderness. The Great Lakes ports of Buffalo, Cleveland, and Chicago all developed as a result of their selection as canal terminals, places where goods and passengers were transferred between lakers and canal boats.[13]

The most successful of the lot was the Illinois and Michigan Canal connecting the river and lake from which it got its

name. Federal involvement in the project was far greater than it had been with most of the nation's other waterways, perhaps because of its strategic significance in connecting the Mississippi and Great Lakes. In any event, Washington took official note in 1810, long before construction had started on the Erie Canal or the Illinois territory had been admitted to the union, when the project was suggested as an addendum to Gallatin's 1808 plan. John C. Calhoun, secretary of war, recommended to Congress in a report on strategic military roads and canals on January 14, 1819, that Jolliet's waterway be built. The bill admitting Illinois to the union in 1818 had been amended at the last minute, moving the state's boundary 41 miles farther north to include the site of Fort Dearborn and the presumed eastern terminus of the proposed canal.[14]

Illinois's first governor, Shadrach Bond, endorsed the idea of the canal in his inaugural address, and the general assembly in its first session asked Congress for the authority to build the project. The problem was money. Sparsely populated Illinois had none and asked Congress for a grant of land for the right of way as well as a diversion of 2 percent of the proceeds from the sale of public land then earmarked for roads. Congress complied with some of the request on March 30, 1822; the grant included the authority to build the canal, a small land grant that consisted of the right of way and a strip of 90 feet on either side, but no financial assistance. Unable to finance the project by itself, the state then incorporated the Illinois and Michigan Canal Company, but it failed to sell its authorized $1 million in capital stock.

That forced the state to go back to Congress for help. In 1827 Congress finally reached a compromise between those who favored public funding of such projects for strategic reasons and those who opposed them on constitutional grounds by granting to the state alternate sections of land for a distance of 5 miles to sell to generate cash for construction. That compromise

became the formula Congress used to painlessly finance various transportation projects during most of the rest of the nineteenth century, including the Illinois Central and transcontinental railroads.[15]

In 1829 the Illinois General Assembly created a public canal commission, and the following year the new agency laid out the towns of Ottawa and Chicago along the 97-mile canal route and began selling lots to raise money for construction. Although the platting of Chicago started a seven-year land boom there, land grant sales were disappointing, and the commission was unable to raise enough money to start construction. Property in what was eventually to become the Loop sold in 1831 for an average of $50 an acre, and some outlying parcels went for as little as $1.25 an acre. That changed quickly once the Black Hawk War of 1832 ended. The frontier community's population jumped from an estimated 50 in 1830 to 3,265 in 1835 but slowed some after the panic of 1837. The inflation of land values was even greater than the population boom; some of the lots sold for $50 an acre in 1831 were going for $85,000 in 1835.[16]

It also appears that Chicago's longrunning system of political graft emerged at about the same time. Shrewd speculators could make their fortunes during the land craze, especially if they had some control over the public works projects being planned to stimulate development. The canal commission spent $40,000 to lay out Archer Road between Chicago and Lockport to the southwest to haul men and construction materials to the project. One of the canal commissioners, William B. Archer, happened to have extensive land holdings in the Lockport area.[17]

Despite the local boom the canal project didn't benefit much from the inflated land values resulting from the speculative craze and was delayed another six years until 1836 while Illinois haggled with financiers in Albany and New York over the terms of a $500,000 construction loan. The money lenders were willing to finance the canal under any of five plans, but were unwilling to give Illinois an outright loan unless it was backed by the full faith and credit of the state, a mechanism known as general obligation bonds. Illinois, which had favored a loan backed by the value of the lands to be sold and future toll revenues, or revenue bonds as they are now commonly called, finally caved in to the bankers in 1836 and construction began on July 4 of that year.[18]

However, the canal still proved to be undercapitalized; estimated construction costs had escalated from $4.1 million a few years earlier to $8.6 million. The panic of 1837, which brought Chicago's first boom to a halt, nearly bankrupted Illinois as a result of its overly ambitious public works program adopted in 1837 to provide a $4 million state loan to the canal as well as build railroads to connect most towns in the state. Continued deterioration of the state's financial situation caused construction of the canal to be halted in 1841, forcing Illinois back to eastern capital markets for another loan to bail out the project. The bankers agreed to refinance with an additional $1.6 million a somewhat scaled-back canal on which $4.6 million had already been spent on the condition that the bonds be secured by a deed of trust and that the canal be completed, owned, and operated by three trustees, two of whom were to be selected by the bondholders.[19]

To cut costs, Illinois agreed to abandon its original plan to dig a deep, 14-foot channel to enable it to be naturally fed by water from Lake Michigan. The "summit" of a midcontinental divide between Chicago and Lockport was 8 feet above the water level of the lake, so any canal that was to use lake water would have to be cut deeper than that through solid limestone for about 34 miles from the Chicago River to Romeoville in modern Will County, at which point the Des Plaines River is at the same elevation (580 feet above sea level) as the lake.[20]

The cheaper alternative ultimately adopted was to climb over the summit by means of locks so that the cut for the channel would need to be only 6 feet, not the 14 feet originally proposed. Two steam pumps were installed to get the water from the Chicago River to the higher canal. Water for the canal west of the summit section was supplied by the Des Plaines River, although a shortage of water impeded traffic in 1848, 1852, and 1856.[21]

The new bonds were ultimately sold in Europe, and work on the canal resumed in 1845. The investment proved to be successful: the Illinois and Michigan Canal posted annual profits from its opening in 1848 until the $4.6 million in bonds were paid off and the trust terminated in 1871. In fact, the canal continued to report profits on its operations until 1879, by which time competition from the railroads had eroded much of its business.[22]

## The Illinois and Michigan Canal

The 97-mile canal was certainly no engineering marvel, especially when compared to the Chesapeake and Ohio and Main Line canals in America and any number of waterways in Europe. Between its terminals in Chicago and La Salle there were only seventeen locks, each 20 feet wide and 100 feet long; four aqueducts; and assorted bridges, dams, canal basins, and towpaths. It was only 60 feet wide at the water line and 6 feet deep, barely deep enough during droughts for a vessel with a 4-foot draft, but artificial basins to serve as harbors were dug at four towns along the route, including Joliet and Lockport. West of Joliet the elevation gradually descended 101 feet in 58 miles to the head of navigation at the Illinois River near La Salle, where there was a drop of 40 feet in only 4 miles that required the construction of four locks.[23]

A 120- to 200-foot-wide turning basin at Morris, Illinois, was the site of an archaeological excavation by the Illinois Department of Natural Resources in 1996 after a dam collapse caused the canal to run dry and expose the skeletons of seven canal boats that had been abandoned there. Apparently the boats had been left to rot and eventually sank. By the time of the excavation, the canal had been converted into a

Swing bridges were used to span rivers and canals in the nineteenth century until the development of bascule bridges. This ca. 1900 swing bridge over the Sanitary and Ship Canal at Romeoville was saved and moved to a nearby nature trail in Will County.

state park and partially restored.[24]

The earliest canal boats were patterned after river keelboats with rounded bow and stern and relatively narrow hulls, but no keel. Their constricting factor was the dimensions of the locks—18 feet wide and 110 feet long, effectively restricting canal boats to a maximum length of slightly more than 100 feet. Passenger boats, or packets, were little more than floating dormitories in which everyone traveled steerage. They were built with large cabins and narrow shelves for bunks, although some had berths that could be folded away during the day. Canal boats had bunks for as many as thirty passengers and also sold deck space. Cargo in bags or crates was stacked in every available space on the deck and cabin roof if bridge clearances permitted it.[25]

Freight boats were even more spartan. Those dedicated to grain service typically had a small house to protect the crew from the elements, but most of the deck was flat and pierced with occasional hatches for access to the cargo hold. The boats carrying stone had open holds, and those intended for trips on the open water of the lakes were equipped with watertight hatches and decks as well as high, upswept sterns. The vessels excavated at Morris all had flat bottoms and lacked keels.[26]

The boats originally were not powered. The I & M Canal was designed with towpaths for mules and horses, although its fleet was converted to mechanical power just after the Civil War, making it the first American canal to extensively use steam power. *General Thornton*, the first boat to make the trip from La Salle to Chicago after the canal opened in April, 1848, took four days to do so. Its cargo was then transferred to the steamer *Louisiana*, which reached Buffalo and the Erie Canal seven days later. Canals were not a particularly fast method of travel even by nineteenth-century standards, although they were considerably more comfortable than stage-coaches, especially in bad weather. Typically, the canal trip between La Salle and Chicago took more than a day, although the *Queen of the Prairies* made the journey in as few as twenty hours.

Although most of the canal boats were locally built and manned, often by families, a few were towed to Chicago from the Erie Canal. Occasionally a traveler would work as a crewman in return for his passage. Although life on the boats could be tedious, for there was no threat from the storms that threatened crews and ships on the Great Lakes and brigands were rare,

This restored I & M aqueduct over a creek in Morris, Illinois, was built largely of stone.

**Above:** Canal builders used aqueducts to span rivers. This one, built on the I & M Canal at Ottawa, Illinois, spans the Fox River and is now used by hikers. (Michael Brown)

**Left:** Many early canal aqueducts were built of wood or stone. This later replacement of a span over the Fox River in Ottawa was made of steel. (Michael Brown)

The Lockport lock on the
I & M was one of the deep-
est to enable canal boats to
begin to descend from the
canal's summit to the Illinois River junction at La
Salle. (Michael Brown)

occasionally a trip had some excitement. Elisha Sly, who had his canal boat, the *G. B. Danles,* towed from Buffalo to Chicago to work on the I & M, wrote his wife about the adventures on his first trip on it:

> I landed at Chicago on the 4th day of May in 1848, there wasn't much doing on the Illinois and Michigan Canal. I took some salt on for LaSalle and then went alongside a steamer off of the river and loaded with Mexican soldiers. Took on 255 for Chicago most of them were down with yellow fever. That was in the spring that the Mexican war broke up.
>
> I made four different graves from LaSale to Chicago. When I had seven or eight of them dead I would run to the bank and dig a hole and put them in.[27]

Although the I & M was able to over-come its own water supply problems, it remained vulnerable to fluctuating water levels on the Illinois River that made navi-

gation almost impossible for months at a time. The drought of 1856 resulted in the formation of the Illinois River Improve-ment Company to maintain a channel by means of locks and wing dams, but those proved ineffective. Attempts to obtain fed-eral funding to improve the Illinois failed, even during the Civil War when the Mis-sissippi River was closed to civil naviga-tion, and in 1867 Illinois was finally forced to act on its own and build locks at Henry and Copperas Creek. When that proved in-sufficient, the federal government in 1880 agreed to build two more locks and dams: LaGrange, which opened in 1889, and Kampsville, which followed in 1893.[28]

By then it was too late. The railroads had become the dominant carriers of pas-sengers and freight in America. Canals were unable to compete with anything but the heaviest of the bulk commodities—sand, coal, and stone. In fact, one of their principal roles by the late nineteenth cen-tury had devolved into providing rate competition for the railroads. Canals simply were too expensive to upgrade or replace to compete with the railroads. The 369-mile Erie Canal cost $7,143,789 to build between 1817 and 1825, the 97-mile Illinois and Michigan Canal two decades later cost almost as much—$6,468,854.

Competition from railroads and the of lack of government support proved fatal to a private venture to make the Kankakee River navigable from the I & M Canal south and east for 40 miles through Kankakee to Momence. The river, which was part of the portage bypass around Chicago during the French colonial period, joined with the Des Plaines River to form the Illinois River near Channahon and was a water feeder to the I & M. In 1847 the state chartered the Kankakee and Iroquois Navigation and Manufacturing Company to build five locks, three dams, and a section of canal to connect Kankakee with the I & M Canal.

The completed project did not live up to the financial expectations of its proponents, primarily because of competition from the railroads, and had its fate sealed in 1882 when its aqueduct over the Des Plaines River to the I & M Canal collapsed. The Kankakee Company, as it was by then

known, didn't have the financial resources to rebuild the aqueduct, and the corps of engineers rejected the Kankakee as a navigable waterway, preventing any federal money from being spent on its rebuilding.[29]

Locks and periods of low water due to drought, especially, were the restrictive factors that limited boat size on the I & M and Illinois River long after more powerful railroad locomotives, coupling systems, and air brakes made possible longer and heavier trains. Low water forced boat operators to lighten their loads to reduce drafts to avoid grounding. Locks proved to be a nemesis to canal boat steam engines, which tended to overheat during the lengthy idling necessary because of the slow locking process. The deepening of the canal between Chicago and Lockport later in the nineteenth century and addition of larger locks at the Chicago River enabled larger canal boats to negotiate that section of the canal, but no farther west. However, as water levels on the western section of the canal declined in the twentieth century because of deferred maintenance, individual boat loads rarely exceeded 100 tons.[30]

The largest I & M boats had a capacity of as much as 150 tons, which could be

A few original locks on the I & M remain. This one is at Lockport. (Michael Brown)

Propeller canal steamer *Niagara* passing through an I & M Canal lock at Lockport ca. 1896. ( Lewis University, Canal and Regional History Collection)

extended to 400 to 450 tons after the conversion to steam by using a steam-powered boat to tow two unpowered boats. Steam power also permitted canal boats to maneuver tows onto Lake Michigan to enable shippers to avoid high railroad switching charges in Chicago. The lake boats were built with high sterns to avoid swamping by waves in following seas.[31]

The I & M was unusual among American canals because it had a dual role as an open sewer and commercial canal. Chicago's principal motive in the 1867–1871 deepening of the eastern section of the I & M was to divert sewage from the badly polluted south branch of the river and the lake. The south branch not only carried the offal and excrement from the Union Stock Yards built in 1865 but coal tar from a town gas plant used to manufacture lighting gas in the decades before electricity became commercially available. The coal tar coated the surface of the river and ships' paddle wheels. The stockyard emptied into the south fork of the river's south branch and became known as Bubbly Creek because of the gas bubbles rising from decomposition.[32]

The pollution problem was so serious following the Civil War that the city agreed to spend $3.3 million in municipal funds to deepen the canal and was given a lien on tolls for repayment, although in 1871 the Illinois General Assembly abated the

lien. The idea was to lower the canal to lake level—approximating what had originally been proposed in the 1830s—but this time to flush the sludge, excrement, offal, and pollution downstream.

Unfortunately, the fix didn't work. By 1881 the canal had become so polluted that the stench was intolerable. Continual complaints by downstream cities like Joliet as well as an 11 1/2-inch rain in August 1885, which caused the Des Plaines River to overflow the watershed divide, back up the Chicago River, and dump pollution into Lake Michigan finally brought the issue to a climax and led to the digging a few years later of the Sanitary and Ship Canal.[33]

The I & M was perhaps most successful as an investment in the development of the wilderness of northern Illinois. The population in the area north and east of Peoria increased fivefold from 21,821 just before the start of construction to 125,708 in 1850, two years after the canal opened. Agricultural products from the Illinois River valley, formerly an economic satrapy of Saint Louis, began to move east on the canal, and manufactured products and lumber moved west. Saint Louis trade declined by 316,625 bushels of corn and 237,000 bushels of wheat in the first year of operation of the I & M Canal, and the diversion increased in 1849.[34]

The I & M Canal also was a major factor in a change of the transportation patterns in the Midwest at midcentury. The trade axis began to shift away from New Orleans and toward New York, giving Chicago its first major boost toward becoming the dominant city of the North American interior over its riverine rivals. The maritime historian K. Jack Bauer called the I & M the most successful of the western canals: "Although the waterway nearly bankrupted the state of Illinois . . . it helped Chicago replace New Orleans as the forwarding point for goods from the East bound for Saint Louis. In 1857 it helped western farmers to ship 20 million bushels of wheat and corn through the Windy City."[35]

# *Chapter Four* Chicago's Rivals

• The earliest American cities of the interior—Pittsburgh and Lexington, for example—were located along roads or trails that led through the gaps in the mountains. Pittsburgh also had the good fortune of being at the head of the Ohio River, because as settlement spread into the wilderness, it did so primarily along the waterways. Louisville; Rock Island, Illinois; and Lafayette, Indiana, sprang up at the heads of navigation of rivers. Green Bay, Cleveland, Chicago, and Toledo appeared at the mouths of rivers emptying into the Great Lakes, and Cairo, Illinois, and St. Louis were at or near river forks. Even fords on smaller rivers, places where wagons or stagecoaches could cross, led to the development of such Illinois towns as Rockford, Dixon, and Elgin.

Before steam engines became ubiquitous, the towns also needed water power to run their mills, as well as flush their sewage. The high-pressure steam engine, when it finally appeared in the interior, freed commerce from the tyranny of the river currents and made it possible to get a crop to export in a matter of weeks instead of months. It also enabled some of the better-situated river towns to develop into cities: Pittsburgh became an industrial city and Cincinnati was a pork-packing center when Chicago was still a fur-trading post waiting for New York to finish the Erie Canal and open the Great Lakes to commerce.

It wasn't until the railroads came upon the scene in the middle of the nineteenth century to provide all-weather, overland

The side-wheeled excursion steamer *Ivanhoe* gave tourist rides along Chicago's lakefront. Note the apparatus just behind the smokestack to transfer power from the steam engine to the paddle wheels and the unidentified schooner under sail in the background. (David R. Phillips Collection)

shortcuts that the importance of the rivers began to decline, but by then the pattern of development was set. So were the economic rivalries between cities in the interior that became as parochial and cutthroat as anything on the Atlantic coast.

The first cities of the interior tended to be migratory gateways, and as the frontier moved west the gateways moved with it. Thus Pittsburgh and Lexington were successively succeeded by Cincinnati, Louisville, and St. Louis on the western rivers, and Buffalo was supplanted by Detroit and Chicago on the Great Lakes.

As the frontier moved on, the gateways became regional centers. Some remained important because they were at major transportation crossroads or convenient transfer points for commerce, and others increased their relative importance because they were able to extend their natural waterways by means of dams, channels, canals, railroads, and highways. Thus the highly competitive nature of American society in today's global economy was well established in the form of municipal rivalries between cities on the seacoast and their wilderness gateways shortly after the ink dried on the Constitution.

## Pittsburgh

The Ohio and Mississippi Rivers were the first water migratory routes, and as their valleys became settled they formed part of a great transportation circle that led to New Orleans, then north by ocean to the eastern ports, and overland back to Pittsburgh. The harvest traveled by flatboat to New Orleans and then by ship to New York, Baltimore, or Philadelphia. Because of the difficulty of traveling upstream against the current, manufactured goods moved by wagon or packhorse overland to the Ohio River.[1]

After 1763 the Lower Mississippi River shifted from French to Spanish control, and the Great Lakes to British. So the Ohio River replaced the great canoe route through Canada as the principal trans-

portation artery to the interior from the East Coast, and it served as the path of migration and settlement in the late eighteenth and early nineteenth centuries as the flatboat supplanted the canoe. The river meandered for about 980 miles from the junction of the Allegheny and Monongahela Rivers at Pittsburgh to its confluence with the Mississippi at Cairo, Illinois and, because it fell only 460 feet over that distance, was navigable for much of the year at least by small steamboats. The major obstruction to river traffic except at the upper reaches was a limestone ridge that ran at an oblique angle through the river at Louisville, causing a 25-foot drop over a distance of 2 miles and creating rapids known as the Falls of the Ohio.[2]

Although the river was adequate for smaller boats, periods of low water hampered its use by larger steamboats until a lock and dam system was completed in 1929. The Portland Canal dug around the falls in 1830 provided some relief but proved inadequate after a few years because of the rapid increase in the size of steamboats. The depth and breadth of the Lower Mississippi south of Cairo permitted the use of larger and more powerful steamboats and towboats than were possible on the Upper Ohio, and its tributaries and often made it necessary for passengers and cargo to change boats in Louisville. The dams common on the upper rivers to control navigable depth were never required on the Lower Mississippi, although in periods of low water caused by drought navigation was somewhat restricted.[3]

The first two cities of the interior and rivals as gateways to the west were Pittsburgh, an economic satrapy of Philadelphia, and Lexington, Kentucky, Virginia's western gateway. The desire of Virginia speculators, who counted George Washington among their ranks, to begin exploiting the interior was one of the reasons the French built Fort Duquesne on the future site of Pittsburgh in 1754. The settlement of Pittsburgh occurred slowly for forty years after the British captured the fort from the

By 1866 the Chicago River was jammed with ships, including lumber-hooking schooners, steamships, and tugs, shown here at Franklin Street. Just north of the river in the background (near the current-day Merchandise Mart) is the Chicago & North Western Railway station and a fleet of open-vestibule passenger cars. (David R. Phillips Collection)

French in 1758. The 1790 census showed only 376 residents, and by 1800 the city still had a population of only 1,565.[4]

Lexington was settled in 1779—four years after Daniel Boone opened the Wilderness Road over Cumberland Gap—and by 1800 was the largest city in the west with 1,795 inhabitants. However, its relative remoteness from the Ohio River, a 2 1/2-day trip by road, was a drawback and caused it to fall behind Pittsburgh in importance early in the nineteenth century. The steamboat rendered Lexington a relative backwater, and the city's efforts to build a railroad line or canal to the Ohio came too late.

Wheeling, a Virginia city downstream on the Ohio, emerged as a rival of Pittsburgh in

The original Fort Dearborn, pictured in this drawing from A. T. Andreas's *History of Chicago,* sat near the mouth of the Chicago River. Its connection to the outside world was by sailing ship, canoe, and Indian trail. The site is now nearly a mile inland on the south side of the river at Michigan Avenue. (Chicago Maritime Society)

1793, and after the completion of the federally financed National Road from Baltimore there in 1818 appeared for a time to be in a position to surpass its older rival. Wheeling's emergence and the threat posed by the National Road caused Pittsburgh's civic leaders as early as 1818 to press for a better transportation route linking it to Philadelphia. The result was Pennsylvania's Main Line Canal. Pittsburgh also sought to improve the Upper Ohio by removing obstructions in the river as far south as Wheeling.[5]

Pittsburgh's relative isolation from competition and its accessibility to iron and coal deposits enabled the city to become a manufacturing center very early in its existence. The city's first foundry opened in 1804, its first rolling mill in 1812, and from 1820 to 1870 Pittsburgh was the largest steamboat builder on the western rivers.

The city got an early lead in boat building when naval carpenters were sent there in the early 1800s in an unsuccessful attempt to build ocean-going ships that could be floated down the rivers to New Orleans.[6]

It was the development of the steamboat or, more particularly, the high-pressure steam engine, which enabled boats to be driven upstream against strong currents, that accelerated the development of the interior. Until then, a round trip by flatboat to New Orleans and back took several months. However, the steamboat in the first few decades of the nineteenth century made Pittsburgh far more accessible to New Orleans, 1,900 miles to the southwest, than it was to Philadelphia, less than 300 miles to the east by foot or wagon.

But as the frontier drifted southwest down the Ohio River valley, the steamboat also made newer rivals, in particular,

Cincinnati and Louisville, which were even more accessible to New Orleans. Pennsylvania's Main Line Canal offered Ohio River valley farmers an alternative outlet for their harvests but was never competitive enough with steamboats to enable Pittsburgh to develop enough of a back haul to make a dent in the trading zones of its newer rivals.

The opening of the Great Lakes to trade after 1825 also posed a threat to Pittsburgh. The state of Ohio built the Ohio and Erie Canal, completed from Cleveland to Portsmouth in 1832, as a bypass around Pittsburgh with the potential of diverting Ohio River valley traffic to New York via the Erie Canal. Pittsburgh was never able to make much of an impact in eastbound traffic from the Great Lakes basin even after it got a direct link by canal to the lake port of Erie, Pennsylvania, in 1844.[7]

## Cincinnati

Cincinnati, 500 miles downstream from Pittsburgh on the Ohio River, was settled in 1788 and by 1830, when Chicago was still a trading post, had grown to twenty-five thousand inhabitants and had eclipsed Pittsburgh as the dominant inland river city. Cincinnati, unlike Pittsburgh before it and Saint Louis later, never developed as much of a frontier gateway but early in its existence had become a flourishing frontier trade center for a growing regional market.

Cincinnati's political leaders, more so than those of any other river city, realized their city's limitations as a transportation center relative to their rivals and acted aggressively to correct them. At various times, to extend Cincinnati's trading area, they proposed digging a canal around the falls of the Ohio on the Indiana side of the river to allow larger steamboats upstream, building a bridge over the Ohio, digging a canal to central Kentucky, building railroads to Lexington and Charleston, South Carolina, and digging a canal the entire length of the state to the Great Lakes at Toledo.[8]

The failure of most of those projects to get off the ground was to a large extent the result of the intensive economic rivalries between states of the interior, none of which wanted to give a competitor any advantage. Only one of Cincinnati's waterway projects, the ambitious proposal to link the Ohio River with the Great Lakes at Toledo, was completed, and it was only partially successful. Construction began on the Miami and Erie Canal in 1825, but only 50 miles to Dayton had been completed by 1834. The panic of 1837 and a border dispute with neighboring Michigan continued to delay its completion until 1845. The southern section of the canal between Dayton and Cincinnati had some success as an Ohio River feeder, but the northern section never lived up to its proponents' optimistic projections.[9]

Cincinnati was probably the only Midwestern city that considered the Atlantic Ocean ports in the Deep South as an alternative to its two main transportation corridors down the Mississippi River to New Orleans and by canal to New York and Philadelphia. In 1835 the citizens of Cincinnati held a mass meeting and approved a resolution supporting a proposal to build a railroad to Charleston, South Carolina. The state of South Carolina favored the proposal as a way to enter the Midwestern market, and Tennessee considered it a way to end the isolation of the mountainous eastern part of the state. However, Kentucky would agree only if a branch was opened to Louisville. Continued bickering by the states doomed the line and only 8 miles were ever built.[10]

Cincinnati's proposal to bypass the falls of the Ohio fared no better. The proposal to build a canal around the rapids on the Indiana bank across from Louisville induced Kentucky for competitive reasons to charter the Louisville and Portland Company to build a canal on its side of the river—the first major project to improve the navigability of the Ohio River system.

Louisville had been founded in 1778 by George Rogers Clark as a base for use against the British in Illinois and Indiana during the Revolutionary War and, alone among the river cities, had a natural harbor to protect boats. Ice jams were more of a threat to river shipping than storms. By 1830 Louisville had become a rival to Pittsburgh and Cincinnati, and Kentucky leaders saw the Portland Canal as a way to improve Louisville's competitive position. The 2-mile canal was completed in 1830 at a cost of $700,000 but did not help the city as much as its promoters had hoped. Louisville's position as a transshipment point where cargoes were transferred between the big steamboats capable of using the Lower Mississippi and the smaller ones that could navigate the Upper Ohio declined after the financial panic of 1837, and the city was never again a threat to Cincinnati or emerging Saint Louis, still farther west.

Cincinnati, possibly more than any other city of the interior, aggressively pursued the new railroad technology emerging in the 1830s in an effort to overcome some of the limitations that slavery to the Ohio River imposed. The city provided a loan of $200,000 to the Little Miami Railroad, chartered in 1836 and completed in 1846, to provide a rail connection to Lake Erie at Sandusky and to get rail connections to Columbus and Pittsburgh. In 1846 a railroad was incorporated to run between Cincinnati and Dayton parallel to the canal and eventually to connect with the Erie Railroad to New York. That was followed in 1851 by construction of a line east to Marietta, Ohio, and Parkersburg, Virginia, to connect with the Baltimore and Ohio, and later the same year a line was started west to Saint Louis with the help of a $600,000 municipal loan from Cincinnati and $500,000 in stock subscribed there.[11]

The irony was that despite its aggressive rail-building policy, Cincinnati's dominant rail connection before the end of the nineteenth century had become Chicago, a city 300 miles to the northwest. Chicago passed Cincinnati in shipping after the Illi-

nois and Michigan Canal opened in 1848, in railroads by 1852, and in pork packing by 1862. Adding to Cincinnati's woes was that it had been eclipsed as the principal inland river city by Saint Louis.[12]

## Saint Louis

The old French town of Saint Louis had developed as a fur trading center and economic satrapy of New Orleans more than 1,100 miles downstream on the Mississippi River. By the mid-nineteenth century Saint Louis had blossomed into the dominant city of the American interior with a population of 77,000, the gateway to the trans-Mississippi West, and a major commercial, transportation, and manufacturing center. The struggle between Saint Louis and Chicago for economic domination of the American interior occupied much of the second half of the nineteenth century.[13]

The struggle, perhaps more than any of the other municipal rivalries, reflected the changing technology, economics, and culture of the increasingly sectionalizing American interior at that time. Saint Louis belonged to the steamboat era of Mark Twain; Chicago to the railroad era of Casey Jones. Both cities strove to be the gateway to the West, but Saint Louis was dominated by the agricultural economy that moved north and south on the river. Chicago became the factory that processed the agricultural bounty of the Midwest and the point at which the harvests of the West and industrial goods of the East were exchanged. Missouri had strong ties to the agrarian, oligarchical South and its port of New Orleans. Illinois was aligned with the industrial, republican North and its emerging financial capital in New York.

Saint Louis was founded almost four decades earlier than Chicago when Pierre LaClede Liguest in 1764 established a fur trading post on the site. The Louisiana Territory was ceded to Spain by France two years later, and the Spanish imposed their mercantile system, which made the outpost dependent upon the royal colony at

**Table 4.1** Population of Midwest Cities, 1830–1890

| City | 1830 | 1850 | 1870 | 1890 |
|------|------|------|------|------|
| Cincinnati | 24,831 | 46,601 | 216,239 | 296,908 |
| Pittsburgh | 12,450 | 115,435 | 186,076 | 238,617 |
| Louisville | 10,341 | 43,194 | 100,753 | 161,129 |
| Saint Louis | 4,977 | 77,860 | 310,864 | 451,770 |
| Detroit | 2,222 | 21,019 | 79,577 | 205,876 |
| Cleveland | 1,076 | 17,034 | 92,829 | 261,353 |
| Chicago | * | 29,963 | 298,977 | 1,099,850 |

* Later estimated to be 40–50.

*Source:* U.S. Census Bureau.

New Orleans. Poor rule by the Americans after George Rogers Clark captured the east side of the Mississippi during the Revolution caused Saint Louis to prosper and establish economic domination over an area that included southern Illinois.

France reacquired the Louisiana colony in 1800, and by 1803, when Napolean sold the territory to the United States, the Saint Louis area was a flourishing frontier settlement of 2,500 residents and predicted by some to become the seat of a vast inland empire. As late as 1870, some local boosters in Saint Louis were suggesting the nation's capital be transferred there. By way of contrast, Chicago consisted at the beginning of 1803 of a single log cabin.[14]

Growth during the first quarter of the nineteenth century was modest, reflecting the fact that Saint Louis was beyond the settled frontier, but accelerated after 1830 (table 4.1) when agriculture began to supplant the fur trade as the principal industry, indicating that the frontier was passing westward, and the stage was being set for commercial and industrial development. The population tripled in each of the two succeeding decades, and on the eve of the Civil War, Saint Louis, with a population of 160,733, was the seventh-largest city in the nation and threatening to eclipse both its patron, New Orleans, and Cincinnati. Missouri by that time was

the most populous slave state in the nation (table 4.1).[15]

The first steamboat had arrived in Saint Louis in 1817, and by the 1830s river trade was flourishing. There was still some traffic in furs, but agricultural products, iron, and lead (being mined on the river to the north in Galena, Illinois) had grown in importance. The city was a thriving entrepôt where goods arriving on small steamboats plying the Upper Mississippi, Missouri, and Illinois Rivers transferred their cargoes to larger steamboats suited for the Lower Mississippi.[16]

By 1844, Saint Louis had passed Cincinnati in steamboat traffic, and by 1855 it had eclipsed even New Orleans. Steamboat landings reported in 1844 included 2,570 in New Orleans, 2,105 in Saint Louis, and 1,922 in Cincinnati. In 1857, the landings included 3,443 in Saint Louis, 2,745 in New Orleans, and 2,703 in Cincinnati. The lists of annual steamboat arrivals in Saint Louis for the period 1849 through 1852 indicates the extent of the city's trade: from the Lower Mississippi the average for the period was 311; from the Upper Mississippi, 696; from the Missouri, 341; from the Illinois, 741; from the Ohio, 469; and from other ports, 344. The annual average total for the period was 3,100.[17]

Competition began appearing in the 1830s in the form of ships visiting the

Great Lakes port of Chicago, but did not become a serious threat to Saint Louis until after 1848, the year both the I & M Canal and the Galena & Chicago Union Railroad began service west from Chicago. They extended Chicago's trading zone more than 100 miles inland—in the case of the railroad all the way to the Mississippi River— to territory that had once been almost exclusively served by Saint Louis. In effect, the canal and railroad were built as extensions of the Great Lakes, extending all the way to the Mississippi the reach of its schooners and steamships, and providing farmers in the Upper Mississippi River Valley with a shorter and faster route to markets in the East. The river cities continued to dominate the commerce in their valleys but began to lose the new markets in outlying areas to the Great Lakes.[18]

The I & M Canal ended Saint Louis's monopoly on trade to and from central Illinois. The implication was that Saint Louis's leaders, lulled by the prosperity of their steamboat trade, were slow to awaken to the threat from the north. Although that may be a factor in Saint Louis's being supplanted as the dominant transportation center and city of the Midwest, the city's fathers were not completely asleep. The problem was that their only option to compete with Chicago for traffic to the East was to build railroads, but rival Illinois blocked the routes east. Only Illinois could charter railroads within its borders or allow railroad bridges from its banks, and it preferred routes that favored Alton, Illinois, over Saint Louis.[19]

Diversions to the Great Lakes route from central Illinois were significant but not as great as Saint Louis merchants had feared. Steamboat arrivals in Saint Louis from the Illinois River, which had increased annually from 298 in 1845 to 690 in 1848, remained about the same (686) in 1849, the first full year of operation of the Illinois and Michigan Canal. They increased to a record 788 in 1850, dropped to 634 in 1851, then set a new record (858) in 1852. However, by 1866 a decline of Illinois traffic was evident: Saint Louis averaged only 370 steamboats a year arriving from the Illinois River in the postwar years, and by the early 1890s the annual average was only 147 steamboats.[20]

As early as 1835, delegates from eleven Missouri counties met in Saint Louis to discuss the construction of railroads and recommended that two be built to link Saint Louis to the interior of the state.

By 1849, Chicago was a boomtown and its once placid river was choked with traffic during a time when the city's skyline signature was a forest of schooner masts. The Chicago lighthouse in this drawing from *History of Chicago* can be seen just to the right of the river, and the lake in the distance beyond it. (Chicago Maritime Society)

One, which much later evolved into the Missouri Pacific, was proposed to Fayette in the central part of the state, and the other was planned to connect Saint Louis with Iron Mountain, an important mining area to the south. The state legislature in its next session optimistically chartered no less than eleven turnpike companies and eighteen railroads, but was unable to provide any funding because of the financial panic at the time. Across the Mississippi at about the same time Illinois was launching its ill-fated, publicly funded internal improvements transportation program, which produced the Illinois and Michigan Canal and one railroad but nearly bankrupted the state in the process.

Attempts by Missouri to tap the federal treasury were thwarted by Illinois politicians, principally U.S. Senator Stephen A. Douglas. He not only adapted the theory of using federal land grants for transportation, which originated with the National

Road in 1811 and was expanded to the Illinois and Michigan Canal in 1827, to the building of railroads in his state, but effectively resisted early attempts by Saint Louis to become the eastern terminus of the proposed transcontinental railroad. With several railroads already under construction or proposed to and from Chicago, including the Chicago and Alton nearly to Saint Louis's doorstep, Missouri in 1851 was finally forced to dip into the public treasury to get its rail system started.[21]

Neither line turned out to be what their proponents envisioned, however. Hannibal and Saint Joseph, which for political reasons bypassed Saint Louis across the northern tier of the state, was quickly gobbled up by the Chicago, Burlington & Quincy Railroad, which promptly diverted its traffic through the Chicago gateway. The underfunded Pacific Railroad, begun in 1851, was plagued by poor construction, the collapse of the Gasconade Bridge in 1855, the

Grain elevators that permitted the bulk loading of grain into ships revolutionized lake commerce at the expense of the river steamboats, which carried grain in sacks that had to be carried onto the vessels by gangs of stevedores. Note in this drawing from *History of Chicago* that the grain fell down a chute into special boxes with handles, which were then dumped into the hold of the schooner *Osceola* bound for the Erie Canal at Buffalo. (Chicago Maritime Society)

There was no aerial photography in 1871, but that did not stop magazine illustrators like *Harper's Weekly*'s Theodore R. Davis from drawing "bird's-eye" views of the city and the assorted schooners, sloops, packets, and tugs that plied the rivers and lakes. (Historic Urban Plans, Ithaca, N.Y.)

failure of the bond market in 1857, financial scandals, a construction stoppage during the Civil War, and sabotage by Confederate sappers, which delayed its completion to Kansas City until 1865. By that time Chicago was already the nation's undisputed railroad capital with lines stretching across the Mississippi River into Iowa, Minnesota, and Missouri.[22]

Iowa and even the New Orleans route became the battlegrounds between the two cities. Saint Louis had the river route south, so Illinois built a parallel railroad.

Early settlements in Iowa along the Mississippi River were dependent upon the steamboats from Saint Louis, but the Chicago and Rock Island reached the river in 1854, quickly followed by several other Chicago lines. When the railroads bridged the river and dashed across the developing state in the 1850s, Iowa and even Omaha, Nebraska, fell into Chicago's economic sphere, and the city succeeded Saint Louis as the entrepôt for much of the trans-Mississippi West trade, although Saint Louis remained the principal gateway to that region. In the waning decades of the century the most precipitous drop in Saint Louis–bound steamboat traffic occurred from the Missouri River, the most difficult of the Mississippi tributaries to navigate as well as the one most vulnerable to interdiction by Chicago railroads.[23]

The steady southward extensions of the Illinois Central Railroad threatened Saint Louis's vital steamboat route to New Orleans. The railroad in the 1850s employed in various capacities a virtual who's who of the time—Abraham Lincoln as a lawyer; future Civil War generals George B. McClellan (as an engineer), Ambrose E. Burnsides (as treasurer), and Nathaniel P. Banks; the detective Allan Pinkerton; and Mark Twain as a steamboat pilot.

By early 1855, the Illinois Central was running trains between Chicago and Cairo, Illinois, and was negotiating with steamboat operators to provide connecting service to New Orleans. When the deal fell through, McClellan set up the railroad's own steamboat packet line, which provided service not only from its Cairo terminal but Saint Louis and Alton as well. Then the railroad began offering connecting sleeping-car service to Chicago.

Although the Civil War interrupted the packet business, the railroad in 1869 built a bridge over the Ohio at Cairo and by 1873 was offering through trains between Chicago and New Orleans. Despite the competition, steamboat arrivals in Saint Louis from the Lower Mississippi remained relatively high—averaging more than eight hundred annually—for most of the rest of the century.[24]

Unable to build its own line across Illinois to the East, Saint Louis businessmen made a substantial financial investment in the Ohio and Mississippi being built west from Cincinnati. It reached Illinoistown

(East Saint Louis) on the east side of the river in 1857, but because of inadequate finances and political rivalry between Illinois and Missouri a railroad bridge spanning the river wasn't completed until 1874.

The Civil War and its disruption of Mississippi River traffic was the most serious single blow to Saint Louis. Although the steamboat had begun losing markets to the railroads for a few years before the war, the Confederacy blocked the Mississippi in 1861, causing Saint Louis to lose its access to New Orleans. Even after the United States reopened the river in 1863, most of the steamboat fleet was used to haul wartime traffic, and considerable quantities of nonmilitary traffic were diverted to the railroads.[25]

Saint Louis's relative industrial growth slowed after the Civil War: it lost market share to Chicago in meatpacking, milling, and wholesaling, and its river traffic went into a long decline that lasted eighty years. Despite the effects of the war, Saint Louis's population of 310,000 in 1870 was still larger than that of Chicago, at 298,000, but Chicago was growing at a faster rate. Chicago passed Saint Louis in population in 1880 as its proliferating railroads fed traffic to and from the Great Lakes.

The rapidly industrializing city in the southwestern corner of Lake Michigan had become in the 1870s not only the nation's railroad capital but one of the busiest ports on earth. It was already the nation's meatpacker and stacker of wheat and by virtue of its location on the Lakes was on its way to becoming a steel manufacturing center. The 1890 federal census gave the final verdict on Chicago's rivalry not only with Saint Louis but the other river cities: with more than a million residents it was double its nearest rival in size.

# *Chapter Five* From Portage to Port

Cross-lake packets, like the Goodrich Transit Company's *Oconto* shown in ca. 1872, had large gangways in the side of the hull for loading the cargo stacked on the dock. (Wisconsin Maritime Museum)

•  Chicago, which the French thought had limitations as a canoe portage, was not a particularly good port for ships either, even by Great Lakes standards. There were few natural anchorages on the lakes, so most of the ports developed at the mouths of rivers, which made navigation vulnerable to the constant forming and shifting of bars. Ice that closed the lakes for at least three months each winter and storms that raked them in the prime autumn shipping season were the hazards that made maritime commerce an adventure. Chicago suffered from all those problems and others attributable to its rapid growth: a severe case of pollution and congestion caused by

the conflicting demands of waterborne and terrestrial commerce to use or cross the rivers—the battle of the bridges.[1]

Despite its drawbacks and isolation from the ocean, the sluggish, meandering stream called the Chicago River was within seven decades of the first recorded visit of a ship one of the busiest ports on earth. Local boosters claimed it was the busiest in terms of ship movements, though not necessarily tonnage. In the 1870s it was the scene of incredible maritime congestion as scores of ships jammed docks on both sides of the river for miles and a fleet of tugs dragged ships, barges, and canal boats to and from berths and around bridge pilings.

It was not long before Chicago was forced to build a second port at the Calumet River on the South Side, and within a few years it rivaled the downtown port in traffic. After the disastrous 1871 fire downtown Chicago had become too expensive a place for heavy industry such as steel mills, so much of it moved to the south side where plentiful and cheap land was available on the banks of the city's other river. A third port also developed deep inland scattered along the banks of the Illinois and Michigan Canal, giving names to such neighborhoods and suburbs as Bridgeport and Lockport.

The battle with nature to keep Chicago a port lasted the entire nineteenth century. Dredging channels through the bars and building breakwaters to create artificial harbors were a constant preoccupation of federal, state, and local governments to keep maritime commerce flowing. Shipwrights, for their part, designed vessels with flat bottoms, shallow drafts, and centerboards that could be raised to clear the bars. Until those innovations appeared, ships were simply unloaded and loaded out in the lake. The first sailing ship to visit the Chicago settlement, the 90-ton government schooner *Tracy,* on its arrival in 1803 bringing supplies to build Fort Dearborn, anchored about half a mile from the beach and sent the cargo ashore in boats. In 1833, some yachtsmen from Oswego, New York, hired a team of oxen to drag their boat, the *Westward Ho,* over the bar and into the Chicago River.[2]

## The Nature of the Lake

Lake Michigan was not an ideal body of water for maritime commerce in the nineteenth century. The lake runs for more than 300 miles in a north-south direction in a climate in which the prevailing weather is west to east. The fact that the lake was (and is) only 118 miles across at its widest point meant that schooner and steamboat captains did not have room to run with a storm by placing their bow or stern into the teeth of the gale. The standard navigational tactic in extreme weather was to hug the leeward (the shore from which the wind is blowing) side of the lake or find a port, although ships heading toward Chicago from Mackinac often would hug the windward side of the lake, using a string of islands as protection, then make a dash across the lake for Chicago or Milwaukee and hope for the best. On the positive side, the winds on Lake Michigan kept it relatively free of fog.[3]

Fort Dearborn was just being rebuilt after the War of 1812 when a couple of shipwrecks demonstrated that Lake Michigan could be as dangerous a place for ships as it was for canoes. The schooner *Hercules,* after picking up a load of passengers for the trip east in November, 1816, was caught in a storm somewhere off the mouth of the Calumet River and destroyed, with the loss of all on board. The following year the schooner *Heartless,* in an attempt to reach the Chicago River, ran aground, possibly on the bar that blocked the river's mouth, and was a total loss.[4]

With a maximum depth of 923 feet and relatively cool water temperatures year round, Lake Michigan has a reputation among mariners as being unforgiving, a legacy of its origins in the Pleistocene Ice Age. Hypothermia has claimed many a mariner or aviator who otherwise would have survived a sinking or crash landing.[5] The benefit of the cool temperatures and fresh water was that hulls tended to last considerably longer on the Great Lakes than in the salt water of the oceans; organisms that damaged wooden hulls of ocean ships were nonexistent in the lakes, and the corrosive effect of salt water on steel hulls was unknown.[6]

Tides, which average only about an inch on the Great Lakes and slightly more on Lake Michigan, are not a factor in navigation. Only rarely were seiches—the term for tsunami-like, sudden increases in shoreline water levels—disruptive to commercial navigation. Over the years seiches, which vary from a maximum recorded 8.4

Canals, rivers, and Great Lakes ports, despite their restricted waters, were able to support a boat-building industry that typically launched its vessels sideways, as in the case of this barge on the Hennepin Canal at Wyanet. (Illinois Department of Natural Resources)

feet on Lake Erie to 2.5 feet on Lake Huron, have proved to be more of an annoyance to small boats, fishermen, and bathers than commercial shipping.[7]

Perhaps the worst seiche recorded on the lakes was the one that hit Chicago on June 26, 1954, killing seven persons along the shore but causing no appreciable damage to shipping. It resulted from a squall line with 60-mile-an-hour winds that swept the lake from northwest to southeast, causing a 6-foot rise in the water level at Michigan City, Indiana. The wave then reflected off the Indiana shoreline and an hour and twenty minutes later hit Chicago with increases in water levels estimated at 10 feet at North Avenue and 8 feet at Montrose Harbor, a refuge for recreational craft.[8]

### The Ice Problem

The Wisconsin glacier was long gone by the time Europeans began to contemplate commerce on the lakes, but they were confronted with the seasonal buildup of ice that still severely restricts navigation about three months of each year. Only about a third of the 96,000-square-mile surface of the lakes would freeze even in the coldest winter, but the ice tended to concentrate in the bays and harbors, sealing off the more important Great Lakes ports. Floes drifted around in the currents and fast ice formed in the shallow water along the shore, sometimes compressed layer upon layer into formations 50 feet high.[9]

Stories abound on the lakes about ships being trapped, damaged, or sunk by ice, and insurers in the nineteenth century typically wrote annual policies that ended with the fall navigation season. That did not stop the local ship operators from braving the hazards for one last cargo even before effective icebreaking hulls were developed. In 1873, when the lake froze solid from shore to shore, the steamers *City of Freemont* and *Wisconsin* in mid-February were unable to make more than 14 miles off Grand Haven, Michigan, before being forced to turn back, and the *Ironsides* and *Messenger* were frozen solid off White Lake.[10]

Perhaps the most damaging single ice event on the Great Lakes, if not the most bizarre, occurred on March 12, 1849, when an ice jam on the south branch of the Chicago River broke loose and moved down the river, destroying almost everything in its path. The destruction and damage included every bridge, many wharves, and the bulk of the vessels in port—four steamboats, four propeller-powered ships, twenty-four brigs, twenty-seven canal boats, and two sloops.

Most of the mass of ice and wreckage was swept into the lake in a single debris field. The death toll was uncertain: two children were known to have been killed, as well as an undetermined number of men working on canal boats that sunk or were washed out into the lake. One man was seen several hours after the jam broke aboard a canal boat adrift 10 miles into the lake, waving a handkerchief as a distress signal, but there weren't any craft available to rescue him.[11]

## The First Ships

La Salle's *Griffon* notwithstanding, sailing ships were somewhat slow to appear on the Great Lakes, probably because there was no navigable access to the ocean and little commerce in the wilderness to sustain them. The opening of the Erie Canal in 1825 created the Great Lakes merchant marine, although there were a few vessels around before then. The U.S. Army was forced to operate its own navy in an effort to establish its presence in an area controlled by Great Britain until John Jay's treaty of 1796. The following year the army built the 150-ton brig *Adams* at River Rouge south of Detroit and soon thereafter built the small sloop *Tracy*. The armed brig for a time was probably the largest vessel on the lakes, and it was Fort Dearborn's principal link with the outside world until 1812, ferrying commercial cargo and passengers as well as military supplies and personnel to and from the outpost.[12]

There was little traffic on Lake Michigan for the first three decades of the nineteenth century, and the few ships that called there usually carried food and provisions to Fort Dearborn and the adjacent trading post and hauled away furs. Milo Quaife spent some time rummaging through the archives of the Detroit Public Library back during World War II and came up with the freight manifests for several vessels that show the nature of the trade at that time. The sloop *General Hunter* left Detroit for Chicago on May 8, 1805, carrying to the Kinzie and Forsythe Trading Post a barrel of gunpowder, 2 bars of iron, a box of tobacco, 19 bags of flour, and 12 containers of undisclosed contents. It returned to Detroit with 321 packs of furs. The sloop *Contractor* less than a month later hauled to Chicago 65 barrels of pork, 120 of flour, and 36 of whiskey, as well as 4 boxes of candles and 4 saddles, returning with 474 packs of furs. Quaife also found that the army's vessels did triple duty as warships, transports, and tramps, often hauling private cargo for a fee.[13]

In the 1820s the increase in volume of Great Lakes trade because of the opening of the Erie Canal made the business lucrative enough that entrepreneur Oliver Newberry moved to Detroit and got into the shipping business by building the 54-ton sloop *Pilot*. Within a few years, Newberry was operating the largest fleet on the upper lakes, including the 107-ton schooner *Napoleon* he had built in 1828. He put an agent at the Chicago trading post that same year, and in 1831, when the tide of settlers quickly outstripped the local food supply, his new agent, George W. Dole, set up a slaughterhouse. It was so productive that Dole was able to export 287 barrels of beef and 14 of tallow and 152 hides—a modest beginning for what was to become a gigantic agricultural enterprise centered on Chicago, causing historian William Cronon more than a century and a half later to dub the city "Nature's Metropolis."[14]

The city's first grain exports occurred in 1838, when Charles Walker shipped 78 bushels of wheat east, and in 1839 Dole sent 3,678 bushels of wheat on the *Osceola* to Buffalo. By then, the number of ships calling at Chicago, primarily supporting the westward population migration, exceeded four hundred each shipping season—double the number arriving in Chicago a few years earlier. The port had become congested as early as 1836, when thirty-two ships showed up in a fourteen-day span in August. With the Illinois and Michigan Canal under construction and expected to generate additional water traffic, it was obvious that something had to be done to improve Chicago's so-called port. The mouth of the Chicago River was habitually blocked by a bar that prevented larger ships from entering the river; even the smaller ships had to offload some cargo in the lake to reduce their drafts to clear the bar. The practice produced a fleet of small boats, called "lighters," sent out to unload ships anchored on the gravel bottom just outside the river's mouth.[15]

The shipwrights went to work on designs for vessels with a shallow enough draft to clear the river bars up and down the lakes but at the same time stable enough to sail in rough weather. The topsail schooner *Illinois,* for example, was designed in the early 1830s specifically for the immigrant trade to Chicago. With dimensions of 80-by-20-by-8 (the common nautical formula of length-beam-draft stated in feet), it was designed to fit through the new Welland Canal connecting Lakes Ontario and Erie and to be capable of being hauled over the Chicago River bar after unloading. Sometime later, sailing ships were equipped with a retractable centerboard that could be raised to enable them to enter shallow harbors. The centerboard was lowered in the lakes to give the ships stability in the wind.[16]

### The Battle of the Bar

Various schemes were considered to eliminate the bar in Chicago, but nothing was done until work had begun on the Illinois and Michigan Canal and engineers on that project offered some suggestions. The first improvement was a lighthouse built in 1831 with a $5,000 appropriation from Congress as part of an early federal program begun in 1820 to reduce the hazards of navigation on the Great Lakes. By 1833, the state's congressional delegation was able to include among federal appropriations $25,000 to open a channel in the Chicago River. Thus began the battle of the bar. The plan was to cut through the existing bar and build piers extending into the lake to bracket the shipping channel and prevent a new bar from forming. The south pier, extending somewhat less than 500 feet, was completed in 1833, and the 1,260-foot north pier, or "weather pier" as it was sometimes called, was finished in 1835. The improvements came none too soon, for by the end of that year more than 212 ships used the harbor.[17]

Within a few months a new bar began to form about a half mile into the lake, so the south pier was extended and the channel dredged. That solution lasted only until 1839, when the persistent bar reestablished itself, choked off the river, and Chicago again appealed to Congress for money. Washington provided $25,000 in 1843 and $30,000 in 1844 and enlisted the efforts of Captain George B. McClellan of the Army engineers to raise and strengthen the piers. He was no more successful at that than he was years later commanding the army of the Potomac in the Civil War, and Chicago appealed to Washington for more money. This time, President Polk, who held to the rather orthodox Democratic view that federal funds for local improvements were not permitted by the Constitution and was concerned over the costs of the Mexican War, vetoed the Rivers and Harbors Act, which contained Chicago's appropriation.[18]

Finally in 1859 the city was forced to act to repair the decaying piers, spending just enough on repairs in that year and successive years to keep them from collapsing while it unsuccessfully appealed to Washington annually for enough money to do the job properly. The Civil War precluded any federal subsidy, even with Abraham Lincoln in the White House. He

was an ardent supporter of waterway projects, including the Illinois and Michigan Canal, when he served in the Illinois General Assembly and of improvements to Chicago's port when he was a congressman. He had attended the Rivers and Harbors Convention in Chicago in 1847 after President Polk vetoed the 1946 harbor improvement appropriation bill.[19]

In 1864–1865 Chicago was forced to spend $75,000 of its own funds extending the north pier another 450 feet and again dredging the channel, this time to a depth of 14 feet. The bar began to reappear in 1866, however. That forced yet another extension of the pier 600 feet farther east after the federal government relented and appropriated $88,000, followed by an additional $35,000 in 1868 and $29,700 in 1869, to fight the battle of the bar.

By that time, Chicago's river harbor had become hopelessly congested. The number of ships using Chicago had increased by 25 percent during the Civil War, and by 1868 more than thirteen thousand ships called on the port. The city by then was the gathering point for the rich Midwest harvest each fall and a dispersal point for whatever manufactured goods flowed west from New York. Until the railroads took that business away, Chicago was also a transfer point for pioneers headed west, as well as for the lumber they needed to build their houses on the treeless Great Plains. Until the forests of Wisconsin and Michigan were exhausted, lumber constituted an intralake trade that helped make Chicago one of the busiest ports in the world, handling nearly a billion board feet of lumber in 1871.[20]

The river and its north and south branches were not only lined with docks, slaughterhouses, lumberyards, and grain elevators, but were prowled by purveyors

Swing bridges were an obstruction to both vehicular traffic and to vessels on the Chicago River. Note the tight squeeze for this Great Lakes packet, which is also equipped with a vestigial mast. The rounded structure visible on the deck is a structural brace used on wooden ships to prevent hogging, or the sagging of the hull. (David R. Phillips collection)

Goodrich Transit Company's
*Comet,* built in 1860, was
typical of the Great Lakes'
side-wheel packets of the
time. It had a main deck
with gangways for cargo, a
passenger deck above, and a
small pilothouse toward the
bow for greater visibility in
maneuvering in the re-
stricted waters of the lake
ports. The Chicago-based
Goodrich Transit Company
typically wintered its fleet in
Manitowoc, Wisconsin. (Wisconsin Maritime Museum)

of all sorts of vice appealing to sailors as well as by drummers hawking legitimate ship supplies. Chicago's saloons were notorious, as were its brothels and muggers, and there were places down along the river where a policeman dared not go alone. The port of iniquity was an exciting stop for young men from the farms seeking their fortune on canal barges and "lumber hookers," as timber schooners were known at the time, so much so that their older, and presumably wiser, vessel masters often came to Chicago armed with pistols.[21]

Although vice was a municipal problem, the federal government, city, and maritime industry all concluded that something had to be done to relieve the congestion on the water, but they were put off by the enormous costs involved in building a lakeside harbor. As early as 1868 the city proposed widening the main branch of the Chicago River to 250 feet and its two branches to 200 feet. The Chicago Dock and Canal Company, then headed by William B. Ogden, was the first to do anything to expand the harbor capacity when it obtained permission to build a slip parallel to and just north of the river. Ogden Slip, as it became known, continued to be used into the second half

of the twentieth century.

The proposed river widening was intended to relieve some of the traffic congestion that had been building since 1848 when the Illinois and Michigan Canal opened. Canal boats for the most part loaded and unloaded at warehouses and alongside ships on the south branch of the Chicago River, although in some cases they were towed the length of the river and even across Lake Michigan to avoid delays in loading and unloading resulting from the congestion. Twenty years later, canal boats were hauling 737,727 tons of cargo each season, much of it beginning or ending its trip in Chicago.[22] The obvious solution to Chicago River congestion was to build a new harbor in the lake. The army engineers then proposed building, beginning in 1870, a 4,000-foot breakwater in the lake to create an outer harbor at an estimated cost of almost $900,000. Despite the migration of industry to the Calumet River, traffic continued to increase on the Chicago River, peaking at 11 million tons in 1889 and inducing both the federal government and Chicago to continue to pour money into downtown river improvements.

At the time, it was expected that the completion of the Sanitary and Ship

Canal, then in the planning stage, to replace the hopelessly obsolete Illinois and Michigan Canal, as well as enlargement of the canals bypassing the Saint Lawrence River rapids in Canada, would result in a substantial increase in maritime traffic. In 1894 Washington appropriated $25,000 to begin improving and deepening to 21 feet the Chicago River (the south branch was deepened to 17 feet), a project that by the time it was completed in 1909 had cost $1.5 million.

## The Calumet River

The first official interest in the Calumet Harbor 13 miles south of the mouth of the Chicago River did not occur until 1870, when the federal government appropriated some money to cut a channel through the bar that threatened to block that river. In fact, it was a river in name only: the geographer David Solzman described it as little more than "a series of sloughs." The industrial migration there was the result not only of the congestion downtown but of the rapid growth in the steel industry after the Civil War and the Chicago fire of 1871, which leveled most of the downtown area and resulted in its rebuilding more as a commercial center than a heavy manufacturing area. Land along the Calumet was both cheap and plentiful.[23]

Chicago produced no iron before the Civil War. The nation's iron and steel industry was concentrated farther east in Pennsylvania and Ohio. Even by 1870 Illinois produced only 25,571 tons to rank fifteenth among the states, but several factors combined to greatly expand the industry in Chicago over the following decade, eventually establishing the south end of Lake Michigan as the nation's largest steel production center. Iron ore deposits discovered in the 1850s on the Upper Peninsula of Michigan, which could be cheaply transported in bulk by lake, the existence of substantial coal deposits to the east, and the giant limestone formation that underlay much of the Midwest provided in relative proximity the three

The companies that competed for business on Lake Michigan advertised their services with drawings of their vessels racing across the lake, like this drawing from a Graham and Morton Transportation Company advertisement for its *City of Benton Harbor*. (Great Lakes Historical Society, Vermilion, Ohio)

The propeller steamer *Holland* had a profile typical of Lake Michigan packets—a small pilothouse near the bow and the bulk of the hull covered with cabins. The cargo was loaded through gangways on the side of the ship, so there was no need for the large deck hatches typical of oceangoing ships. (Great Lakes Historical Society, Vermilion, Ohio)

Some freighters came in strange shapes to haul specialized cargo. The whaleback steamer *Samuel Mather* was built for the iron ore trade. (Beaver Island Historical Society)

principal raw materials necessary for steel production.

The rapid expansion of the nation's railroad network west after 1870 provided a customer for much of the steel, and Chicago in 1872 accounted for a third of the nation's production of steel rails. By 1880, Illinois produced 417,967 tons of iron and steel to rank fourth among the states.[24]

The Chicago Iron Company was organized in 1868, and the Chicago Rolling Mills, which would eventually evolve into the nation's largest steel producer (U.S. Steel Corporation), came into existence in 1870. By the late 1870s, Chicago Rolling Mills had become Illinois Steel Company and was looking for a site for a giant new mill. The site selected for what became known as the South Works was along the shore of the lake north of the mouth of the Calumet River. Iroquois Company (later Youngstown Sheet and Tube) relocated on the opposite side of the Calumet a few years later, followed by various coal,

steel, grain, and shipbuilding facilities along the 6-mile stretch of the river. By 1900 the facilities at Lake Calumet accounted for 3.5 million tons of shipping— about 2.5 millions tons of it were iron ore—and by 1906 it had surpassed Chicago's downtown port in tonnage.[25]

In the twentieth century the Calumet area became important enough to the economy for Chicago's planners to begin to take note of it, and the Metropolitan Sanitary District dug a canal westward to provide it with its own connection to the Mississippi River and its tributaries. The decline of the downtown port was a long, slow process. The ore boats and colliers were the earliest users of the Calumet River, but the smaller packets, lumber hookers, and grain schooners stayed downtown. Gradually, as steel construction techniques made larger ships possible, the schooners became obsolete and the big new steel ships favored Chicago's south side port.

# *Chapter Six* Schooners and the Reign of Sail

• In 1860, the Chicago steamship captain Albert Goodrich plunked down $32,000 for the 165-foot-long, 350-ton wooden paddle-wheel steamer *Comet* to expand his fleet to serve the growing cross-lake market and within a year overhauled the vessel to add four watertight compartments. The addition may have extended *Comet*'s life because in 1865, when it was driven onto the rocks in a storm and lost its $10,000 cargo, Goodrich was able to refloat and salvage the vessel. The ship steamed across the lakes for another four years under his flag.

Great Lakes ship owners were notori-ously frugal, so when a vessel finished its useful life, it was often cannibalized to provide parts for other ships. Engines, es-pecially, were often too valuable to be scrapped and wound up in other hulls, which sometimes were salvaged from older ships as well. It was common to upgrade a hull with a new propulsion system, as in the case of the Buffalo-based side-wheeler *Globe,* built in 1848 and converted to a propeller-driven ship eight years later.

Thus when *Comet*'s profitable tenure as a Great Lakes steamer ended in 1869, it was decommissioned and its machinery

Sailing ships negotiating constricted and busy ports like Chicago often did so behind tugboats, but skilled captains could lighten their sails considerably to reduce speed if the Chicago River wasn't too crowded and could use the wind to get to the dock. (Painting by Charles Vickery, courtesy of the Clipper Ship Gallery)

was removed. Goodrich then found a buyer for $1,000 for the still useful hull: it was converted to a barge in Chicago on May 21, 1870, then rigged as a schooner four years later. *Comet* plied the lakes for another nine years as a sailing ship before being abandoned in 1883.[1]

Despite the advances made in maritime propulsion during the previous half century, a relic from the age of sail—the two- and three-masted sailing schooner—by the time of the Civil War had become the dominant commercial vessel on the Great Lakes. Long after the steam engine revolutionized travel on the western rivers, the schooner persisted on the lakes in competition with steam because of its excellent economics. Schooners could be operated with crews of as small as five people, and if the cargo was in no particular hurry, they were a cheap way to ship. When the schooner finally did succumb, it was to the superior economics of the big steel hull, not any efficiency of mechanical propulsion over the gaff and topsail.

The fore-and-aft-rigged schooner was one of the end products of the centuries-long evolutionary process in hulls and sail configurations that in the nineteenth century also led to the fast clipper ships, the epitome of the square-rigger. The rigging of sailing ships was a topic of minimal public interest at the end of the twentieth century, except perhaps to yachtsmen, readers of Horatio Hornblower novels, and visitors to occasional exhibitions of "tall ships," but for hundreds of years it was of vital concern to mariners who depended wholly upon the winds.

La Salle's *Griffon*, the first sailing ship on the Great Lakes, had square sails, a configuration that had served New World explorers for 186 years in crossing the Atlantic Ocean. La Salle was a promoter, not a mariner, so the *Griffon* in 1679 was square-rigged even though the geography of the lakes made them friendlier to the type of fore-and-aft rigging—the triangular sail arrangements carried perpendicular to the hull, as in the case of modern recreational sailboats—that the Portuguese before Columbus had found useful in the African coastal trade. Columbus wanted to take advantage of trade winds to cross the Atlantic Ocean, so he rigged his caravels with square sails fixed to yards perpendicular to the center line of the hull to take maximum advantage of the following winds.[2]

Although no plans and specifications or contemporary drawings of the completed *Griffon* exist, there is general agreement that it was a square-rigger. It supposedly was a 60-ton barque, which carried its square sails on a foremast and mainmast, although some reconstructions show it as a brigantine with a mainmast and mizzen. Both classes are square-riggers but with somewhat different masts and configuration. In any event, the *Griffon* disappeared with all hands on its second voyage, so it did not contribute as much to commerce on the lakes as it did to historical curiosity. It is significant that by the time regular maritime commerce began on the Great Lakes almost a century after La Salle, the square-rigged sail configuration had been largely, though not entirely, discarded. Thus the first technological innovation in transportation affecting Chicago was the reinvention of the wheel, in this case fore-and-aft rigging.[3]

## The Search for a Practical Ship

The maritime industry that developed on the Great Lakes in American times was for the most part entrepreneurial in the tradition of La Salle. But the Michigan woodsmen, Wisconsin farmers, and Chicago merchants who went off to the Inland Seas were a more pragmatic bunch. They were not zealots on a mission; they simply wanted to make money. Although all sorts of crazy inventions appeared on the lakes, the realities of commerce quickly discarded them in favor of devices that worked and did so cheaply. They settled on the single-masted sloop and its larger cousin, the schooner, vessels that had been

refined in New England in the eighteenth century for the coastal trade.

The Dutch a century earlier were using small, two-masted ships with triangular sails called *speeljaght* (from which the English word "yacht" derives) as pleasure craft. The vessels were also known as *sloepe,* or sloops. According to maritime tradition the term "schooner" was born in 1713 in Gloucester, Massachusetts, when a spectator watching one being launched remarked, "Oh, how she scoons," and the term caught on.[4]

At first the New England schooner was popular among fishermen, but as trade with the West Indies increased, larger models were built for that market. Because of their speed they later became popular as blockade runners, revenue cutters, slave ships, and privateers. The Royal Navy bought six in 1767–1768. However, their

principal benefit to the merchant marine was their economy; their crews were a fraction of those of square-rigged ships of similar dimensions.[5]

Surprisingly schooners showed up on the western rivers almost before they did on the Great Lakes. Possibly as early as 1761 Pittsburgh began building them for the ocean market and sailing them down the Ohio and Mississippi Rivers to New Orleans, although the first known seagoing vessel (of uncertain class) from the western rivers was the 1792 *Kentucky Gazette.* Somewhat later the *Monongahela Farmer,* a 100-ton schooner, was loaded with 750 barrels of flour and sent downstream, picking up additional cargo on the way, but was delayed for three months until the Ohio had risen sufficiently to carry it over the falls at Louisville. The vessel was still in service between the East Coast and West

Great Lakes schooners typically had their masts rigged with fore-and-aft sails for running at right angles to the wind—a far more efficient sail configuration than square-rigging for coastal and lakes sailing. (Painting by Charles Vickery, courtesy of the Clipper Ship Gallery)

Lake schooners frequently carried two masts, like the *C. L. Johnson* shown at dock, but three-masters were common. A few larger ones with as many as four masts were built but proved impractical. (Wisconsin Maritime Museum)

Indies in 1808. By the first decade of the nineteenth century there was between the Monongahela River above Pittsburgh and Marietta, Ohio, a small, but active, industry building sloops, schooners, and brigs for the ocean trade, some as large as 200 tons burden.[6]

The existence of large forests and availability of skilled craftsmen who built flatboats and keelboats as well as sailing ships sustained a modest shipbuilding industry on the Ohio and its tributaries in the first decade of the nineteenth century. Leland D. Baldwin estimated that as least sixty-seven ships worth more than half a million dollars were built then. Ocean ship building on the rivers began to decline after 1808, when three ships were wrecked trying to shoot the falls of the Ohio, although a few vessels were built afterward, one as late as 1817. The shipwrights then turned their attention to barges, keelboats, and, after 1811, steamboats.[7]

The schooner also made its appearance shortly after commerce developed on the Great Lakes. The small Great Lakes fleet in the eighteenth century consisted primarily of dual-service vessels intended to sustain whatever commerce existed as well as maintain the military presence of the various belligerents in their struggle for control of North America. The British in 1755 began building small warships on Lake Ontario to interdict French supply lines to the interior. Between the fall of New France in 1763 and the end of the War of 1812, the British built twenty-eight ships on Lake Ontario and an additional twenty vessels, including schooners, sloops, and brigs on Lake Erie. A few visited Lake Michigan late in the century, including fur trader Robert Askin's fore-and-aft-rigged *Archange* in 1778 and the sloops of war *Welcome* and *Felicity* in 1779. The first American ship on the lakes, the 50-ton sloop *Detroit*, was purchased from the British in 1796, but when it proved to be too small for military duty, the United States built the 150-ton brig *Adams*.[8]

It was not until after the United States

crushed British naval power on the Great Lakes in the battle off Put-in-Bay on Lake Erie in 1813 that commercial sailing vessels of any size and number appeared on the lakes. The first U.S. merchant brig on the lakes, the 96-ton *Union,* was in 1814 considered too large for the available traffic and was laid up to await the growth of trade. However, schooners began to appear in numbers soon thereafter. Customs manifests in Detroit indicate that in 1816 three small schooners cleared Detroit for Lake Michigan, including the *Blacksnake* (21 tons burden and a crew of two), *Diligence* (32 tons), and *Eagle* (20 tons). From that modest beginning, the commercial schooner survived for seven decades in competition with the steamship (1818), the screw propeller (1841), the iron ship (1843), and the railroad (1828).[9]

The schooner *General Wayne* in 1816 brought the garrison and provisions for the rebuilding of Fort Dearborn, which had been abandoned after the massacre of 1812. Later that year the schooner *Hercules* became Chicago's first shipwreck when it foundered in a storm. The first steamer, *Sheldon Thompson,* did not arrive until 1832, bringing troops for the Black Hawk War. By 1836 there were 211 schooners totaling 15,030 tons operating on the Great Lakes, in contrast to only forty-five steamships with a combined tonnage of 9,017. Four years later the lakes' merchant marine had grown to 225 schooners with an aggregate tonnage of 35,123 and sixty-one steamships totaling 17,324 tons. That fleet had a combined value of $2.4 million and employed about three thousand persons.[10]

Although the first two ships of any importance built in Chicago were both steamers, the *James Allen* in 1838 and *George W. Dole* in 1840, the city's shipyards within a few years were concentrating on schooners. Ironically, the *James Allen,* which had been built on Goose Island on the Chicago River's north branch for a group of Chicago investors who wanted to provide cross-lake service to Saint Joseph, Michigan, to connect with a stagecoach

and mail line there, proved to be underpowered and, like the *Comet* somewhat later, was converted to a sailing ship in 1840. Within seven years Chicago shipyards had built or had under construction 80 schooners, a brig, and a propeller-driven ship on any available riverfront land.[11]

James Averell established a shipyard beneath the Rush Street bridge in 1842 and launched the sailing ship *Independence,* which at 262 tons was extremely large for its time and was equipped with a small engine and propeller in case of headwinds. In the succeeding years, Averell built a variety of vessels, including the brigantine *S. F. Gale,* the schooner *Maria Hilliard,* the brigs *Sultan, Minnesota,* and *Mary,* the barque *Utica,* and the scow *Ark.* However, by 1845, schooners were the preponderant product of Chicago's shipyards; of the ten vessels built that year, eight were schooners.[12]

## The Golden Age of Schooners

Schooners were so popular that their numbers on the Great Lakes doubled between 1840 and 1848 to form one of the largest merchant marines on the globe. The Great Lakes fleet in 1848 consisted of 548 schooners, 226 sailing ships of other configurations, and 140 steamships of all types. By 1870, there were nearly 1,700 schooners registered on the lakes, almost three times the number of steamers.[13]

The schooners built in the lakes' shipyards originally were similar to their coastal cousins on the oceans, but as both sailors and builders gained experience, they began to make adaptations for special conditions on the lakes. For one thing, masts were taller on the lakes because the prevailing winds were not as strong as on the ocean and more sail could be carried. For another, lake schooners tended to have modest drafts and retractable centerboards to negotiate the shallow harbors and often were boxy in shape to fit through canal locks.[14]

The *Illinois* (not to be confused with the steamship of the same name built a few years later), a 100-ton topsail schooner

Schooners used in the lumber trade were called "hookers." The *Rouse Simmons,* shown with a heavy load of lumber, was built for that business in 1868, although it ended its long career in 1912 carrying Christmas trees. (Milwaukee Public Library)

built in 1834, had a box-shaped hull 80 feet long and 20 feet wide and drawing only 8 feet of water to enable it to navigate the Welland Canal between Lakes Ontario and Erie. It was the first commercial sailing ship to get over the bar and into the Chicago River. Such ships over the years acquired the nickname "canallers" because of their design.[15]

A number of Great Lakes schooners wound up on the oceans; some were built for salt water and others designed to lake specifications were simply sold to international shippers. International traffic via the Saint Lawrence River, although it began as early as 1844 with the voyage of the brigantine *Pacific* from Toronto to Liverpool, did not pick up until after the schooner *Dean Richmond,* one of three vessels to bear that name, sailed from Chicago and Milwaukee to Liverpool with 14,320 bushels of wheat in 1856.[16]

However, international trade was not a major factor on the lakes until Canada enlarged the Welland and Saint Lawrence canal systems over a thirty-year period ending in 1901. The first Saint Lawrence

canals were completed in 1783, but at only 40 feet long and 6 feet wide were too small for ships. The system was enlarged and expanded between 1806 and 1847 to a standard length of 100 feet, a width of 25 feet, and a depth of 9 feet to permit small ships to make the transit between the lakes and the ocean. The Welland Canal was built between 1825 and 1829 to those dimensions to bypass Niagara Falls and provide a connection between Lake Ontario and the upper lakes.[17]

Although some schooners were built for speed, like William W. Bates's 1854 *Clipper City,* and were capable of 18 to 20 miles an hour (speed on the lakes is measured in miles per hour, not knots) with a strong, favorable wind, most were plodding vessels. Two weeks was considered a fast round trip between Chicago and Lake Erie, and the average was longer than a month. During the Black Hawk War of 1832, General Winfield Scott chartered steamships to take his army from Buffalo to Chicago because they could make the trip in seven days, but a sailing ship typically took twenty-five.[18]

The best-known of the schooner builders was William W. Bates (1827–1911), who designed and built the high-speed "clipper schooners" first in Manitowoc, Wisconsin, and later Chicago. He was a prolific writer on maritime topics and from 1889 to 1892 served as U.S. commissioner of navigation. He learned the trade and the skills in designing schooners while growing up in a shipbuilding family in Calais, Maine, where his father, Stephan, was a master builder. In 1849, at age twenty-two, the younger Bates headed west to seek his fortune and wound up in Manitowoc, which at the time was developing as a major supplier of ships for Chicago's growing markets.[19]

It was in 1852 in Manitowoc that Bates introduced his clipper class of schooner adapted for the Great Lakes, not to be confused with the Baltimore clipper class of schooner used on the oceans. The *Challenge* had a retractable centerboard, which could be raised to allow the vessel to enter shallow harbors and lowered when at sea to function as a keel and prevent the vessel from drifting off course in a crosswind. The 110-ton, 85-foot vessel had an exceedingly long life for a wooden sailing ship on the lakes. It was reported destroyed in a storm on September 10, 1910, while hauling a load of lumber from Manitowoc to Chicago.[20]

Bates stayed a few more years in Manitowoc but in 1854 left the shipyard business in the hands of his father and moved to New York to write for the Nautical Magazine and Naval Journal. When it folded in 1859, he wound up back at the family shipyard, but two years later he closed it, enlisted his workers, and marched them off to Civil War as Company K of the Nineteenth Wisconsin Volunteers. After being mustered out in 1864, he reestablished his shipyard in Chicago. For the next fifteen years he

The *Rouse Simmons,* shown in 1912, possibly at Two Rivers, Wisconsin, shortly before it was lost with all hands in a storm. (Milwaukee Public Library)

built ships in Chicago and as a spokesman for the maritime industry lobbied Congress on a number of issues.

He was nearly ruined when the Chicago fire of 1871 destroyed his business, but rebuilt it and continued to launch ships in Chicago until 1881. However, the shipbuilding business was changing. Schooners were losing their attraction and economic advantages as ever larger iron and steel ships appeared on the lakes. By the time he left the shipyard in 1881 to take a succession of maritime jobs and write, the average tonnage of the fifty-two sailing ships built on the lakes was almost 250 tons, but twice as many steamships were built that year, and they averaged 451 tons apiece. The *Onoko,* an iron-hulled bulk steamer launched in 1882, had a capacity of 3,000 tons of ore, the equivalent of twelve to fifteen midsize schooners.[21]

Thirty years earlier the schooner had held a substantial cost advantage over its competitors. Data extrapolated from the registry of Great Lakes ships in antebellum times gives an indication why the vessel was so popular among ship owners. The average value of the 974 schooners and sloops registered on the Great Lakes in 1858 was $6,352, in contrast to an average of $30,413 for side-wheelers and $19,439 for propeller-driven ships. The steamship *Illinois* cost $120,000 to build in 1838, including $45,000 just for the engine. The German engineer Franz Anton Ritter von Gerstner, who visited the United States to study its railroads and their competition in 1838-1839, concluded that the twenty-five largest steamships on the lakes cost an average of $50,000 to build.[22]

Schooner operating costs also were considerably lower. A midsize schooner, typically 125 feet long and with a cargo space rated at 200 tons, could be safely operated with a crew as small as five—a master, mate, two seamen, and a cook. On the other hand, in 1839 the paddle-wheel steamship *Erie,* operating between Buffalo and Detroit, required a crew of thirty-four and an annual payroll of $7,670. However, the largest operating cost was fuel (wood) at about $315 per round trip, in contrast to the $192 per round trip cost of the crew. The somewhat larger *Illinois* with a crew of forty had operating costs of $3,523, including depreciation, per round trip between Buffalo and Chicago.[23]

## The Decline

The slow decline of commercial sail on the Great Lakes began a few years after the Civil War when larger and better steamships appeared and the use of iron and steel allowed a substantial increase in the size of vessels beyond what was practical to power by sail. The construction of steamships passed that of sailing ships in 1875, and after reaching a postwar peak of 130 in 1874, the construction of sailing ships declined to negligible levels by the end of the century. The sailing fleet was surpassed by steamships in total tonnage in 1884 and in the number of hulls by 1888.[24]

By then, many of the vessels registered as schooners were in fact nothing more than barges towed around the lake by tugs. In 1869 James Norris of Saint Catherines, Ontario, as an experiment, hired the American tug *Sampson* to tow three of his schooners to Chicago and back. Cordwood stacked on the schooners was used as fuel on the tug. The sortie was so successful that within a few years it was being imitated all over the lakes, and in some cases the old schooners were demasted. As the century began to wane, schooner owners and masters, usually the same person, were able to survive by tramping from harbors too small for steamships or operating in niche markets, like the Lake Michigan lumber trade or stone hooking (salvaging stone from the lake bottom) on Lake Ontario.[25]

August and Hermann Schuenemann were brothers and Chicago schooner captains who attempted to survive in the dying age of sail by finding such a niche—in their case the annual Christmas tree market. Late each shipping season in the late 1800s and early 1900s, when the weather

Schooners and sea gulls were grist for the mill of Chicago artists long after the ships disappeared from the Great Lakes. This pen-and-ink drawing decorated a local bank's Christmas card in the early twentieth century. (Great Lakes Historical Society, Vermilion, Ohio)

on Lake Michigan got nasty and old schooners were being laid up for the winter, the Schuenemanns would buy or charter one, sail to northern Wisconsin or the Upper Peninsula of Michigan, and return with a load of yule trees to sell off their ship at its dock on the Chicago River. The Christmas tree trade was not so lucrative that a mariner could make a living at it, but it could provide a nice supplement to the dying business of tramping around the lakes, looking for cargoes of opportunity. In the end, both men prematurely went to watery graves in separate storms, and in time Hermann Schuenemann became something of a local legend—the captain of the ill-fated "Christmas Tree Ship."[26]

The brothers grew up near Ahnapee (now Algoma), a small Wisconsin port, the sons of a German immigrant who went blind during the Civil War and was forced to give up the farm. Suddenly bordering on poverty, the older brother, August, worked as a hired farmhand and finally got himself a job as a member of the crew of the locally owned schooner *Ella Doak*, hauling lumber

to Chicago and occasionally hooking stone from the lake bottom to build breakwaters in other ports. In 1875 he bought an interest in the schooner *W. H. Hinsdale* and became its master. Late that year he proved his skills by managing to sail the old ship, which had lost one anchor in a previous storm and had a hold filled waist-deep with water, safely through a gale and into Sheboygan's harbor. A year later, the *Hinsdale* was wrecked in a storm at South Haven, Michigan.[27]

By then, a Christmas tree market had begun to develop in Chicago and Milwaukee, probably because of the large German immigrant population and their traditions revolving around the *tannenbaum*. Local merchants in towns along the northern shores of the lake would have them cut and shipped south by schooner, and finally some shipmasters set themselves up in that business. They were looking for a big score, which in some cases could double what they made the rest of the year in the declining lake trade.[28]

The older brother had done well

William Bates was Chicago's master schooner builder in the era after the Civil War. (Wisconsin Maritime Museum)

enough on the lake that by 1884 he decided to seek his fortune in the big city. With too many schooners chasing too few cargoes in competition with the newer steamships, dilapidated old schooners were a glut on the market and could be bought cheaply. In 1889 August Schuenemann sold his scow-schooner *Supply* for $650 and paid $1,400 for the schooner *Josephine Dresden.* By then, Hermann Schuenemann had joined him in the business, for he was listed as owner and manager of that ship from 1890 to 1893. In the late fall, when other lake traffic began to fall off, the brothers always sailed north to get Christmas trees. They may not have been able to support themselves entirely on the lake, however. Hermann tried his hand unsuccessfully at the grocery business in Chicago in the 1890s.[29]

However, in 1897 he paid $1,400 for the schooner *Mary Collins,* and the next year August Schuenemann bought for only

$250 the decrepit old schooner *S. Thal.* It had been built in 1867 at Oshkosh on shallow Lake Winnebago as a two-masted schooner with a draft of only 4.8 feet. Hermann, who had newborn twin daughters, decided not to make the Christmas tree trip north with his brother that year and was at home with his family when a gale dashed the returning *S. Thal* onto the beach at north suburban Glencoe. Residents of the area saw the struggling ship offshore late in the afternoon of November 9, but the next morning could only find "wreckage being made sport of by the surf," including the ship's nameplate. No bodies were found.[30]

Despite his brother's fate, Hermann Schuenemann carried on the family's annual Christmas tree business. To increase his revenues he not only bought his own Christmas tree farm near Manistique, Michigan, and continued to buy or charter old schooners, but sold the trees retail from the deck while docked at the southwest corner of the Clark Street bridge to avoid giving wholesale discounts to stores and having to pay teamsters to haul them away. In 1900 he bought the old lumber hooker *Truman Moss* and in 1903 paid $377.68 for the schooner *George L. Wrenn.* By 1910 that vessel was in such sad shape that he had to charter the aging schooner *Rouse Simmons,* the vessel that two years later would become his coffin.[31]

The three-masted *Rouse Simmons* had been built as a lumber hooker for $17,000 for a group of Kenosha businessmen, including its namesake, in 1868. The 123.5-foot-long vessel had a cargo capacity of 205 tons or 350,000 feet of lumber, but by 1912 it was showing its forty-four years. Schuenemann agreed to rent the vessel from M. J. Bonner, the three-fourths owner of the ship, for only $187.50, although Bonner claimed after the wreck he wanted $1,125, its presumed value, for failing to return it.

Hermann Schuenemann's probate records indicate he borrowed heavily in

hopes of making a big profit on a single load of perhaps 5,000 Christmas trees. He had borrowed $750 over seven months from his assistant Philip Bausewein and owed the ship's crew and woodcutters (or their estates) a total of $1,588.53. Apparently they were to be paid from the proceeds of the tree sale in Chicago. Aggregate claims against the estate, which had a value of $3,250.32, came to $5,000 to $6,000.[32]

The Schuenemanns' biographer noted that Hermann on his 1911 voyage on the *Rouse Simmons* had stopped in Sturgeon Bay and had the ship recaulked. Probably because of Schuenemann's financial condition he did not have it caulked on his way north in 1912. Heavily laden with trees, the vessel foundered in a storm off Two Rivers Point, Wisconsin, on November 23, 1912, with the loss of all eighteen persons aboard. Schuenemann's widow, Barbara, for years continued to sell Christmas trees from the deck of a ship but had them shipped to Chicago by railroad.[33]

Life on a lakes schooner was somewhat different from what a seaman would find on the ocean. The voyages were short,

In the last quarter of the nineteenth century, many schooners ended their careers as barges, towed across the lakes by tugboats. In this somewhat fanciful drawing the tug *Champion* is towing a string of sailing ships off Windmill Point, Michigan. (Wisconsin Maritime Museum)

In the late twentieth century, schooners made a
modest comeback on the
Great Lakes as excursion
vessels. The design of the
four-masted *Windy,* shown
here hoisting sails off Navy
Pier in 1999 with a load of
tourists aboard, was based
on European coastal
schooners with a forecastle
(pronounced fo'c's'le) and
poop, the raised sections of
the hull fore and aft. Great
Lakes schooners typically
lacked such configurations
and had a single deck the
length of the ship with a
small house toward the
stern to provide shelter for
the crew.

rarely more than a few weeks in duration;
as a result there were few amenities aboard
ship. The only shelter was a small cabin,
usually near the stern. For a farm boy from
Wisconsin who ran away to sea, the most
exotic port he was likely to encounter was
Buffalo, although Chicago by the end of
the century had eclipsed it. The fact that
schooners operated night and day meant
that the crew of five was kept busy on
shifts, so much so that the cook, often a
woman, had to lend a hand on deck when
things got hectic.

The master (captain) and mate alter-
nately would steer, and the three crewmen
would handle the rigging and lookout
chores. Although there was always the
danger of a fall from the rigging or injury
by a shifting load, the greatest danger was
from the weather. Violent storms and cold
water were unforgiving even though the
ships rarely got out of sight of land. Toward the end of the sail era on the lakes,
when the aging schooners were being

squeezed for an extra year of two of service, much of the crew's work consisted of
making repairs to keep the ship afloat. In
the winter when the lakes were closed seamen had to find whatever other jobs they
could to make ends meet.[34]

The number of schooners rapidly dwindled in the closing years of the nineteenth
century. Some were wrecked and not replaced; others were burned in public spec-
tacles; many had their masts removed and
were towed about the lakes as barges; and
scores, perhaps hundreds, of them were
simply abandoned and left to rot in small
ports scattered around the Great Lakes.
The *Lucia A. Simpson,* which was wrecked
in 1929, and *Our Son,* which sank in a
storm in 1930, are sometimes considered
to be the last schooners under sail in commercial service on the lakes, but other
maritime historians claim that a few
schooners continued in service on the
lakes in the 1930s.[35]

# Part Two

## Life and Death on the Waters

Maritime America
1900's

r.sweitzer

Beaver Island
Duluth
Sault Ste. Marie
Montreal
Boston
Milwaukee
Detroit
Buffalo
Cleveland
New York
Chicago
Pittsburgh
Philadelphia
Peoria
Sandusky
Baltimore
Cincinnati
St. Louis
Louisville
Savannah
Cave-in-Rock
Memphis
New Orleans

# *Chapter Seven* Traveling by Water

• The first Europeans to enter the interior of North America, although they had traveled by coach on Europe's highways and crossed thousands of miles of ocean on ships, found that the best way to get around in the vast wilderness was on foot or by means of a handy conveyance used by the natives—the canoe. However, it wasn't long before they began to experiment with all sorts of watercraft to make the task of traveling easier. Thus *pirogues* gave way to river rafts and eventually steamboats on the rivers and birchbark canoes were succeeded by sailing ships and finally steamships on the Great Lakes.

With each development the watercraft became larger and the task of operating them required less individual muscle power. More important, they permitted the vessels to carry passengers who didn't have to serve as members of the crew. The early canoes required that almost everyone aboard paddle if any sort of progress was to be made, but thirty or more people could buy passage on a nineteenth-century sloop and watch a crew of five operate the ship. As the interior was settled and the demand for travel and commerce increased, the people of means began demanding vessels with cabin shelter from

The whaleback excursion ship *Christopher Columbus* was a popular way for tourists and Chicago residents to get from downtown to the Columbian Exposition in Jackson Park in 1893. (Chicago Maritime Society)

The Chicago River in the 1880s in this drawing from A. T. Andreas's *History of Chicago* was the scene of a variety of vessels—schooners, steamers, tugs, and canal barges. (Chicago Maritime Society)

storms, meals they didn't have to prepare themselves, and, eventually, private rooms. The poor, traveling steerage, as always, plopped down in whatever space they could find.

Sometime during the nineteenth century, speed of travel became a paramount concern of the public. Fewer people were willing to spend months on a flatboat traveling down the Mississippi River to New Orleans when they could make the trip by steamboat in a week. Sailing time between Buffalo and Chicago ostensibly was six days in 1841, although unfavorable winds often made it nine days or more. Steamships the following year advertised they could make the same round trip in sixteen days.[1]

By 1847, the maritime industry was boasting that the travel time from Buffalo to Chicago, using a combination of railroad and ship, had been reduced to three days. The railroads were faster yet and took most of the passenger traffic away from the Great Lakes steamers and canals, and the motorcar finished the job in the twentieth century. Dwindling numbers of passenger ships survived in niche markets or as plea-

sure craft catering to the cruise market.[2]

When Henry R. Schoolcraft circumnavigated Lake Michigan by canoe in 1820, an average-day paddling for an eight-man crew was 40 to 50 miles. That required being on the lake by dawn and paddling until dusk—a fifteen-hour day in summer. Schoolcraft, a chronicler of Indian lore and secretary of the federal commission negotiating with the Indians over land forfeiture, was somewhat more literate than the earlier French explorers and published his diary of the journey in 1821. Nothing spectacular occurred, so the twenty-one-day voyage was about as average a trip by canoe on the lake as was possible.[3]

The group of sixteen men in two canoes left the mouth of the Fox River at Green Bay at 2:30 P.M. on August 20 and managed to make 25 miles before dark. The next day, after paddling for 35 miles and completing a three-hop portage across the Door County peninsula to Lake Michigan, the crew arrived in the early afternoon but was kept on the beach by a strong headwind. By Schoolcraft's estimate they made 40 and 43 miles in each of the next two days, only 35 on the third day because of headwinds, and 40 miles on the fourth day. They crossed the bar into the Chicago River at 5 A.M. on August 29 after paddling 10 miles. The 275-mile, uneventful voyage had taken nine full days.

They spent the second day (September 1) of the 400-mile trip from Chicago to Michilimackinac sitting on the beach because of strong headwinds but managed to make 70 miles with strong following winds by putting in a long workday on September 5. Ten days after leaving Chicago they were on the beach, staring across the stormy straits at their destination on Mackinac Island. Some of the more experienced and braver canoists finally made a successful crossing later in the day when the winds ebbed somewhat. Perhaps the most interesting passages in Schoolcraft's diary were his accounts of the evidence he saw of the lake's violent nature:

> In walking along some parts of the shore, I observed a great number of skeletons and half consumed of the pigeon, which, in crossing the lake, is often overtaken by severe tempests, and compelled to alight upon the water, and thus drowned, in entire flocks, which are soon thrown up along the shores. This causes the shores of Lake Michigan to be visited by vast numbers of buzzards, eagles, and other birds of prey. The Indians also make use of these pigeons, as food, when they are first driven ashore, preserving such in smoke, as they have not immediate occasion for. Vast broods of young gulls, are also destroyed during the violent storms, which frequently agitate this lake.

On the return trip on the windward (eastern) shore of the lake he found evidence of two shipwrecks, the *Hercules* of 1816 near modern Michigan City, Indiana, and an unidentified British vessel near Grand Haven, Michigan. "The mast, pump, and some fragments of spars, scattered along the shore, still serve to mark the spot, and to convey some idea of the

dreadful storms which at certain seasons agitate this lake. The voyageurs also pointed out to us, the graves of those who had perished, who appear to have been buried at different places, along the shore, where they happened to be washed up."

## Charles Dickens in Illinois

By the time the English author Charles Dickens showed up on America's shores in 1842, among other things to check on his land investments, the canal age was in progress, steam-powered vessels were common on the rivers and Great Lakes, and some railroads were operating in the East. The travelogue he wrote about his long journey as far inland as Saint Louis and Cahokia, Illinois, in 1842, while creating an uproar in the United States at the time, is a glimpse of how people got around in the canal, steamboat, and stagecoach eras while railroads were still in their infancy. *American Notes for General Circulation* is as good a commentary as exists on travel in America in the 1840s from the standpoint of a tourist.[4]

The democratic American railroads, in which everyone sat in a classless coach without interior compartments, did not impress him. Then again he had not yet ridden on a canal boat:

> There are no first or second class carriages as with us; but there is a gentlemen's car and a ladies' car: the main distinction between which is that in the first, everyone smokes; and in the second, nobody does. As a black man never travels with a white one, there is also a negro car. . . . There is a great deal of jolting, a great deal of noise, a great deal of wall, not much window, a locomotive engine, a shriek, and a bell.
>
> The cars are like shabby omnibuses, but larger; holding thirty, forty, fifty people. The seats, instead of stretching from end to end, are placed crosswise. Each seat holds two persons. There is a long row of them on each side of the caravan,

a narrow passage up the middle, and a door at both ends. In the center of the carriage there is usually a stove, fed with charcoal or anthracite coal; which is for the most part red hot. It is insufferably close; and you see the hot air fluttering between yourself and any other object you may happen to look at, like a ghost of smoke.

Dickens also was intrigued at how the rural American trains stopped almost anywhere to pick up and discharge passengers. "The train calls at stations in the woods, where the wild possibility of anyone having the smallest reason to get out, is only to be equaled by the apparently desperate hopelessness of there being anybody to get in."

The trip in Pennsylvania between York and Harrisburg was by stagecoach: "There came rumbling up the street, shaking its sides like a corpulent giant, a kind of barge on wheels. . . . However, they packed twelve people inside; and the luggage (including such trifles as a large rocking-chair, and a good-sized dining-table) being at length made fast upon the roof, we started off in a great state." Dickens and another passenger, a drunk, wound up atop the coach next to the driver. Of course, it rained: "I was glad to take advantage of a stoppage [to change horses] and get down to stretch my legs, shake the water off my great coat, and swallow the usual anti-temperance recipe for keeping out the cold."

At Harrisburg they switched to a canal boat—"a barge with a little house on it"— on Pennsylvania's Main Line. His account of the trip, with thirty passengers crammed into the cabin as the boat crept down the canal at 2 or 3 miles an hour behind a tow of three horses, is similar to less literate accounts of travel on the Illinois and Michigan Canal a few years later:[5]

> As it continued to rain most perseveringly, we all remained below; the damp gentlemen around the stove, gradually becoming mildewed by the action of the fire; and the dry gentlemen lying at full length upon the seats, or slumbering uneasily with their faces on the tables, or walking up and down the cabin, which it was barely possible for a man of middle height to do, without making bald places on his head by scraping it against the roof. At about six o'clock, all the small tables were put together to form one long table, and everybody sat down to tea, coffee, bread, butter, salmon, shad, liver, steak, potatoes, pickles, ham, chops, black-puddings, and sausages.
>
> I have mentioned my having been in some uncertainty and doubt, at first, relative to the sleeping arrangements on board this boat. I remained in the same vague state of mind until ten o'clock or thereabouts, when going below, I found suspended on either sides of the cabin, three long tiers of hanging book-shelves, designed apparently for volumes of the small octavo size. Looking with greater attention at these contrivances (wondering to find such literary preparations in such a place), I descried on each shelf a microscopic sheet and blanket; then I began to dimly comprehend that the passengers were the library, and that they would be arranged, edge-wise, on these shelves, till morning.

The passengers drew lots for bunk assignments, and a red curtain was drawn to separate men's and women's sections. Dickens discovered in the morning that the washroom consisted of a tin ladle with chain attached that enabled passengers to draw canal water to fill the wash basin outside on the open deck. Breakfast was the same fare as the supper the previous night. For exercise and a diversion, passengers could get off the boat and walk along the towpath beside it.

The canal boat, which left Harrisburg on Friday morning, by Sunday morning had reached the first mountain in western Pennsylvania. The mountains were scaled by the canal by means of ten inclined railways with stationary engines to drag the carriages over the mountains. By Monday night the lights of Pittsburgh were in sight.

The Dearborn Street draw-bridge built in 1834 and shown in this drawing by A. T. Andreas was an early attempt by the booming town of Chicago to enable its population to cross the increasingly busy river. (Chicago Maritime Society)

The 204-mile trip—now possible in 3 1/2 hours by automobile—had taken Dickens about 3 1/2 days, at an average speed of slightly less than 3 miles an hour.

> We tarried here three days. Our next point was Cincinnati; and as this was a steamboat journey, and western steamboats usually blow up one or two a week in season, it was advisable to collect opinions in reference to the comparative safety of the vessels bound that way, then lying in the river. One called *Messenger* was the best recommended. She had been advertised to start positively, every day for a fortnight or so, and had not gone yet, nor did her captain seem to have any fixed intention on the subject.[6]
>
> Impressed by the deep solemnity of the public announcement, I (being ignorant of these usages) was for hurrying on board in a breathless state, immediately; but receiving private and confidential information that the boat would certainly not start until Friday, April the First, we made ourselves comfortable in the meanwhile and went on board at noon that day.

On the *Messenger,* Dickens finally got some privacy in the form of a small stateroom near the stern and as far, he noted, from the dangerous boilers as he could get. Steerage passengers rode in the open on deck. The staterooms opened onto a central cabin with a ladies' room at one end and a bar at the other. The central cabin had a long table in the center and stoves at both ends. Aside from the omnipresent danger from the boilers hissing in the bowels of the steamboat, the skimpiness of the meals on the three-day trip seemed to intrigue Dickens the most: "fancy slices of beet root, shred of dried beef, complicated entanglements of yellow pickle, maize, Indian corn, apple-sauce, and pumpkin."

"At dinner, there is nothing to drink upon the table, but great jugs full of cold water," he reported. Through service was uncommon for steamboats on the Ohio in 1842, so at Cincinnati Dickens switched to the steamboat *Pike* for the twelve- to thirteen-hour trip to Louisville. There he changed again, this time to the *Fulton* for the four-day trip to Saint Louis.

But what words shall describe the Mississippi, great father of rivers, who (praise be to heaven) has no children like him! An enormous ditch, sometimes two or three miles wide, running liquid mud, six miles an hour: its strong and frothy current choked and obstructed everywhere by huge logs and whole forest trees: now twining themselves together in great rafts, from the interstices of which a sedgy, lazy foam works up, to float on the water's top; now rolling past like monstrous bodies, their tangled roots showing like matted hair; now glancing singly by like giant leeches; and now writhing round and round in the vortex of some small whirlpool, like wounded snakes. The banks low, the trees dwarfish, the marshes swarming with frogs, the wretched cabins few and far apart, their inmates hollow-cheeked and pale, the weather very hot, mosquitoes penetrating into every crack and crevice of the boat, mud and slime on everything: nothing pleasant in its aspect, but the harmless lightning which flickers every night upon the dark horizon.

For two days we toiled up this foul stream, striking constantly against the floating timber, or stopping to avoid those more dangerous obstacles, the snags, or sawyers, which are hidden trunks of trees that have their roots below the tide. When the nights are very dark, the look-out stationed at the head of the boat, knows by the ripple of the water if any great impediment be near at hand, and rings a bell beside him, which is the signal for the engine to be stopped: but always in the night this bell has work to do, and after every ring, there comes a blow which renders it no easy matter to remain in bed.

On the return trip Dickens discovered what every American already knew: travel by water, however bad, was preferable to overland travel by stagecoach. He wanted to visit Canada, so he took a shortcut by stagecoach the length of the state of Ohio to get to the Great Lakes. On the canal boat he complained about the potability of the water; on the stagecoach, potables were the issue at an otherwise unidentified inn on the road to Columbus: "We dine soon afterwards with the boarders in the house, and have nothing to drink but tea and coffee. As they are both very bad and the water is worse, I ask for brandy; but this is a Temperance Hotel, and the spirits are not to be had for love or money."

After an all-night stage ride to Columbus, he chartered a coach from there to the railhead at Tiffin and stocked it "with a hamper full of savory cold meats, and fruit, and wine. . . ." Unfortunately, the road was a little rough:

> At one time we were all flung together in one heap at the bottom of the coach, and at another we were crushing our heads against the roof. Now, one side was down deep in the mire, and we were holding onto the other. Now the coach was lying on the tails of the two wheelers; and now it was rearing up in the air, in a frantic state, with all four horses standing on the top of an insurmountable eminence, looking coolly back at it, as though they would say 'Unharness us. It can't be done.' The drivers on those roads, who certainly get over the ground in a manner which is quite miraculous, so twist and turn the team about in forcing a passage, corkscrew fashion, through the bogs and swamps. . . ."

The otherwise unidentified, 500-ton steamship arrived at Sandusky late in the afternoon and after stops at several places in between arrived in Cleveland—a distance of only 55 miles—at midnight and stayed overnight. It was not unusual in those days for steamships on the lakes to sail only during daylight hours. The ship left Cleveland at 9 A.M., and got to Erie, Pennsylvania—another 102 miles—at 8 P.M. After a layover for an hour, the vessel steamed the remaining 78 miles to Buffalo, arriving between 5 and 6 A.M. the next day. If Dickens's notes are correct, the steamship took twenty-five hours to steam 235 miles—an average speed of about 9 miles an hour. The 120-mile stagecoach trip between Cincinnati and Columbus took twenty-three hours with various stops to change teams and drivers and feed the passengers, an average speed of just over 5 miles an hour.

## Abraham Lincoln's Travels

Abraham Lincoln at age nineteen and while a resident of Indiana made his first flatboat trip down the Mississippi River to New Orleans, and in 1831, after moving to Decatur, Illinois, he and two other young men agreed to haul a load of hogs from Springfield to the market in New Orleans on a flatboat. The heavy snow that winter and spring rains had left central Illinois flooded and the roads impassable, so he bought a canoe and paddled down the Sangamon River from Decatur to Springfield. He, his stepbrother, and a friend then built the flatboat at Sangamon Town 7 miles north of Springfield and floated the hogs to New Orleans.

After moving to New Salem, Illinois, Lincoln invested in the small steamboat *Talisman,* with which the local promoter Vincent A. Bogue hoped to establish steamboat service on the Sangamon River. Both Lincoln and a friend were the pilots on the craft's trip on the river to Bogue's mill in March 1832. As backers of the scheme, Lincoln and his partner in a New Salem tavern, Nelson Alley, were forced to cough up $147.87 seven months later when Bogue went bankrupt.[7]

In the 1980s the Lincoln archivist Wayne C. Temple reconstructed the probable details of a number of trips Honest Abe made on stagecoaches, canals, and Great Lakes steamboats 120 years earlier. Temple's reconstructions, although they might be open to debate over some details and are admittedly a little speculative in others, give a glimpse of what travel was like in 1847 and 1848. Lincoln's trips home to Springfield from Chicago in those years indicate the lengths to which people would travel by water to avoid stagecoaches.[8]

Lincoln, a Whig congressman-elect needing some national exposure, attended and spoke at the River and Harbor Convention in Chicago in 1847. The Illinois and Michigan Canal, which Lincoln had supported when he was in the state legislature in the 1830s, was under construction at the time, so when he made his return trip home to Springfield it was by a combination of stagecoach and steamboat. The 225-mile route in 1847 involved changing from stagecoach to steamboat at La Salle for a trip down the Illinois River to Peoria, where stagecoaches handled the final leg of the trip.[9]

A Boston newspaper reporter traveled the same route at the same time, a portion of it with Lincoln as a fellow passenger, and left a published account. The reporter, four other men, and three women were packed into the overnight stage that left Chicago at 9 A.M. and reached La Salle at noon the next day—a trip of approximately 100 miles that took twenty-seven hours, at an average speed of less than 4 miles an hour. It included a stop at an inn in Dresden south of Joliet at which a supper of "codfish" and hashed potatoes was served them, a rest stop to change horses in Morris, and a breakfast stop in Ottawa farther down the line.

> At a small place called Morris, at half past eleven o'clock, we again stopped to change horses, and remained an hour in the most uncomfortable place you can conceive of; the tavern-keeper and all his people were in bed, but we succeeded, after some difficulty, in getting into the house, and had the luxury of two tallow candles, and a little water, which was warm, and not very palatable. . . .
>
> The rest of our ride during the night was as uncomfortable as any enemy, if we

had one, could desire. We made progress at the rate of less than three miles an hour; the weather was intensely hot, and not a breath of air was stirring; the horses and carriage raised any quantity of dust, which, of course, rose only high enough to fill the carriage. . . .

Following a 6 A.M. breakfast at Ottawa, the stagecoach got to La Salle, the head of navigation of the Illinois River, three hours before the scheduled departure of the steamboat *Dial*. It took eleven hours to steam 65 miles downriver to Peoria, including a three-hour stop at Lacon to take on freight. The travelers arrived at 2 A.M., in plenty of time to make the scheduled departure of the stagecoach to Springfield two hours later, but not long enough to book into a hotel for a nap.

At Peoria the travelers were joined by Lincoln and another congressman. With six passengers in a coach built for four, the stage crossed the Illinois River on a ferry, but its passengers were obliged to dismount on the far bank and walk up a steep bluff because the horses were incapable of pulling the loaded stage up the escarpment. Lunch in Delavan was the usual stagecoach inn fare: beef swimming in fat, fried eggs, hashed potatoes, and bread.[10]

"We started in a grumbling humor, but our Whig congressman (Lincoln) was determined good natured, and to keep all the rest so if he could; he told stories, and badgered his opponent, who it appeared was an old personal friend, until we all laughed, in spite of the dismal circumstances in which we were placed," the reporter wrote in his dispatch back to Boston.

In all, the 2 1/2-day trip from Chicago to Springfield was excellent by the standards of the day in the Midwest. There were no accidents, the delays were minimal, and the connections were about as good as could be expected. But Lincoln, like most travelers in his day, was quite willing to take a longer route if he could avoid stagecoach travel. So in 1852, when

he was a member of the Illinois and Michigan Canal Commission and had to attend meetings in Ottawa and Chicago, he took a 100-mile-longer route than he had five years earlier. That meant traveling 53 miles in the wrong direction (west) to Naples on the Illinois River where he could catch a steamboat upriver to La Salle. He then took the I & M Canal the remaining 15 miles to Ottawa.

The 1852 trip to Chicago was exactly 325 miles; we know because Honest Abe on his expense account billed the commission for a 650-mile round trip. Shortly thereafter, Lincoln also joined the growing legion of train travelers. When the Chicago & Alton Railroad was completed through Springfield to Chicago in early 1858, it cut the trip between the two cities to 185 miles and reduced the one-way travel time to six hours or less. On November 21, 1860, Lincoln and his wife took the morning train to Chicago on business, making three whistle-stop speeches in towns along the route.[11]

His trip from Boston back to Springfield in 1848 is representative of travel at the end of the canal age, when railroads were just starting to invade the market. Congressman Lincoln, after making some political appearances on behalf of the Whigs, left Boston by train for Albany on September 23 with his wife and two sons in tow. After a brief stop in Albany the next day to visit Millard Fillmore, they headed west, probably by train, because they reached Buffalo the next day. Lincoln then went aboard the new 251-foot-long, 1,300-ton paddle-wheel steamship *Globe* and booked stateroom passage for Chicago the next day. Independently owned ships like the *Globe* typically didn't have offices and required passengers or shippers to come aboard to book space.

The ship sailed on September 26 and three days later was in the Detroit River, unsuccessfully attempting to help refloat the grounded steamship *Canada*. Lake vessels then as now typically assisted each other in trouble even if there was no danger of foundering. However, the *Globe* was unsuccessful and steamed on its way.

To stave off the boredom of the long voyage, some passengers arranged a political debate, and Lincoln wound up defending the Whig cause. The excursion ships of the next century featured entertainment for the passengers, but the *Globe* in 1848 was offering basic point-to-point transportation, so the debate dragged on for two days as heavy weather slowed the vessel's progress. She finally arrived in Milwaukee on October 4—eight days after leaving Buffalo—and after a brief stop headed down the lake for Chicago. She finally arrived in Chicago in the early morning hours of October 6 to end a ten-day voyage that was scheduled to take only seven.[12]

The Lincolns checked into the Sherman House and the next day headed for the Chicago terminal of the newly completed I & M Canal to resume their trip. Three canal boats left Chicago that day, and Temple speculated that the congressman and his family took the *Chicago,* which specialized in passengers at $4 per person. The *Oswego,* which left earlier, carried twenty-seven passengers as well as 100 pounds of lead, 6,000 pounds of salt, and 5,232 board feet of lumber. The *Chicago,* which had thirty-five passengers and made no stops en route, apparently reached La Salle in time for breakfast on October 7, and the Lincolns a few hours later boarded one of two steamboats for the nine-hour trip to Peoria. They booked into a hotel for the night and left two days later on the 4 A.M. stagecoach for Springfield, which got them home by 9 P.M.[13]

## Rudyard Kipling and the Railroads

As the century neared its end, railroads so dominated passenger travel that the British author Rudyard Kipling made his

Entire families lived on and crewed the smaller vessels on waterways. This rude stern-wheeler, the *M & W,* with family aboard was photographed on the Hennepin Canal early in the twentieth century. Note the Tin Lizzy in the background. (Judi Jacksohn Collection)

**Right:** The *Christopher Columbus* was later sold to the Goodrich line and steamed the lake in excursion service between Chicago and Milwaukee. (Chicago Maritime Society)

For many small Great Lakes towns like Saint James, Michigan, the only communication with the outside world was lake packets. The steamer *Eugene Hart* ran such a local service between Detroit and Chicago. (Beaver Island Historical Society)

**Left:** As the nineteenth century progressed, passenger steamers supplanted grain schooners at the docks along the Chicago River near its mouth. They were later moved to Municipal (Navy) Pier after it was completed in 1916. (Great Lakes Historical Society, Vermilion, Ohio)

four-month tour of the United States in 1889 almost entirely by train, even to the gates of remote Yellowstone Park in Montana. The crack trains by then had almost every accommodation that half a century earlier had made the luxury excursion steamers a preferred mode of travel. There were sleeping cars, a business that Chicago's George Pullman was beginning to dominate; smoking and lounge cars with bars; and dining cars. There was even steerage—the so-called immigrant cars:

> It was like a nightmare, and not one in the least improved by having to sleep in an immigrant car; the regularly ordained sleepers being full. There was a row in our car toward morning, a man having managed to get querulously drunk in the night. Up rose a Cornishman with a red head full of strategy, and strapped the obstreperous, smiling largely as he did so, and a delicate little woman in a far bunk watched the fray as he did so and called the man a 'damned hog,' which he certainly was, though she didn't have to put it quite so coarsely. Immigrant cars are clean, but the accommodation is as hard as a plank bed.[14]

Kipling preferred Pullman sleepers, which at the time consisted of a car in which day seats folded down into beds and upper berths folded down from the top of the car. Heavy curtains hung along either side of the aisle provided the only privacy.

> When the negro porter bedded me up for the night and I had solved the problem of undressing while lying down,—I was cheered by the thought that if anything happened I should have to stay where I was and wait till the kerosene lamps set the overturned car alight and burned me to death. It is easier to get out of a full theater than to leave a Pullman in haste.

Trains traveled at high speeds by 1889, and Kipling was concerned about the possibility of accidents, as Dickens had been obsessed with steamboat boilers' exploding. Railroad cars were still made of wood at that time, and passengers who survived a crash often died in the resulting fire that spread from the wood-burning stoves. The worst railroad accident in Illinois history occurred on August 10, 1887, when a small bridge collapsed beneath a Toledo, Peoria & Western Railroad excursion train, killing eighty-two, and perhaps as many as a hundred persons trapped in the wreckage, which caught fire.[15]

Kipling wrote that he had been told of the dangers of wrecks:

> Take up—you can easily find them—the accounts of ten consecutive railway catastrophes—not little accidents, but first class fatalities, when the long cars turn over, take fire, and roast the luckless occupants alive. To seven out of ten you shall find appended the cheerful statement: 'The accident is supposed to have been due to the rails spreading.'

### Twentieth-Century Travel

The railroads had taken their toll on long-distance travel by river steamboat and Great Lakes passenger ships by the time the twentieth century dawned, although some cross-lake vessels and small river packets continued for a few decades serving isolated markets until the automobile and motor truck put them out of business. The surviving maritime companies turned to excursion markets, pleasure travelers who considered the voyage itself a vacation. After that market disappeared at midcentury, the only passenger ships left on the lakes were the ferries.

Dr. Frederick L. Whitlark, a maritime buff who worked on several Great Lakes cruise ships while a college student just before World War II, in 1991 published his recollections of a 2,100-mile composite voyage of the *Seeandbee,* a side-wheeler built in 1912 for overnight express service on Lake Erie but during the Depression converted into service on week-long excur-

sion cruises between Chicago and Buffalo. Because such travel was discretionary, there was no steerage on the *Seeandbee* and the dozen or so other such excursion ships on the lakes, which were fitted out to emulate the lakes' great passenger ships of a century earlier and the first- and second-class accommodations on contemporary ocean liners. Meals and entertainment were an important part of the atmosphere, and their quality was a considerable improvement over what Dickens had endured in the 1840s.[16]

The Marine dining room was done in Adams style with columns, mahogany panels and silver candelabras. It was glass enclosed with great views of the water. Passengers were summoned to meals by a waiter walking the decks with a chime

box, announcing each sitting. Fresh bakery was a tradition and dinner featured duck, lake trout, and steak.

Passengers might spend the evening listening to Chicago's famous organist, Ken Griffin, in the grand saloon, enjoy a cocktail in one of several bars, take in the night's professional entertainment, the *Seeandbee* Review, or dance to the ship's orchestra. In the evening men wore white jackets and dark pants, or vice versa; ladies dressed in cocktail dresses or gowns.

The *Seeandbee* left from Chicago's Navy Pier at 8 P.M. Saturday and paddled 330 miles up the lake at 18 miles an hour to Mackinac Island. After a stop there for shopping the ship did a night crossing of Lake Huron and made stops in downtown Detroit and Cleveland on Monday. The

The busy port of Chicago was an exciting place for kids in the 1900s. (Chicago Maritime Society)

outbound voyage ended in Buffalo on Tuesday with side trips to Niagara Falls. The return voyage's itinerary was identical except for a detour to the Soo locks.

By the time the twentieth century ended, the only surviving passenger vessels on the Great Lakes were fifty ferries of assorted sizes, most of them less that 100 gross registered tons (GRT). The largest of them in the U.S. fleet at 4,244 tons (GRT) and the only one offering scheduled cross-lake passenger service on Lake Michigan was the car ferry *Badger,* which made a daily round trip across the northern end of the lake between Ludington, Michigan, and Manitowoc, Wisconsin. Originally designed in the early 1950s to handle railroad cars, its new owner in the 1990s modified the coal-fired ship to carry as many as six hundred passengers and 120 automobiles or a smaller number of trucks and buses on a four-hour trips across the lake.[17]

In that respect the *Badger* was more like the cross-lake packets early in the century, although the ship's owner, Charles F. Conrad, said just after he bought the vessel in 1991 that his intention was to operate four-hour "minicruises" appealing to vacationing families and bus tours. The vessel accepted freight traffic only on a space-available basis and did not operate in winter, even though it had an icebreaking hull, because tourism was minimal.[18]

Although private cabins were available for rent, the *Badger* had none of the opulence of the 1930s cruise ships. It was reconfigured and priced for the age of Disneyland—families traveling with children—with such things as an electronic game room, a gift shop, a small movie theater, and television sets playing videotapes. The ship had a bar and two restaurants; one served fast food and the other was a buffet with two main entrees on a steam table and a dozen side dishes.

To those who have never seen the Great Lakes the idea of taking a pleasure cruise in the middle of a continent might seem far fetched. The *Badger*'s course (279 degrees westbound on the compass and 99 degrees eastbound) is only 60 miles in length, but for two of the four hours it takes the ship to make the transit it is entirely out of the sight of land. The only sight is the ship's wake fanning out astern and an occasional passing freighter or sailboat.

Herman Melville, the great chronicler of the oceans in such novels as *Moby Dick* and *Billy Budd,* had heard stories about the Great Lakes more than 150 years ago. He knew of the dangers of sailing them and of the terrible shipwrecks and loss of life that occurred more than 1,000 miles from the ocean, yet out of the sight of land. Travel on the waters, whether in the seventeenth century or the twentieth, involved a degree of risk.

# *Chapter Eight* Disasters

• Sagas of the sea have tended to ignore or downplay the rigors and dangers of sailing on fresh water, barely, if ever, out of view of land. But two of the worst maritime disasters in United States history were both on fresh water, rivers no less, with insufficient depth for the vessels involved to sink out of sight. A boiler explosion destroyed the steamboat *Sultana* on the Mississippi River north of Memphis, killing 1,547 and possibly 1,643 persons aboard, and the lake steamship *Eastland* capsized at its dock in the Chicago River in 1915, drowning 844.

From pre-Columbian times, when a flotilla of Winnebago canoes was swamped in a sudden storm, drowning several hun-

dred of their occupants, to 1975, when the 729-foot leviathan ore boat *Edmund Fitzgerald* foundered on Lake Superior, the Great Lakes and western rivers have been the scene of fatal snaggings, groundings, explosions, collisions, capsizings, and gales comparable to anything on the oceans. The number of such disasters has declined in recent years because of improved rescue techniques; better weather forecasting to warn of storms; the development of radar, radio, sonar, and satellite global positioning systems; more stringent licensing of ships and crews; and advances in ship design. There are also far fewer ships on the lakes and relatively little passenger traffic.

Substantial investment by the federal

The *Eastland* disaster, because it occurred in downtown Chicago in 1915 within a few blocks of the offices of all the newspapers, is photographically one of the best documented maritime disasters. The death toll was 844 although the ship capsized only a few feet from shore and tugs and other watercraft immediately came to the rescue. (Great Lakes Historical Society, Vermilion, Ohio)

government in the form of safety regulations; navigation aids, such as lighthouses
and channel markers; establishment of a
lifesaving service; and the building of such
things as breakwaters and locks around
river obstructions have made the waterways less dangerous to travel. Improvements in steam engines and safety valves
have reduced the risk considerably, as did
steel hulls and watertight bulkheads.

Herman Melville, a saltwater sailor
turned novelist, knew of the dangers of
the Inland Seas, and when he wrote his
masterpiece *Moby Dick* included a passage
about them. Ishmael is spinning yarns in
the Golden Inn in Lima and tells his lis-
teners the tale of the whaling ship *Town-
Ho,* its encounter with the great white
whale and three of its inland crewmen, a
lake man named Steelkilt and two (Erie)
canallers:

> Now, gentlemen, in square-sail brigs and
> three masted ships, well-nigh as large and
> stout as any that ever sailed out of your
> old Callao to far Manila; this Lakeman in
> the land-locked heart of our America, had
> yet been nurtured by all those agrarian
> freebooting impressions popularly con-
> nected with the open ocean. For all their
> interflowing aggregate, these grand fresh-
> water seas of ours,—Erie, and Ontario,
> and Huron, and Superior, and Michigan—
> possess an ocean-like expansiveness, with
> many of the ocean's noblest traits; with
> many of its rimmed varieties of races and
> of climes. They contain round archipela-
> goes of romantic isles, even as the Polyne-
> sian waters do; in large part are shored by
> two great contrasting nations, as the At-
> lantic is; they furnish long maritime ap-
> proaches to our numerous territorial
> colonies from the East, dotted all round
> their banks; here and there are frowned
> upon by batteries, and by the goat-like
> craggy guns of lofty Mackinaw; they have
> heard the fleet thunderings of naval vic-
> tories; at intervals, they yield their
> beaches to wild barbarians, whose red-
> painted faces flash from out their peltry

> wigwams; for leagues and leagues are
> flanked by ancient and unentered forests,
> where the gaunt pines stand like storied
> lines of kings in Gothic genealogies; those
> same woods harboring wild Afric beasts of
> prey, and silken creatures whose exported
> furs give robes to Tartar Emperors; they
> mirror the paved capitals of Buffalo and
> Cleveland, as well as Winnebago villages;
> they float alike the full-rigged merchant
> ship, the armed cruiser of state, the
> steamer, and the beach canoe; they are
> swept by Borean and dismasting blasts as
> direful as any that lash the salted wave;
> they know what shipwrecks are; for, out
> of sight of land, however inland, they
> have drowned many a midnight ship
> with all its shrieking crew.[1]

There is no way of knowing how many
persons died in accidents on the inland
waters over the years, or even how many
vessels were destroyed. The death tolls of
many disasters, even into the twentieth
century, are little more than guesses. The
remoteness of many of the accidents, swift
currents that carried bodies away, and the
cold lake waters, which retarded the decomposition that causes corpses to float to
the surface, made accurate body counts
impossible. The lack of passenger manifests also made impossible the process of
calculating a death toll by subtracting the
survivors from the number of persons
known to have been on board. Even in the
case of the *Eastland,* a vessel that capsized
in the middle of downtown Chicago and
from which all bodies presumably were re-
covered because the hull was refloated, the
death toll was in some dispute (table 8.1).[2]

## The Rivers

The price of the dramatic increases in
speed and capacity made possible by mechanical traction had a liability measured
in mortality tables; the inevitable accidents occurring on vessels equipped for
higher speeds and increased passenger
loads were likely to result in a greater

**Table 8.1** Worst North American Merchant Marine Disasters

| Vessel | Date | Location | Fatalities Toll | Cause |
|---|---|---|---|---|
| *Sultana* | April 22, 1865 | Mississippi River (Memphis) | 1,547–1,653 | Boiler explosion |
| *Empress of Ireland* | May 29, 1914 | Saint Lawrence River | 1,012–1,024 | Collision |
| *General Slocum* | June 15, 1904 | East River (New York) | 957 | Fire |
| *Eastland* | July 24, 1915 | Chicago River (Chicago) | 812–844 | Capsizing |
| *Lady Elgin* | Sept. 8, 1860 | Lake Michigan (Glencoe) | 279 | Collision |
| *G. P. Griffith* | June 27, 1850 | Lake Erie, off Cleveland | 250–296 | Fire |
| *Monmouth* | Oct. 30, 1837 | Lower Mississippi River | 235–400 | Collision |
| *Phoenix* | Nov. 21, 1847 | Lake Michigan (Sheboygan, WI) | 190–250 | Boiler fire |
| *City of Portland* | Nov. 26, 1898 | Atlantic, off Cape Cod | 157 | Storm |
| *Moselle* | April 25, 1838 | Ohio River (Cincinnati) | 150 | Boiler explosion |
| *Morrow Castle* | Sept. 8, 1934 | Atlantic, off New Jersey | 134 | Fire |
| *Noronic* | Sept. 17, 1949 | Lake Ontario (Toronto) | 130 | Fire |

*Sources:* Charles Hocking, *Dictionary of Disasters at Sea During the Age of Steam* (London, 1969), 266–267, 671; Mansfield, *History of the Great Lakes,* 610–671; James Croall, *Fourteen Minutes: The Last Voyage of the 'Express of Ireland'* (New York, 1979), 147; Hilton, *Eastland,* 134–136; Hunter, *Steamboats on the Western Rivers,* 271–304. The death toll estimates were culled from local newspapers. Some steamboat accidents have been excluded from the list because of the uncertainties over the death tolls.

number of deaths and injuries. Slow-moving flatboats and keelboats undoubtedly had their share of mishaps—collisions with other craft and snags, fires, and swampings on swollen rivers—but because crews were small there were few casualties in any single accident. The steamboat changed all that within a few years.

An admittedly incomplete compilation of data between the beginning of steam navigation on the rivers in 1811 and the end of 1851 indicates there were nearly 1,000 accidents of which somewhere between 33 and 40 percent resulted in a total loss of the vessel. Fire accounted for 166 accidents (21%), explosions for 209 (32%), and snags and other obstructions for 576 (42.5%). Although snags claimed more boats, explosions, primarily of boilers, were the deadliest. Between 1816 and 1848, more than 1,443 fatalities were attributable to explosions.[3]

Despite their rarity, the worst disaster on

the rivers in antebellum times was the result of a collision. The *Monmouth,* carrying an estimated 500 Creek Indians being relocated to the West and packed into its small cabin, was steaming upstream on the Mississippi River after dark in 1837 and was hit by the *Warren* headed downriver. The force of the impact caused the *Monmouth*'s cabin to separate from the hull and break apart as it floated off downstream. The vessel sank, taking with it anywhere from 235 to 400 of the persons aboard.[4]

Although they rarely had a large death toll, snags resulted in more complaints from the steamboat industry because of the considerable damage they caused, especially to the paddle wheels. As early as 1824 the War Department began a concerted effort to remove the sunken tree trunks and within ten years declared that the worst of the problem was largely solved, although the war on snags was a continuing one. From late 1842 to mid-1845 government

Most of the *Eastland*'s victims drowned when trapped below decks. Rescuers spent most of the day dragging bodies out of the hull through open gangways. (*Chicago Tribune*)

snag boats pulled 21,681 snags and 36,840 roots, logs, and stumps from the rivers; and felled 74,910 trees on the banks that were in danger of toppling into the water. Snag boats were essentially self-propelled, twin-hulled double rams equipped with a crane to remove the snags once they had been loosened by ramming.

Although the snag removal program reduced the risk, as the steamboats got larger and faster, snaggings became deadlier. Only 16 persons were killed in the thirty-eight reported snaggings between 1830 and 1840, but between then and the Civil War there were ten disasters, usually on upstream trips and at night, that occurred with such violence that the steamboats sank within three to five minutes. A snag cut the *John Adams* in half when it was steaming up the Mississippi about 200 miles south of Memphis in 1851; the boat

sank so quickly that only 107 of the 230 persons aboard survived.[5]

Surprisingly one of the worst disasters caused by a snag did not occur until July 5, 1918, more than half a century after the traveling public and most freight shippers abandoned the rivers for the railroads, when the twenty-year-old Illinois River excursion steamer *Columbia* with 496 passengers, returning to Pekin from a day trip to an amusement park in Peoria, just before midnight hit a submerged tree trunk on the river south of Peoria. The snag tore an 11-foot gash in the hull, causing an immediate list and the collapse of some structural beams on the main deckhouse. Although the wooden, stern-wheel steamboat sank only up to the hurricane deck, 87 persons, mostly women and children, were drowned.[6]

In 1892 the Peoria area also was the site

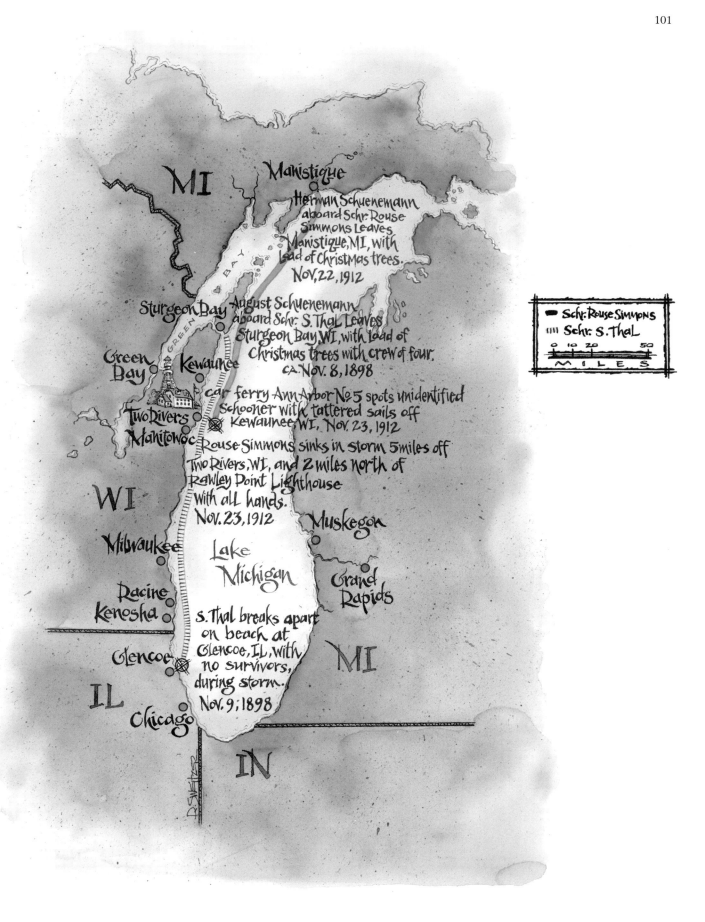

MI

Manistique

Herman Schuenemann aboard Schr. Rouse Simmons Leaves Manistique, MI, with load of Christmas trees. Nov. 22, 1912

Sturgeon Bay

August Schuenemann aboard Schr. S. Thal Leaves Sturgeon Bay, WI, with load of Christmas trees with crew of four. CA. Nov. 8, 1898

Green Bay

Kewaunee

car ferry Ann Arbor No. 5 spots unidentified schooner with tattered sails off Kewaunee, WI, Nov. 23, 1912

Two Rivers

Manitowoc

Rouse Simmons sinks in storm 5 miles off Two Rivers, WI, and 2 miles north of Rawley Point Lighthouse with all hands. Nov. 23, 1912

WI

Muskegon

Milwaukee

Lake Michigan

Grand Rapids

Racine

Kenosha

S. Thal breaks apart on beach at Glencoe, IL, with no survivors, during storm. Nov. 9, 1898

MI

Glencoe

IL

Chicago

IN

GREEN BAY

Schr. Rouse Simmons
Schr. S. Thal

0 10 20    50
MILES

The *Eastland* accident attracted a huge crowd of spectators as word of the disaster spread through the Loop and workers left their offices to watch. (*Chicago Tribune*)

of an accident more typical of the Great Lakes than the western rivers. The steamer *Frankie Folsom,* also on an excursion, was hit broadside by a violent windstorm, capsized, and sank. The death toll has been estimated at anywhere from 12 to 27 persons.

Fires were a major cause of disaster on the rivers, resulting in the deaths of 444 persons between the beginning of steam navigation and 1840. The flimsily constructed wooden steamboat superstructures were tinderboxes. Fuel wood stacked aboard and various combustible cargoes, even straw used for packing, added to the hazard. The high-pressure engines, which got exceedingly hot with little or no insulation to separate them from the wooden parts of the vessel, and sparks spewing from the smokestacks were often a source of fires. The standard emergency procedure on the rivers and Great Lakes in the nineteenth century when a fire broke out was to steam at full speed to shore, but fires often burned the tiller ropes, leaving the pilot without the ability to steer. Few people could swim in those days, and lifeboats were unknown.[7]

The fire aboard the *Ben Sherrod,* which killed between 120 and 175 persons in 1837 was one of a succession of disasters

that finally prodded Congress into action the next year to attempt to impose some safety regulations on steam-powered vessels on the rivers, lakes, and oceans. The *Sherrod*'s captain was supposedly racing another boat home to Louisville when a fire spread from the furnace to a pile of cordwood nearby. There followed a succession of blunders that turned the accident into a disaster. The crew was slow to spread the alarm to the 200 sleeping passengers aboard, the pilot failed to head for shore until the tiller ropes had burned, making steering impossible, the engineer fled his post leaving the engine at full speed ahead, and the captain of the passing steamboat *Alton* refused to stop to assist the survivors in the water.[8]

Boiler explosions were the greatest fear of steamboat passengers and crew, however. They came without warning and often scalded their victims to a slow, agonizing death. Charles Dickens was well aware of the danger when he arrived on America's shores (see chapter 7), and Mark Twain described in *Life on the Mississippi* the death of his brother, Henry, a pilot aboard the *Pennsylvania,* when her boilers blew up in 1858 about 60 miles south of Memphis, hurling him into the river.

Samuel Clemens, long before he adopted the nom de plume of Mark Twain, at the time was steaming north on the *A. T. Lacey* two days behind the *Pennsylvania,* but he was able to reconstruct the details of the accident after interviewing many of the survivors when he reached Memphis to visit his dying brother:

It was six o'clock on a hot summer morning. The *Pennsylvania* was creeping along, north of Ship Island . . . on a half head of steam, towing a wood flat which was fast being emptied. The wood being nearly out of the flat now, [George] Ealer [the pilot] rang to 'come ahead' full of steam, and the next moment four of the eight boilers exploded with a thunderous crash, and the whole forward third of the boat was hoisted toward the sky! The main part of the mass, with the chimneys, dropped upon the boat again, a mountain of riddled and chaotic rubbish—and then, after a while, fire broke out.

By this time the fire was beginning to threaten. . . . Shrieks and groans filled the air. A great many persons had been scalded, a great many crippled; the explosion had driven an iron bar through one man's body—I think they said he was a priest. He did not die at once, and his sufferings were very dreadful. A young French naval cadet of fifteen, son of a French admiral, was fearfully scalded but bore his tortures manfully.

In a temporary hospital in Memphis, Twain found his dying brother:

By this time Henry was insensible. The physicians examined his injuries and saw that they were fatal, and naturally turned their main attention to patients who could be saved.

The sight I saw when I entered that large hall was new and strange to me. Two long rows of prostrate forms—more than forty in all—and every face and head a shapeless wad of loose raw cotton. It was a gruesome spectacle. I watched

there six days and six nights, and a very melancholy experience it was. There was one daily incident which was particularly depressing: this was the removal of the doomed to a chamber apart. It was done in order that the morale of the other patients might not be injuriously affected by seeing one of their number in the death-agony. The fated one was always carried out with as little stir as possible, and the stretcher was always hidden from sight by a wall of assistants; but no matter: everyone knew what the cluster of bent forms, with its muffled step and slow movement, meant; and all eyes watched wistfully, and a shudder went abreast of it, like a wave.

Dr. Peyton . . . did all that educated judgement and trained skill could do for Henry; but, as the newspapers had said in the beginning, his hurts were past help. On the evening of the sixth day his wandering mind busied itself with matters far away, and his nerveless fingers 'picked at his coverlet.' His hour had struck; we bore him to the death-room, poor boy.[9]

From the 1816 explosion aboard the *Washington* at Marietta, Ohio, that killed 13 to the end of 1853 when the second steamboat inspection act took effect, an estimated 7,000 persons died in explosions on steamboats—600 of them in the eight months prior to adoption by Congress of the new act.[10] The law and Steamboat Inspection Service that it created did little to help the *Sultana* when wartime exigencies often took precedence over safety. The death toll from the boiler explosion that destroyed the vessel on the Mississippi north of Memphis on April 27, 1865, was more than 1,500, most of them repatriated Union prisoners of war. The disaster still stands as the worst in U.S. maritime history.[11]

The *Sultana,* which had a registered capacity of 376 persons, already had 100 civilian passengers and a crew of 85 aboard when its captain, J. Cass Mason, agreed to make a big score and haul back north an additional 1,800 Union soldiers repatriated

Divers were necessary to remove many of the bodies trapped below decks of the *Eastland*. (*Chicago Tribune*)

from Southern prison camps. It was never made clear in the subsequent hearings why U.S. army officials tried to jam all the soldiers on one vessel instead of sending some home on other steamboats available in Vicksburg at the time. The vessel also had a bulging seam on its middle larboard boiler repaired at Vicksburg before taking the soldiers on board and steaming north, and the commission investigating the disaster concluded that the explosion was due to insufficient water in the boilers.[12]

## Safety Regulations

As early as 1826 Alabama passed a law requiring steamboats to be inspected annually, followed by Kentucky (1836), Illinois (1837), and several other states, but the state statutes were nearly impossible to enforce because the major rivers were the boundaries of many states, making jurisdiction a difficult issue. Finally the rash of fires and explosions in 1836–1837 caused Congress to act by adopting the largely toothless Steamboat Act, which did little but establish the principle of safety regulation of steam-powered vessels on all navigable waterways, not just the rivers. It did not even require vessels to carry life preservers for passengers, although that issue had been debated.[13]

After another rash of disasters between 1847 and 1852, Congress put some teeth into the law by mandating on all fresh- or saltwater passenger vessels such things as testing of boilers, maximum allowable pressures, passing rules, and life preservers and lifeboats. The law also required the testing and licensing of both engineers and pilots and the hiring by the new U.S. Steamboat Inspection Service of boiler and hull inspectors, who had the power to suspend or revoke licenses for violations of the law. The result was an immediate and dramatic decline in accidents and fatalities; from fifty explosions and 1,155 resulting deaths in the four years prior to the new law (1848–1832) the toll dropped to twenty explosions causing 224 deaths in the four years after the law had been enacted (1854–1858).[14]

The Steamboat Inspection Service was one of five separate federal agencies concerned with marine safety that ultimately wound up being merged into the U.S. Coast Guard in the twentieth century. Although the Coast Guard didn't come into existence until 1915, its oldest constituent member traces its roots back to 1716, when the colony of Massachusetts set up a lighthouse at the entrance to the Boston harbor. One of the first transfers of power from the states to the new federal government created by the 1789 Constitution was the twelve colonial lighthouses.

The resulting U.S. Lighthouse Service, which was transferred to the Coast Guard in 1939, ultimately built more than a thousand of the structures to mark dangerous obstacles, channels, points of land useful for navigators, and harbor entrances. It also built a lighthouse at Natchez on the Mississippi, although the preferred method of marking the courses of the western rivers

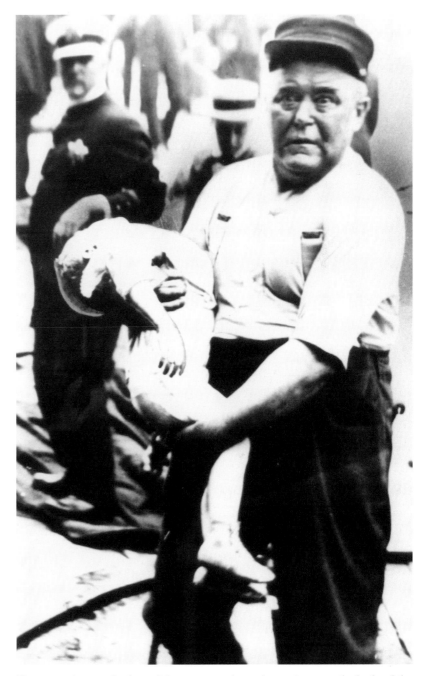

The expression on the face of the rescue worker as he carries away the body of the child tells the story of the *Eastland* disaster better than words. The impact on the public was such that the Goodrich line was forced to conduct stability tests on its excursion steamer *Christopher Columbus* in the aftermath, not because regulators required it but to reassure the public the vessel was safe. (*Chicago Tribune*)

The *Eastland,* shown on the Chicago River sometime before the disaster. Note the open starboard gangways that, when the ship began to capsize, contributed to its rapid flooding. (*Chicago Tribune*)

The *Eastland* suffered almost no structural damage in the accident and was refloated and later converted into a naval training vessel, the *Wilmette.* The vessel was finally scrapped, beginning in 1946. (*Chicago Tribune*)

was by unmanned post lights and channel buoys. The first of more than a hundred lighthouses on the Great Lakes and Saint Lawrence River was built in 1819 on Presque Isle near Erie, Pennsylvania. By 1832 maritime traffic had increased to the point that Chicago rated its first lighthouse to mark the mouth of its river.[15]

The Revenue Cutter Service had been created in 1790 by Treasury Secretary Alexander Hamilton to curb smuggling at a time when duties on imports were an important source of federal revenue. However, the cutters, which appeared on the Great Lakes in the 1820s, were probably more useful in assisting ships and sailors in distress than in law enforcement. The Treasury Department's revenue cutter *Ingham* was conspicuously absent during most of the navy frigate *Michigan*'s skirmishes with the timber poachers on Lake Michigan.[16]

The Revenue Cutter Service wound up being merged with the now largely forgotten Life-Saving Service in 1915 to become the Coast Guard. Lighthouses were added in 1939, and the Steamboat Inspection Service and Bureau of Navigation were moved to the Coast Guard in 1942.

The Life-Saving Service, beginning in 1848, grew out of volunteer efforts along the coasts of Long Island and New Jersey to save people from ships wrecked within sight of land but who drowned in the surf trying to reach shore or when the ship broke up. Immigrant ships blown ashore in storms while trying to reach New York were a major cause of marine fatalities in the nineteenth century, and beach shipwrecks were a serious enough problem on the Great Lakes that after a particularly bad storm in 1854 Congress appropriated $12,500 to buy lifeboats for twenty-five points on Lake Michigan, generally near lighthouses. Lake Ontario got nine boats, Lake Erie fourteen, and Lake Superior one. Lake Michigan got the biggest allotment because it was (and is) considered the most dangerous of the Great Lakes with a relatively narrow, north-south configuration with few natural harbor refuges. More than half of the thirteen worst disasters on the Great Lakes in terms of loss of human life occurred on one lake—Michigan.[17]

It was the task of the life savers to row, or motor, in small boats into stormy seas to rescue survivors. Possibly the most famous of them on the Great Lakes was Lawrence O. Lawson, a native of Sweden, who immigrated to the United States and wound up commanding for twenty-three years the Life-Saving station on the grounds of Northwestern University in north suburban Evanston, manned almost entirely by college students. The impetus for the station had been the heroic efforts in 1860 of the Northwestern student Edward Spencer and some of his colleagues in rescuing from a pounding surf some of the estimated 150 survivors of the *Lady Elgin*. About 300 of the survivors of the steamship's collision with a schooner off Chicago's northern suburbs had survived the night by clinging to wreckage.[18]

By one estimate Lawson's crews for the twenty-three years after he took over the station in 1880 rescued more than 447 persons from thirty-five shipwrecks. His finest hour was on November 28, 1889, when the steamer *Calumet* ran aground off Fort Sheridan and Lawson's crew and boat were hauled by train as close as the railroad could get to the scene. Then the crew had to maneuver the boat down a steep bluff and into the teeth of a gale to successfully rescue all 18 crewmen.[19]

## The Violent Lakes

The wreck of the *Lady Elgin* was for fifty-five years, until the *Eastland,* the worst disaster on the Great Lakes: 297 persons died. Like many disasters on land, sea, or in the air, it was the result of a succession of causes—a collision that occurred during a storm made worse by some poor decisions. Storms were the most common cause of disasters on the lakes, not just in the age of sail, although fires and collisions took their toll. Boiler explosions were less of a problem on the lakes, though not unknown, because low-pressure steam

River steamboats were vulnerable not only to fires and boiler explosions but to hitting snags—underwater tree stumps. The wreckage of the *Columbia* on the Illinois River near Peoria in 1918, in which eighty-seven persons died, shows the disastrous effects of snaggings on wooden steamboats. (Peoria Public Library)

Rescue workers inspect the *Columbia*'s collapsed superstructure after the vessel hit a snag on the Illinois River in 1918. (Peoria Public Library)

engines were predominant.

The *Lady Elgin* was returning to Milwaukee with a group of militia members who had attended a political rally in Chicago when a storm broke over the lake. The paddle-wheel steamship was weathering the storm well and making progress, but in the other direction the schooner *Augusta* was in trouble; its load of lumber had shifted, causing a list, and the crew was having trouble keeping control, with most of the vessel's canvas still flying. Rules of the sea give sailing vessels the right of way over steamships, and a prudent pilot even in 1860 should have steered a course wide of another vessel when in difficulty, especially in a storm. The *Augusta* plowed into the *Lady Elgin* just aft of the port paddle wheel about seven miles off Winnetka. Although it is not entirely certain that the schooner's crew under the circumstances could have conducted a rescue, they lost sight of the *Lady Elgin* shortly after the collision and sailed on to Chicago to later face considerable public outcries when news of the disaster got out.[20]

The *Lady Elgin* was in compliance with the Steamboat Inspection Act of 1852 in that she carried both lifeboats and life jackets, but her sinking illustrates the problem maritime safety officials were still confronting at the time of the *Titanic, Eastland,* and *Empress of Ireland* disasters more than half a century later: having adequate lifesaving equipment aboard a ship does not ensure there will be time to use it. The *Lady Elgin,* whose captain, first mate, and most passengers had been asleep in their cabins at the time of the 2:30 A.M. crash, by most accounts broke apart and sank within twenty minutes. Attempts to launch two lifeboats were unsuccessful, and the breaking up of the ship separated the passengers from the life preservers.[21]

The *Titanic* in 1912, because of adept handling by its crew, took a leisurely two hours to sink after striking an iceberg in mid-Atlantic but didn't have sufficient lifeboats aboard because the British Board of Trade's rules on lifeboat capacity were based on the assumption that an incident catastrophic enough to sink the ship would do it so quickly that all the boats couldn't be launched. That was the case two years after the *Titanic* disaster when the Canadian Pacific Railway's *Empress of Ireland* ocean liner outbound from Quebec was hit by a collier and sank in the Saint Lawrence River in just fourteen minutes, killing 1,012 of the 1,477 persons aboard. The ship had lifeboats with a combined capacity of 2,000 persons, but the portside boats were useless because of the collision-induced list.[22]

It was the "lifeboats-for-all" movement, which picked up speed after the *Titanic* sinking, that, George W. Hilton has argued, contributed to the *Eastland* disaster in 1915; additional lifeboats required by post-*Titanic* regulations probably made the lake excursion vessel top-heavy under maximum load.

The *Eastland* is certainly one of the most bizarre disasters in maritime history. It occurred in the central business district of one of the largest cities on earth when a ship loaded with Western Electric Company employees on their way to a company picnic capsized in slow motion at its moorings in a barely navigable river with insufficient depth to sink the ship. Yet 844 persons were drowned in what is still the worst disaster on the Great Lakes.[23]

The United States' version of the lifeboats-for-all reforms following the *Titanic,* known popularly as the La Follette Seamen's Act after the progressive Wisconsin senator Robert M. La Follette, was signed into law in early 1915. Among other things it required lifeboats for three-fourths of the passenger capacity and rafts or collapsible craft for the rest on any passenger ship that operated more than 3 miles from shore, including Great Lakes excursion ships.

The *Eastland,* which had a draft that could be adjusted by pumping water into and out of ballast tanks to clear shallow harbors, had exhibited some stability problems early in its existence in 1903–1904. On July 2, 1915, the ship had additional lifeboats and rafts installed on her hurricane deck, adding an estimated 14 to 15 tons of weight, to conform to the new regulations. The refitted vessel made twenty trips between then and July 23, but never carried even half of its rated capacity of

Because they often occurred in storms, at night, far from land, and when photography was in its infancy, there are few photographs of Great Lakes disasters. The light at Rawley Point, near Two Rivers, Wisconsin, originally stood in Chicago and was moved in 1893. The *Rouse Simmons*, the "Christmas Tree Ship," sank with all hands about five miles off this light in 1912.

The artist Charles Vickery did three canvases of the *Rouse Simmons,* this one at the dock in Chicago with a load of Christmas trees. The vessel became something of a Great Lakes legend—the "Christmas Tree Ship"—when it mysteriously disappeared with all hands in a storm off Rawley Point, near Two Rivers, Wisconsin. (Painting by Charles Vickery, courtesy of the Clipper Ship Gallery)

2,500 passengers. Then on July 24, the first time it was loaded to capacity with 2,501 passengers, it capsized, trapping and drowning most of the victims below deck.[24]

The Chicago River also was the site of other, less deadly, disasters. Boiler explosions, the plague of river steamboats, were infrequent but deadly on the lakes. The vintage 1837 steam tug *Seneca* blew up in the river on October 16, 1855, while steaming by the Randolph Street bridge. The explosion destroyed the superstructure and killed the captain and engineer but no one else.[25]

A potentially deadlier explosion on November 8, 1860—two months to the day after the *Lady Elgin* collision—destroyed the *Globe,* the vessel Lincoln had ridden with his family from Buffalo to Chicago

back in 1848, at its dock in Chicago. The explosion and flying debris killed as many as sixteen persons, three of them bystanders, including a fifteen-year-old girl gleaning apples that had fallen out of broken barrels on the dock, and heavily damaged the nearby canal boat *Alonzo.* The blast would have been deadlier, but the passengers aboard the *Globe* had already left the vessel.

In 1856 she had been converted from a side-wheeler to a propeller, and new high-pressure boilers were installed to provide the higher revolutions necessary to turn the screws. As was frequent in such explosions, the boilers blew up when the engine was at rest or slow speed and the steam pressure built up. The *Globe* had docked from Buf-

falo at 4 A.M. below the Wells Street bridge and discharged its passengers. Her apparently unattended larboard boiler blew up five hours later. As was common on the lakes, the sunken hull was later raised, salvaged, and converted to a barge.[26]

## Fires

Although the Chicago fire of 1871 was not a maritime disaster in terms of death toll, it was in terms of property damage. The new propeller *Naravino* worth $75,000 was a total loss, as were the schooners *Glenbula, Eclipse,* and *Butcher Boy,* and the bark *Fontanella.* The loss of vessels would have been far worse had not Captain Joseph Gilson of the tugboat *Magnolia* been awakened by the glare of the fire and steamed up the river to pull several vessels to the safety of Lake Michigan.

As the fire intensified, Gilson's mission changed: refugees from the flames crowded onto the propellers *Ira Chaffe* and *Skylark* and the side-wheeler *Manitowoc,* which the tugboat then towed out into the lake. Later Gilson towed some flaming schooners into the lake in an ill-fated effort to save the warehouses at which they were docked. At dawn he discovered eight to ten thousand people crowded along the lakeshore north of the lighthouse and with the help of other tugs moved them to safety.[27]

Individual ship fires at sea often were deadlier. The Chicago-bound *Seabird,* a Goodrich ship headed home on April 9, 1868, is often cited as an example of a disaster caused by carelessness when a porter dumped a coal scuttle with embers overboard into the wind, although the cause was never officially determined. According to the most popular account, the hot embers landed on the deck below and set some freshly varnished tubs packed with straw afire.[28]

The usual procedure in emergencies on the Great Lakes was to steam for shore and the captain of the *Seabird* tried to do just that, but the northeast wind fanned the flames the length of the vessel. Most of the passengers and crew who leaped overboard to escape the flames quickly succumbed to hypothermia in the icy water. Only three of the 73 to 100 persons aboard survived.[29]

Far worse were the tolls aboard the *Phoenix,* a steamer bound from Buffalo to Chicago with a load of Dutch immigrants in 1847, and aboard the *G. P. Griffith* on the same route with immigrants three years later. Heat from the boiler set the deck afire on the *Phoenix* off Sheboygan, Wisconsin, and 250 died. The *G. P. Griffith* in 1850 near Cleveland bolted for shore only 2 miles away after a fire of unknown cause was discovered in the hold but ran aground on a bar a half mile from safety. At that point the captain and everyone else aboard panicked and leaped overboard. Only 31 of the 326 persons believed to have been aboard the vessel survived.[30]

There is a tendency among Great Lakes historians to group weather-related disasters by storms, not individual ships. A. T. Andreas mentioned the storm of April 27, 1854, as causing the loss of 7 ships on the lake near Chicago, killing 7 persons and resulting in the acquisition of the city's first two lifeboats. J. B. Mansfield refers to a succession of storms in 1852 that caused the loss of or heavy damage to 229 vessels, 55 of them during a single gale on November 11–12, and the death of 296 persons. Two storms in 1869—September 16–20 and November 16–19—resulted in the loss of another 68 ships. Robert J. Hemming wrote an entire book about the four-day gale in 1913 that claimed 12 ships, seriously damaged 25 more, and drowned 250 to 300 persons. In Chicago the storm swept at least two spectators on land to their deaths and caused hundreds of thousands of dollars in damage to roads, parks, and seawalls.[31]

## Disappearances

The tendency of ships in the years before the wireless telegraph was invented (1895) to disappear with little or no trace spawned a succession of local "Flying

Dutchman" legends and became the grist for popular historians writing maritime mysteries. The *Rouse Simmons,* lost in 1912, was memorialized for a time as the "Christmas Tree Ship" that somehow had sailed through a hole in the lake. Barbara Schuenemann, the widow of the ship's master, somewhat exploited the legend for years to attract public attention to the fact that she was continuing her husband's annual Christmas tree business despite his mysterious disappearance; but she filed a probate petition in Cook County Court on January 20, 1913, claiming that her husband had died intestate two months earlier, on November 23, 1912.[32]

Although sailing ships were generally considered more vulnerable to storms than steamers, Goodrich and the Graham and Morton Transportation Company, rival cross-lake shipping companies, both lost steamships with all aboard to storms in 1880 and 1895, respectively. In 1868 Goodrich bought for $80,000 the year-old, wooden, side-wheel steamer *Alpena* to replace the ill-fated *Seabird,* which had burned earlier in the year. The *Alpena* disappeared on a run between Grand Haven, Michigan, and Chicago during an unexpected storm on October 16, 1880. In 1892 Graham and Morton took delivery of a new wooden propeller, the *Chicora,* to compete with Goodrich. The vessel disappeared in a storm on a midwinter run in 1895 while carrying flour from Milwaukee to Saint Joseph, Michigan, after a telegram from the frantic owner warning the master not to sail because a falling barometer indicated an impending storm was delivered a few minutes after the ship sailed.[33]

Neither steel hulls nor the giant vessels that appeared on the lakes in the twentieth century were completely inured to the infamous lake gales. The wooden-hulled *Alpena* was registered at only 653 gross tons (100 cubic feet per gross ton) and the *Chicora* at 1,122 tons, but by the early twentieth century Great Lakes shipyards were turning out sturdy steel car ferries of

nearly 3,000 tons to enable railroads to bypass the Chicago rail bottleneck. Since the vessels were intended to haul small railroad trains across the lakes year round, they had powerful, 3,000-horsepower engines and hulls designed to plow through ice and operate under almost any conditions.

However, two almost identical vessels built for different owners in 1902–1903 at the American Ship Building Company yard in Cleveland both foundered in storms, sinking by the stern under circumstances that have not been fully explained. Hull No. 412 was named *Pere Marquette 18* when acquired by the railroad of that name in 1902 and put in service on cross-lake runs with summer excursion charters from Chicago. On September 9, 1910, while on a run from Ludington, Michigan, to Milwaukee during a storm she radioed a CQD[34] distress signal that she was taking water from the stern. Another car ferry had reached the scene and was standing by to help when the *Pere Marquette 18* unexpectedly plunged beneath the waves, taking twenty-seven or twenty-nine persons with her. Another thirty-five were picked up by the rescue vessel.[35]

The Cleveland yard's almost identical Hull No. 413 was named the *Manistique, Marquette and Northern I* after it was delivered to the new railroad of that name in 1903 but was renamed *Milwaukee* after being sold to Grand Trunk Railway in 1908. As late as 1929 she was not equipped with a radio and disappeared without any alert after leaving Milwaukee for Grand Haven in a storm on October 29 of that year with twenty-five railroad cars and a crew of forty-seven. The only indication of her fate was a note found five days later in the ship's message case, written by A. R. Sadon, the ship's purser, saying that the "flicker"—the stern compartment aft of the engine and boiler rooms used as the crew's living and sleeping quarters—was flooded and that "things look bad."[36]

The 640-foot-long *Carl B. Bradley,* built

Despite such improved navigation technology as global satellite positioning systems, a lighthouse still stood on the breakwater off Navy Pier in the year 2000 to guide ships to the mouth of the Chicago River. Like almost all contemporary Coast Guard lighthouses, this one was automated.

in 1927 and capable of carrying more than 18,000 tons of limestone for its owner, a subsidiary of U.S. Steel Corporation, dwarfed the car ferries. She had delivered the final load of the season to Buffington, Indiana, and was heading back up the lake for the annual winter lay-up in Rogers City, Michigan, in November 1958 when a storm began to build. At about 12 miles south of Gull Island at the northern end of the lake, the *Bradley* abruptly split in half and sank, killing thirty-three of its crewmen. Two, including the first mate Elmer Fleming, who had broadcast the ship's "M'aidez!" distress call as the vessel's stern began to sag a few minutes before she foundered, somehow survived to be rescued by a Coast Guard ship responding to the distress call.[37]

The last major Great Lakes disaster was

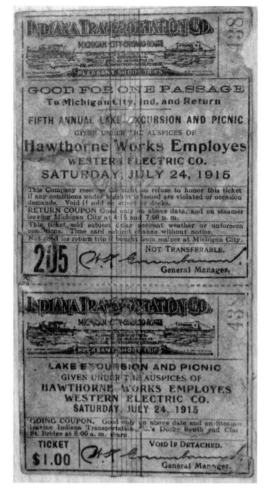

The people who died on the *Eastland* paid a dollar apiece for their tickets and were forbidden to buy them from scalpers. This ticket belonged to the author's grandfather and father, who escaped the disaster because they were late and literally missed the boat.

the 1975 sinking of the ore ship *Edmund Fitzgerald* with all twenty-nine hands aboard during a gale about 17 miles from the relative safety of Whitefish Bay on Lake Superior. The disaster has attained something of a legendary status after the popular singer Gordon Lightfoot recorded a song about it. The *Fitzgerald,* which holds the dubious distinction of being the largest vessel to sink on the Great Lakes, was 711 feet long, and when she foundered November 9, 1975, was carrying 26,116 tons of taconite pellets. Despite being equipped with radio and radar, the ship sank so quickly that her crew was unable to make a distress call and was reported missing after she disappeared from the radar aboard the U.S. Steel Corporation's *Arthur M. Andersen* steaming about 10 miles astern.

The lack of disasters in the last quarter of the twentieth century is probably the result of improved communications, global positioning, and weather forecasting as well as a substantial decline in the number of ships. More than 5,000 ships were registered on the Great Lakes between the Civil War and 1875. In 1958, the year the *Edmund Fitzgerald* was launched, there were 699 commercial vessels registered, 415 U.S. and 284 Canadian.[38]

Although the lakes and rivers were as dangerous a place for mariners as the oceans, they did not suffer from another plague common for a time on salt water—piracy. There was some piracy and brigandage on the inland waters, but it was relatively rare, especially after steam-powered vessels became common.

# Chapter Nine Pirates

"He would be a pirate! That was it! Now his future lay plain before him, and glowing with unimaginable splendor. How his name would fill the world and make people shudder! How gloriously he would go plowing the dancing seas, in his long, low, black-hulled racer, the *Spirit of the Storm,* with his grisly flag flying at the fore!"
　　　　　　　　　　　　　　　—Tom Sawyer[1]

• Soon after commerce began on the western rivers and as early as 1760, miscreants were finding ways to prey on it. The Great Lakes also had their share of piratical incidents, though not on the scale of the oceans and not nearly as well documented in popular literature. There were no Jean LaFittes or Blackbeards on the inland waters primarily because there were no Span-

ish galleons laden with gold and Chinese porcelains; the flatboats and schooners for the most part carried bulk cargoes like corn and lumber. The wars that spawned privateering on the high seas were far removed from the rivers and lakes. Nevertheless, there was sufficient value to such things as lumber and fish, and especially personal belongings of travelers, to cause some piracy.

The term itself conjures up a popular image of cutthroats looting ships on the high seas, but most inland piracy bordered on brigandage, looting vessels lured to shore, which by definition of the Law of Nations is piracy. In some cases, the definition gets a little fuzzy: looting a shipwreck could be considered piracy by the victim

The *Michigan* never fought a battle. One of its major duties in the 1850s and 1860s was to combat piracy and keep the peace on the Upper Great Lakes. The vessel was equipped with masts at a time when steam engines were not reliable but proved to be a better steamer than a sailer and rarely used its canvas. (Great Lakes Historical Society)

but salvage, which is legal, by the looters. Some of the so-called piracy on the Great Lakes was poaching—the stealing of timber from federal lands by ship; other cases involved turf wars by local fishermen or, late in the nineteenth century, independent fishermen trying to make a living in competition with a Chicago company trying to monopolize the catch or prevent the extinction of certain types of fish, depending upon whose point of view is accepted.

The Barbary Coast of the western rivers was the Ohio River palisades in southern Illinois, from which gangs pillaged flatboats and murdered their occupants in a manner as brutal as anything on the high seas. Lawlessness was a serious enough problem on Lake Michigan that in the 1850s the federal government assigned its first iron warship there to bring order. Somewhat later the state of Michigan leased and armed a tug to enforce the Booth monopoly on Lake Michigan and put local fishermen out of business. Perhaps the only documented case of high-seas style piracy in which a vessel was taken on the open waters occurred during the Civil War on Lake Erie when Confederate agents from Canada commandeered two ships in an effort to free prisoners of war being held at Sandusky, Ohio.

### The River Pirates

*The Adventures of Tom Sawyer* is scattered with boys' dreams of piracy and buried treasure along the Mississippi River obviously drawn from Samuel Langhorne Clemens's early life along the river. Although the story is fiction, the idea of piracy and buried treasure is not so far-fetched: the western rivers were rife with land pirates a few decades before Clemens's birth in 1835 in Florida, Missouri. Writing forty-one years later as Mark Twain, he had Tom Sawyer and Huck Finn innocently looking for buried treasure in a haunted house when the nefarious Injun Joe and an accomplice showed up unexpectedly, looking for the real thing:

Injun Joe took the pick, looked it over critically, shook his head, muttered something to himself, and then began to use it. The box was soon unearthed. It was not very large; it was iron-bound and had been very strong before the slow years had injured it. The men contemplated the treasure awhile in blissful silence.

"Pard, there's thousands of dollars here," said Injun Joe.

"Twas always said that Murrel's [sic] gang used to be around here one summer," the stranger observed.[2]

Although less well known than the brigand Jesse James, John A. Murrell and his clan were notorious, land-based pirates on the Mississippi River in Arkansas early in the nineteenth century. A gang of Englishmen and renegade Indians under James Colbert preyed on Spanish shipping on the Mississippi south of Natchez in the 1780s, and there were reports of boat plunderings on the Ohio as early as 1760.[3]

They apparently operated independently of another group of pirates using Cave-in-Rock in Illinois overlooking the Ohio River about 20 miles south of modern Shawneetown. Inland piracy along the Ohio occurred off and on for about thirty years until steamboats became dominant. Probably because of the paucity of traffic before the steamboat era, piracy on the Illinois River was negligible.[4]

Cave-in-Rock was an ideal site for pirates: anyone standing in its mouth could see for miles up the Ohio, but flatboat crews couldn't see the cavern until they were almost upon it. The serpentine channel and a bar in the river made navigation difficult for 8 miles below Cave-in-Rock to Hurricane Island. Some pirates hired themselves out as pilots for this dangerous channel, then ran the flatboats aground so they and their crews could be plundered by confederates. Another ploy involved some gang members, often women, standing on shore and pretending to be stranded. When the flatboat came to their assistance, crew members would be made hostage or murdered. Pirates working upstream would get aboard flatboats when they docked at shore and poke holes or remove caulking so the vessels would run aground in the shoals.[5]

Undoubtedly the most inventive ruse was used by Samuel Mason, a Revolutionary War veteran, who headed a gang using the cave beginning in 1797. He posted a sign outside the mouth of the cave that year: Liquor Vault and House for Entertainment. When the bored flatboat crews came ashore for some recreation, he and his gang robbed them. Mason abandoned the cave after two years to become a brigand, robbing travelers on the Natchez Trace, the trail many flatboatmen used to return home with the proceeds of the sale of their goods in New Orleans. Mason was hatcheted to death in 1803 near Natchez by two of his confederates, including the infamous serial killer Wiley Harpe, trying to collect a reward on his head.[6]

Harpe, known popularly as "Little Harpe," and his older brother Micajah, or "Big Harpe," were perhaps the nation's first recorded serial killers, and during their brief stay at Cave-in-Rock in 1798 or 1799 they so repelled the pirates with their brutality and notoriety that they were ostracized. Their trail of terror, killing and mutilating victims, often without robbing them, began near Knoxville, Tennessee, in 1797 or 1798 and continued north and west through Kentucky. The Harpes finally sought refuge at Cave-in-Rock, but quickly alienated the pirates there with a particularly brutal murder: a captive young man was stripped and tied to a blindfolded horse, which was then driven off a cliff. After their ostracism they returned to Kentucky, where Big Harpe was killed by a posse and beheaded in 1799. Little Harpe was hanged in Mississippi on February 4, 1804, after killing Mason.[7]

The tavern ploy had worked so well for Mason that by 1810 a gang leader known as Jim Wilson was again using it at Cave-in-Rock. With a gang estimated at as many as forty-five men, Wilson preyed on flat-

boats at nearby Hurricane Island, seizing the vessels, killing or impressing the crews into his gang, and sailing the boats to New Orleans to sell them and their cargoes. Shippers in Pittsburgh became so concerned with the disappearance of boats in the vicinity of Wilson's Tavern, as it had become known, that they posted a reward. Later that year a posse led by John Waller and posing as a flatboat crew surprised and slew Wilson.

Some of the river pirates were in fact counterfeiters who bought goods from unsuspecting boatmen with phony money. Other cases of piracy often consisted of little more than local residents preying on targets of opportunity, often a grounded vessel. Thus when the sailing ship Tuscarora grounded on Flint Island about 100 miles below Louisville, it was stripped by thieves of $2,000 worth of equipment.[8]

## Chicago's Timber Pirates

Chicago's so-called timber pirates operated on such a large scale that the federal government sent its iron paddle-wheel frigate *Michigan* to Lake Michigan to put them out of business. The lumber barons in Chicago and Milwaukee in the 1850s began poaching timber from federal lands to feed the growing demand for construction materials that was to make the Windy City the world's largest lumber emporium during the last half of the nineteenth century, supplying lumber not only for its own rapid growth but for the settlement of the treeless plains to the west. Gangs of lumberjacks, often idle mariners during the winter, would cut the timber and float it on the rivers to the lake where schooners known as lumber hookers hauled it to Chicago for shipment west on the railroads. By the early 1850s, more than 50 million board feet of lumber a year were passing through the city.[9]

Although laws prohibiting poaching federal timber, initially to protect the navy's supplies of live oak and red cedar, had been passed in 1817, 1822, and 1831,

Wrecked ships were often plundered by local residents, giving rise to tales of piracy on the Great Lakes. Beaver Island was supposedly a center of such impromptu salvage operations. William Chapman of the Beaver Island Historical Society in 1999 examined the skeleton of a wreck of an unknown ship near Saint James exposed by the falling lake level.

the federal government didn't become concerned enough to take action for two decades. The General Land Office of the Department of the Interior finally sent the revenue agent Isaac Willard to investigate and take whatever action was necessary to put an end to the poaching. Even before he arrived, the timber pirates had become brazen, murdering one federal agent in Iowa, burning government boats and buildings, and stealing back timber that had been seized. The inn in which Willard and a fellow agent were sleeping soon after he took the assignment was burned, although both men escaped.

Willard, the long-forgotten Eliot Ness of his day, after his escape seized a pile of poached lumber from the timber baron

Benjamin Bagnell in the Manistee River valley of lower Michigan and shipped it to Chicago, where he intended to hold a government auction to sell it. But an armed mob met Willard's agent with the first load and drove him off. Bagnall escaped during the raid in Michigan, but Willard arrested several schooner captains, who were sent to Chicago, released on their own recognizance by judges, and promptly disappeared. For the most part Chicago, including several of its newspapers, was sympathetic to the "free market" timber pirates.[10]

The situation had deteriorated to the point that Washington decided to send in the navy. Its only vessel available on the Great Lakes was the *Michigan,* an iron-hulled, paddle-wheel frigate launched in 1843 as an experiment and in anticipation of a war with British Canada that never occurred. The *Michigan* was the fastest and most heavily armed vessel on the Great Lakes and, as the opening shot of the pirate war was to prove, was relatively invulnerable even to ramming.

The timber pirates apparently learned the vessel had sailed for Lake Michigan from its home port of Erie, Pennsylvania, and on Lake Huron before dawn one morning she was rammed under mysterious circumstances by the big propeller ship *Buffalo.* The *Michigan,* which was lighted according to regulations, was forced to take several evasive changes in course to avoid a collision with the *Buffalo,* which was running without lights and changed her course to intercept the warship. Although the two ships collided, neither suffered anything more than moderate damage, and they were able to continue on to their destinations. Commander Abraham Bigelow, the *Michigan*'s captain, who made his home with his family in Chicago during the winter when the lakes were frozen, was never able to convince federal authorities to try the master of the *Buffalo* for any violations of maritime law.

The warship and its platoon of marines,

once they reached Lake Michigan, surprised a crew of poachers and their ships on September 9, 1853, at the Herring River, then steamed off to Milwaukee, where Bagnell had fled from Chicago. He was arrested and ultimately tried in Detroit, where the judges were not as forgiving of timber poaching as their counterparts in Illinois and Wisconsin. For the remainder of the year, the frigate steamed back and forth on Lake Michigan, making additional raids and assisting Willard. By the end of the sailing season, the federal effort had nearly put the pirates out of business.[11]

The lumber barons, unable to beat the navy, in 1854 modified their strategy and went to Congress. The ploy worked. At the behest of the lumber industry, Congress in 1855 withdrew funding for the Timber Agencies, which had been set up to enforce the federal poaching laws. With no agency or money to enforce federal laws, the timber poaching resumed until the forests were exhausted later in the century.[12]

## Beaver Island War I

The *Michigan*'s next trouble spot was Beaver Island at the northern end of Lake Michigan where a splinter sect of Mormons trying to set up a colony had become embroiled in a running dispute with local Irish fishermen and those on nearby Mackinac Island to the north. Although there were accusations but little documentation that the Mormons had committed piracy on passing ships, it seems more likely that the two groups robbed each other, including some fishing boats, as a method of intimidation rather than for financial gain.

Not long after James Jesse Strang appeared on Beaver Island in 1847 with his first band of Mormons, the tales of piracy began. Strang, who had lost a power struggle with Brigham Young for leadership of the Mormon Church after the murder of the church founder Joseph Smith in Nauvoo, Illinois, in 1844, was looking for a utopian setting in which his group could prosper somewhat isolated from mainstream society. The subsequent, documentable, violent crime seems to have resulted more from a political and economic power struggle between the settled Irish fishermen and commercial interests on Mackinac Island on one side and the Mormon newcomers on the other than any freebooting.[13]

Stories abounded about how the Mormons set up a phony navigation light on Indian Point, the northwestern corner of the island, to lure ships onto the rocks to be looted or, in one instance, cut the anchor chains of a brig that was bound for Chicago but had been forced to wait out a storm under the protection of the leeward side of the island. Most probably, the inhabitants of the island simply "salvaged" cargoes from ships that ran aground in storms, a practice common on the Great Lakes and western rivers as late as 1937, when several Beaver Island residents were killed in an explosion while removing gasoline from the tanker *J. Oswald Boyd,* which had run aground on nearby Simmons Reef.[14]

The grounding of the schooner *J. I. Case* in 1884 is an example of how a rescue-salvage operation was sometimes interpreted as piracy. The ship went aground in a spring storm off Hog Island about 10 miles northwest of Beaver Island, whose fishermen managed to rescue all nineteen persons aboard the stranded vessel. But the islanders returned for the next few days and helped themselves to the grain aboard. Accusations of piracy also followed the grounding of the schooner *Lafriner* in 1886 at the same place, and again in 1894 when islanders helped themselves to $3,000 worth of barrels filled with lard.[15]

By 1850, Beaver Island with its protected harbor at Saint James had become a refueling point for some wood-burning steamers traveling to and from Chicago 294 miles to the south. The leaders of Mackinac Island, which had been the commercial center of northern Lake Michigan since the fur-trading days, had become

concerned that the Mormon population of Beaver had grown to 680, in contrast to only 100 "gentiles" as the Mormons called non-believers. There was at least one skirmish between the two groups in 1850, the year Strang had himself crowned king of the island. More incidents of looting and battery caused Strang the following year to declare a "Holy War" on the gentiles.[16]

The non-Mormons induced the federal government to charge the Strangites with several crimes, including timber poaching from federal land and counterfeiting, and in 1852 President Millard Fillmore ordered the *Michigan* to Beaver Island to take the Strangite leaders to trial in Detroit. They were acquitted and soon thereafter ordered the eviction of all gentile families from the island and took control of the adjacent fishing grounds. Reports of fish piracy—the beating and robbing of the Irish fishermen—by the Mormons became so widespread that Charles H. McBlair, the *Michigan*'s new skipper, on June 6, 1856, warned the governor of Michigan, "I have every reason to believe that the greater part of the community has been for a long time engaged in a system of plunder upon the property of fishermen and others who may arrive at the island, and such as may be within reach of boat expeditions to the Michigan and Wisconsin shores."[17]

By then, some of King Strang's high-handed tactics were beginning to wear thin on his followers, and he retaliated by stripping several of them of their ecclesiastical roles in the church-state. In Chicago, McBlair met with a number of Strangite dissidents and took their depositions. On the return to Beaver Island on June 16, the *Michigan* docked at a wharf owned by two of the dissidents, and McBlair sent for Strang to come on board the ship for a conference. But as he approached the vessel, he was mortally wounded by two dissidents, who were then given asylum on the ship. The coincidence led the historians Milo Quaife and Bradley Rodgers to conclude that the captain of the *Michigan* must somehow have been an accomplice, if unwittingly, in the assassination plot.[18]

The Strangite colony collapsed quickly after his death. An Irish mob from Mackinac and nearby islands quickly descended on Beaver Island and forced the Mormons to flee, looting them of their possessions and property. The steamers *Keystone State* jammed 490 of them on its decks and the *Buckeye State* another 350 for the trip to Chicago, where they arrived destitute and sat on the dock until city officials offered them assistance. Beaver Island once again became a backwater until its Irish fishermen became embroiled in another war with the fish barons of Chicago later in the century.[19]

## Civil War Privateers

The *Michigan* steamed off on her regular peacekeeping and lifesaving duties and was not involved in another act of piracy until the Civil War. Early in the war the vessel had been used on recruiting visits to major cities, like Chicago, under a program that resulted in four thousand enlistments for both the saltwater and western rivers fleets. But by 1863 it had been relegated to helping guard Confederate prisoners at Johnson's Island near Sandusky, Ohio. Early that year the Confederate government in Richmond began hatching plots to disrupt the northern rear on the Great Lakes by raiding prisoner-of-war camps and freeing their inmates. Besides Johnson's Island, there was Camp Douglas on Chicago's south side where a plot in late 1864 by Confederate agents and sympathizers to raid the camp and free the prisoners was thwarted by the Federals.[20]

A year earlier twenty-two Confederates under Lieutenant John Wilkerson had been smuggled into Canada with the intention of commandeering a steamship between Chicago and Saint Catherines, Ontario, and using it to ram and board the *Michigan* in Sandusky. That scheme collapsed when Canada Governor-General Lord Monck got wind of it and warned the United States.[21]

A year later Confederates in Canada were reviving the plot. Jacob Thompson, an agent, who had funded peace rallies by the Sons of Liberty in Chicago, Peoria, and Springfield without a notable effect on the Union's war effort, decided to go after the *Michigan* again. This time he sent Captain Charles H. Cole, an escaped prisoner living in Canada, to Sandusky to ingratiate himself to officers aboard the warship. The idea was to have Cole get the officers drunk or drugged and then send a signal to other agents aboard a commandeered ship to attack. Once the *Michigan* was under their control, they would use her to attack the Johnson's Island camp and free the prisoners.

Meanwhile, twenty-five Confederates under Acting Master John Y. Beall, in small groups to avoid suspicion, boarded the steamer *Philo-Parsons* at various ports on its trip east from Detroit and on September 19 seized her at gunpoint. They then steamed to Middle Bass Island near Sandusky for fuel, but while there the steamer *Island Queen,* loaded with Union soldiers, pulled alongside for fuel. After a brief firefight the Confederates overpowered the surprised soldiers, stranded them on the island, and scuttled the *Island Queen.*

They then awaited Cole's signal to attack. But, unknown to them, he had been arrested after a Canadian informant told the United States of the scheme earlier in the day. When no signal came, Beall gave up the plot, steamed back to Sandwich, Ontario (now Windsor), and looted and scuttled the *Philo-Parsons.*[22]

The *Michigan* was promptly relieved of guard duties and began aggressively patrolling the lakes, searching ships for guns and ammunition in various ports. That diligence resulted in thwarting yet another Confederate plot later in the year when federal agents got wind that the rebels had purchased the Canadian propeller *Georgian* and intended to use her in yet another attack on the *Michigan.* The captain of the *Michigan* got two of his sailors posing as merchant seamen on board the *Georgian* to spy on her activities. When they reported that the vessel was being fitted with a ram, the State Department protested to Canada, which seized the ship, ending Confederate activity on the Great Lakes.[23]

## Pirates versus the Chicago Fish Monopoly

Fishing was largely a cottage industry on Lake Michigan until 1872 when steam tugs were developed, permitting fishermen to operate as much as 100 miles from port and set 5 1/2 miles of nets. The introduction of twine gill nets also increased the catch. A few years later the A. Booth and Sons Packing Company in Chicago and its competitors began to apply some of the refrigeration and mass-processing techniques to seafood that had been adapted by the city's meatpacking industry a few years earlier.

Alfred A. Booth, who had been born in 1828 in England and immigrated to the United States twenty years later, started out in Chicago selling fresh vegetables and

some fish. By 1851 he had bought a store and was importing fresh oysters from Chesapeake Bay and fish from the Atlantic. Booth had expanded to three stores by the time the fire of 1871 burned him out, but he quickly rebuilt and within nine years was the largest seafood processor and distributor in the nation. He built refrigerated warehouses and processing plants in several Great Lakes cities and operated his own fleet to bring the catch to Chicago.

In season, as much as 10 tons of fresh fish a day went through his operation there. Saint James, the only port on Beaver Island as well as the center of one of the best fishing grounds on the lake, was added to his shipping routes in 1884. The next year, Beaver Island sent 289 tons of fresh fish to Chicago and 495 tons of salted fish to various markets. Salted fish had been the principal export before refrigeration permitted the development of markets for fresh and frozen fish.[24]

The Booth expansion on the lakes also coincided with a noticeable drop in fish

The *Michigan* (later renamed *Wolverine*), a paddle-wheel frigate, was the U.S. Navy's first iron warship nearly two decades before the famous Civil War *Monitor*. Its relative obscurity is probably due to its being consigned to duty on the Great Lakes. (Great Lakes Historical Society, Vermilion, Ohio)

catches on Lake Michigan, a phenomenon some local officials attributed to the company's voracious consumption of fish, and others to overfishing by the local fishermen. An investigation by John W. Milner, a Waukegan, Illinois, scientist hired by the federal government to look into the situation, produced the shocking revelation that populations of whitefish and trout, the two principal food fish in the lake, had declined 50 percent in ten to twelve years.[25]

As the annual catches fluctuated and began to dwindle, Booth began to press for restrictions on the fishing industry, including following the lead of Canada and banning fishing during the spawning season in the late fall—the so-called closed season. The company in 1893 organized fish wholesalers into a lobby called the Michigan Fisheries Association and succeeded two years later in inducing the Michigan legislature to impose a closed season between November 1 and December 15.

If that wasn't enough to enrage local fishermen, in 1897 it was disclosed that Booth's company in May had called a meeting in Chicago of fish dealers to discuss forming a combine in trust form to consolidate the industry. The resulting trust the next year had forty-three U.S. and Canadian companies as members and William Vernon Booth, Alfred's son, as its president and principal stockholder with 20,000 of the 25,000 outstanding shares. Shortly afterward F. B. Dickerson, a member of the Michigan Fish Commission, who had been trying to crack down on Lake Michigan fishermen during the closed season, admitted publicly that he owned $17,500 worth of stock in the Manitoba Fish Company, a Booth subsidiary.[26]

It wasn't long thereafter that Booth's hidden agenda became public: the company's detractors claimed the company wanted a closed season so it could sell at higher prices in Chicago when fresh fish were not available its reserve of frozen fish caught on Lake Winnepeg in Manitoba. The remoteness of Lake Winnepeg, more than 900 miles northwest of Chicago,

made it difficult to ship fresh fish. The suspicions about Booth's motives increased in 1896 when the company took over its largest Chicago rival, R. Connable and Sons, after a default on an $11,000 loan.[27]

The next year Booth pressured Michigan Fish and Game Warden Charles S. Osborn to crack down on the Beaver Island "fish pirates." Late in 1898 during the closed season his deputy, Charles E. Brewster, chartered the tug *Parmelee* from the Booth company, armed it, and steamed off in pursuit of the pirates. He encountered the fisherman Frank Left aboard the *Ciscoe* checking his nets under a full moon off Beaver Island, gave chase, and began firing away. The *Ciscoe* was captured, and Left was arrested, as were six other Beaver Island fishermen before the season ended. The fish pirate war continued off and on for several years with mixed results; some fishermen were convicted or pleaded guilty, whereas others were acquitted. As late as 1907, while a deputy warden was processing some arrested fishermen in Saint James, the engine of his unattended boat was smashed, and the vessel was set afire at its moorings.[28]

There also were skirmishes between American fishermen and Canadian authorities on other Great Lakes into the twentieth century. Ultimately the war was settled by Mother Nature. As fish populations continued to decline in the twentieth century due to overfishing, pollution, and predation by the saltwater lamprey eel, accidently introduced into the lakes, the fish pirates met the same fate as the timber pirates: they exhausted the natural resource on which their income depended.[29]

## Rum Runners and Cap'n Streeter

Rum running during prohibition (1920–1933) produced the last spate of piracy on the Great Lakes when rival gangs preyed on each other while trying to sneak liquor into the United States by boat. The most active rum running apparently occurred in narrow channels and on the Detroit and Saint Lawrence Rivers, where the distances between Canada and the United States were shortest and the dangers from storms were not as great as on open water. Chicago gangsters were involved in some of the rum running even in places as distant as Upstate New York, where the notorious Stephen Wesley transported booze across the Saint Lawrence until he disappeared in 1929 while trying to haul a load across the ice-choked river.[30]

The best-documented cases of piracy occurred on a 70-mile stretch of the Detroit River where entrepreneurs based around the downriver suburb of Ecorse in 1920 began running liquor from Windsor, Ontario, in motorboats in warm weather and on iceboats when the river froze. That year alone it was estimated that Canadian distillers and breweries shipped 900,000 cases to border cities for smuggling into the United States. By 1921 pirates appeared, not only robbing and killing the bagmen who were carrying cash to Canada but the rum runners bringing booze back across the river. The alleged leader of the pirate gangs, a man known only as the "Gray Ghost," was later assassinated after bouncing a check on his Canadian suppliers.[31]

Possibly the most interesting case of piracy, if that is what it could be called, was an attempted theft not on the high seas but of its shores. Cap'n George Wellington Streeter—variously, in his long career, a showman, circus promoter, steamboat operator, and excursion guide—in 1886 accidently grounded his steam launch *Reutan* on a bar about 400 feet off Superior Street on what is today the near north side of Chicago. As the lake deposited sand and contractors willingly dumped debris in the shoal, Streeter became the squatter on 100 acres of newly created and prime lakefront fill.

He declared the reclaimed land to be his, announced the formation of the District of Lake Michigan, and disannexed it from both Chicago and Illinois before proceeding to sell parcels of it to anyone willing to pay. A succession of lawsuits involving Streeter, his heirs, and assorted property owners of the former shoreline were not resolved in the former shoreline owners' favor until 1940.[32]

# *Chapter Ten* Steam and Steel

• At a time when rockets carry men to the moon and supersonic jets span the Atlantic in a few hours, it is hard to imagine the impact that the steam engine, which we now consider a relic, had on transportation in the first half of the nineteenth century. In 1800 the fastest and most efficient way to travel in the American interior was still by canoe. Canals were the technological marvel of the early Industrial Revolution, but travel on them was barely faster than a man could walk or paddle. Their advantage, aside from comfort, was that they could operate twenty-four hours a day and carry tons of freight. A pedestrian could do neither.

Horses and sails, when they appeared in the Midwest a few years later, also permitted travel in considerably more comfort than walking and at about twice the speed of canals. By midcentury the steam engine and mechanical traction again doubled the average speed of travel, with a quantum leap in cargo capacity. A man was capable of walking briskly at 4 miles an hour, but his average speed while carrying an 80-pound pack and taking into account such things as rest stops, bypassing obstacles, looking for river fords, eating, and sleeping was considerably less. The average speed of a freight train in North America in the second half of the century was only 10 miles an hour, but the trains averaged thirty cars and 313 tons of cargo. Passenger trains were considerably faster.[1]

River commerce proved to be a problem for street traffic in downtown Chicago because bridges had to be raised to let ships pass slowly up the narrow river. Note the elevated train (far left) and pedestrians waiting at the Van Buren Street bridge for the steamer to pass. (Lewis University, Canal and Regional History Collection)

The Chicago River congested in the 1800s even in the winter when ice reduced commerce to a minimum. Tugs and packets sometimes tied up three and four abreast for the season. The Union Steamboat Company, whose two packets are shown tied up next to North Western Station (background center), was owned by the Erie Railroad at a time when that industry owned many of the fleets on the Great Lakes. The practice was later banned by federal law. (David R. Phillips Collection)

The steam engine made it possible to reduce the round trip travel time by river between Cincinnati and New Orleans, a distance of 1,484 miles by flatboat, from six months to about three weeks. The railroads after midcentury cut the distance to 922 miles and reduced the round-trip travel time to five days. Voyageurs took almost six months to make a round trip over the 900-mile canoe route between Montreal and Chicago, but by the middle of the nineteenth century it was possible to make the round trip over the 1,250-mile route between Chicago and New York by Great Lakes steamship, Erie Canal boat, and Hudson River steamboat in less than a month. Before the century ended, high-speed overnight trains on a more direct

route of just over 800 miles made a round trip possible in three days.

The steam engine also made travel considerably more comfortable for passengers and more efficient for freight. The stage-coach was no match for the steamboat or even the canal packet, which in turn succumbed to George Pullman's sleepers and dining cars pulled by steam locomotives. Equally important, the steam engine made possible a revolution in freight transportation: the technology developed for the steam-powered grain elevator in the 1840s eventually made possible bulk shipments of grain, coal, and ore, eliminating the costly and inefficient handling of it in small quantities in bags or boxes.

The conversion to steam on the rivers

was abrupt by any historical standard. Within a decade and a half of the introduction of such a vessel on the western rivers in 1811, Fulton's 371-ton *New Orleans,* steamboats were the dominant form of transportation with more than seventy in service, and by 1850 their numbers had swelled tenfold. The steam conversion took longer on the Great Lakes—almost half a century—and on the canals, where steamboats could not provide any great increase in speed or cargo capacity, conversion was surprisingly slow. The Illinois and Michigan Canal opened in 1848 but did not convert from equine traction to steam until after the Civil War.

## The Steam Engine

Although the steam engine was known in the ancient world, attributed to Hero of Alexandria in the second century B.C., the Greeks and Romans considered it a curiosity and never put it to mechanical use. The modern steam engine was developed as a machine to pump water from mines in seventeenth-century England. Its application to traction was evolutionary—the work of a number of inventors, each improving earlier versions, over a period of years. The early steam pumps developed by Thomas Savery (1698) and Thomas Newcomen (1712) were not very efficient because they relied on alternate heating and cooling of the cylinder, so James Watt separated the condenser from the cylinder, greatly reducing the fuel consumption. It was left to Richard Trevithick, another Englishman, to develop a high-pressure engine capable of developing 30 pounds per square inch, versus 15 in a Watt engine, and Oliver Evans, an American, to increase the steam pressure to the point (100 pounds) that it could drive a steamboat upstream against considerable current.[2]

Because of the size, weight, and fuel consumption of early steam engines, they were used predominantly as stationary power sources. As traction engines, they were too large for anything but ships, and

it was the United States, a new and largely undeveloped nation that had few roads but a massive river system, that for a time led the world in the development of the river steamboat. On the other hand, the United States lagged behind Great Britain in the development of the oceanic steamship.[3]

After some early experimentation in 1783 by Jouffroy d'Abbans in France, the American John Fitch built a successful steamboat, *Experiment,* in 1790 that logged 2,000 miles up and down the Delaware River between Philadelphia and Trenton. That was followed by steam-powered vessels by Samuel Morey (1797) on the Connecticut River, Robert Livingston (1798) on the Hudson River, Oliver Evans (1802) on the Mississippi River, and Robert Fulton (with Livingston) in 1807 on the Hudson. Steam navigation is generally dated from Fulton's 1807 *Clermont* because reliable and continuous service began with her.[4]

The business end of a low-pressure engine consisted of a cylinder into which the steam flowed and a condenser in which it was converted back to water, producing a partial vacuum that supplied much of the power. In a high-pressure engine the steam was used solely to drive the piston and was then vented into the air, eliminating the condenser. As a result, low-pressure engines were larger and more expensive than high-pressure types of comparable power.

As it turned out, the low-pressure engine developed by Watt and used by Fulton was adequate for the oceans and Great Lakes, but Evans's high-pressure engines were a necessity in bucking strong river currents. High-pressure engines were also favored on early Great Lakes' propellers because they developed more revolutions per minute than the low-pressure engines used on side-wheelers, although by the end of the century condensing engines were standard on both types of ships. River steamboats generally were designed to have their wheels operate independently to increase maneuverability, but Great Lakes side-wheelers typically operated both wheels on a single shaft because short turning radiuses were not necessary on the open waters.

## The Rivers

Since river steamboats were designed for their operating environment with long and relatively narrow hulls for speed and shallow draft, they, in effect, were little more than steam engines sitting on rafts. The engine, substantial apparatus necessary to transmit power from the engine to the wheels, and the paddle-wheels themselves consumed a good deal of the combined main and boiler decks, which on the typical steamboat of the 1850s were 20 feet high. Above that was a 10-foot-high passenger, or "hurricane," deck, often extending the entire length of the ship. Many steamboats also had a "Texas" deck above the hurricane deck to provide rooms for the vessel's officers and some passengers.[5]

After some experimenting with both types in the early steamboat era, side-wheels became the favored system of propulsion because they increased maneuverability, enabling the boat to make a quick turn to put its bow up to the bank to lower a gangplank for loading, the typical technique used on the rivers because of the shallow banks. Steamboats with two engines could operate their side-wheels in opposite directions, permitting the vessel to turn in its own length. Side-wheels were also easy to repair, a major consideration, since paddle wheels suffered frequent damage from things like floating logs.

The stern-wheel, which because of its location at the rear of the vessel was not as vulnerable to damage from floating debris, made a comeback after the Civil War once the railroads took away passenger traffic and speed was no longer a preoccupation on the rivers. By the end of the century, river boats were relegated to pushing chains of barges laden with bulk commodities.

The screw propeller appeared on the rivers in the 1850s but was consigned to small vessels for harbor use because the

shallow rivers inhibited their efficiency and the high number of revolutions needed to drive the propeller would have required the development of a different engine. Propellers capable of fitting between the bottom of the steamboat and the bed of the river were too small to generate the needed power for the upstream trips unless they could be made to turn at a much higher rate than the standard river engine of the day would allow.[6]

With the dramatic decline in river traffic in the last decades of the nineteenth century, there was little financial incentive on the part of waterways operators to experiment, and the rivers became a technological backwater. The coal-fired, steam-powered stern-wheeler remained a fixture on the rivers into the 1950s, although some stern-wheelers were reequipped with propellers in the late 1930s.

The screw propeller didn't come into wide use until after World War II, when the river traffic returned and the fleet was converted to diesel power; dependable reversing reduction gears were developed to increase horsepower; hulls were built with spoon-shaped recesses for propellers to prevent them from being damaged on the shallow river bottoms; and Kort nozzles, funnel-shaped devices fit around the propellers to concentrate the flow of water, were installed on towboats.[7]

## Canals

The Illinois and Michigan Canal built more than two centuries after Canal de Briar was not all that much technologically advanced over its European predecessors, although the steam engine was in the process of revolutionizing transportation even before the first spade of dirt was turned in Chicago. In fact, the state had debated whether it was better off building a railroad or canal. James M. Bucklin, the chief engineer for the canal commission, in 1833 estimated the canal would cost $4.1 million but a railroad could be built for a fourth of that.[8]

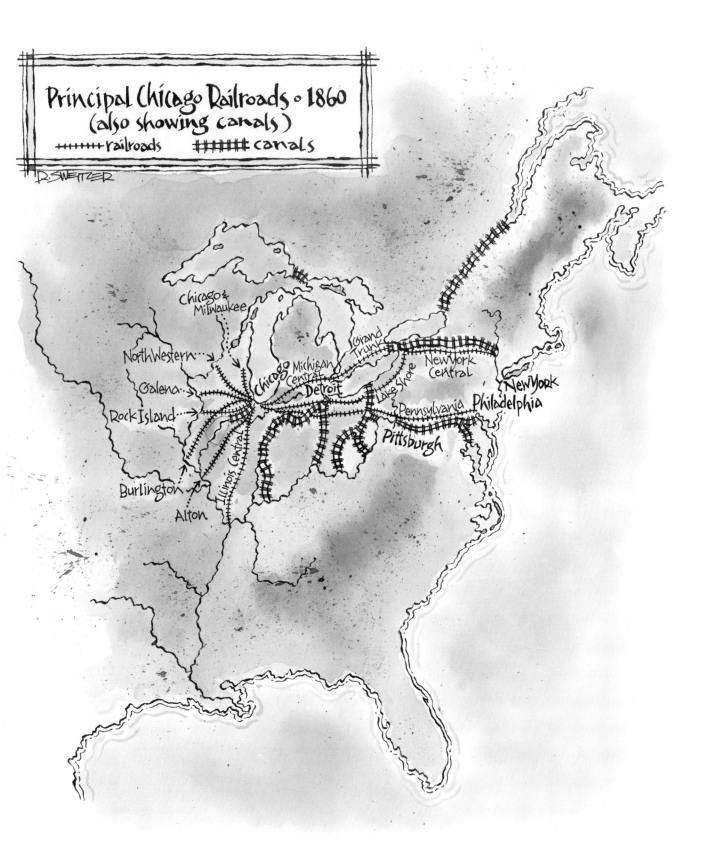

Principal Chicago Railroads • 1860
(also showing canals)
┼┼┼┼┼ railroads    ╫╫╫╫╫ canals

R. SWEITZER

Chicago & Milwaukee
NorthWestern
Galena
Rock Island
Burlington
Alton
Illinois Central
Chicago
Michigan Central
Detroit
Grand Trunk
Lake Shore
New York Central
New York
Pennsylvania
Philadelphia
Pittsburgh

The I & M was designed for equine traction with towpaths for mules and barns every 15 miles, and frequent changes of teams were necessary when the canal had a passenger trade that demanded overnight travel. Three to six equine teams were used to pull boats. Although steamboats could travel only marginally faster than mule tows because of the potential damage to the canal banks from wakes, the conversion to steam power had important advantages. It improved the efficiency of the canal as well as the average travel times of boats by eliminating the need to feed and water the animals and periodically change teams. Most important, it permitted a single steamer to tow two unpowered boats.

Mules remained the principal method of traction in the canal's early years despite the availability of steam propulsion. In fact, the first canal boat, *General Fry,* was towed on April 10, 1848, into Chicago from the canal by the steam propeller tug *A. Rossitor,* although the first vessel to travel from La Salle to Chicago, the *General Thornton,* did so behind mules. Side-wheeled canal boats equipped with outriggers to prevent damage to the paddles in the narrow channel were tried but proved impractical because of the damage they sustained. Eventually stern-wheelers and especially propellers were the power system of choice on the canals, where there was minimal current to buck and there were tight clearances.[9]

Although there were several steampowered boats on the canal in the 1850s, the conversion of the bulk of the fleet to steam occurred just after the Civil War, making the I & M one of the first American canals to extensively use steam power. The fact that the canal was built over relatively level terrain meant it needed only seventeen locks over its 97-mile length, an average interval of 5.7 miles between locks, and made conversion to steam easier because locks were a nemesis to steam engines, which tended to overheat during the lengthy idling during the slow locking process. By way of contrast the average interval between locks on Pennsylvania's Main Line Canal was only 1.7 miles, the Chesapeake & Ohio 2.5, and the Erie 4.3.

The use of steam tows meant a nearly threefold increase in the capacity of a single transit, and powered canal boats were often pressed into service on the Illinois River and, with special modifications to raise the stern to prevent swamping in high seas, on Lake Michigan as well. The latter practice enabled canal boat operators to compete with the railroads by enabling shippers to avoid high railroad switching charges in Chicago.

The largest boats on the canal had a capacity of as much as 150 tons, although those equipped with engines typically did not exceed 90 tons burden. The dimensions of the canal locks effectively prevented anything larger. One of the best documented canal boats, the *City of Pekin,* which was built in 1875 in Chicago without power, was later converted to a steam barge and finally rebuilt as a steamboat for use on the Illinois River before the turn of the century.[10]

## The Great Lakes

The Great Lakes by the middle of the nineteenth century had become a technological battleground between advocates of the four different types of ship propulsion—sail, side-wheels, stern-wheels, and screw propellers. Since there were no strong currents and tides, the most important consideration on the lakes was the oceanlike swell and waves. Stern-wheels because of potential damage from rough seas were an early casualty, although sidewheelers and sail persisted well into the twentieth century. The screw, which appeared on the lakes before it did on the oceans and as early as 1848 powered 45 of the 914 registered hulls in the lakes fleet, ultimately won out and became the favored mechanism of propulsion.

The steam engine appeared on the lakes soon after it showed up on the rivers and

**Above:** The *Seeandbee*, a four-stacked luxury excursion side-wheeler shown in this painting, operated between Chicago and Buffalo. (Great Lakes Historical Society, Vermilion Ohio)

**Left:** The *Seeandbee* ended its career on Lake Michigan converted to a training aircraft carrier during World War II. (Great Lakes Historical Society, Vermilion, Ohio)

demonstrated to the maritime industry the adaptability of that form of propulsion to deep-water commerce. A few side-wheelers were operated on the lakes shortly after the War of 1812, but they did not proliferate until after the Erie Canal in 1825 opened the region to development. The deeper drafts and greater freeboard (distance between the deck and waterline) required on lake ships meant that steam engines could be mounted below the main deck, leaving more room for cargo and passengers.[11]

The screw propeller was introduced to the lakes in 1841 and became popular because it greatly reduced the size of the engine and mechanical gear necessary to run a ship, giving ship owners more cargo space in the same hull. Propeller ships also required proportionally less fuel than paddle-wheelers of comparable size. By the end of the nineteenth century, when iron and steel ships became common, the screw propeller was the predominant system of propulsion in almost all new cargo hulls and proved to be the most efficient way to drive the evolving giant bulk carriers—ore boats that by 1900 had grown to 500 feet in length and 10,000 tons of cargo capacity. On the other hand, the largest schooner built on the lakes was the *David Dows,* a 278-foot five-master built in 1881 and rated at 1,418 tons. She was lost in a gale off Whiting, Indiana, in 1889, after being converted to a steamship.[12]

The Fulton-Livingston monopoly granted by New York, the most important of the Great Lakes states from a maritime standpoint in the first half of the nineteenth century, slowed somewhat the development of steamships on the lakes. There were only 4 steamers in service on the lakes as late as 1820, as contrasted to 71 on the western rivers and 52 on the Atlantic Coast where other states simply ignored the New York-granted monopoly. In fact, the first steamers on the lakes were both Canadian—the *Frontenac* in 1816 and the *Ontario* a year later—but they demonstrated to the skeptics the practicability of

the use of such vessels on open waters. In the United States, the inertia persisted until 1824, when the U.S. Supreme Court in *Ogdon v. Gibbons* ended the monopoly, and by 1848 the number of steamships registered on the lakes was 140, or more than 15 percent of the merchant marine (table 10.1).[13]

**Table 10.1** Great Lakes Fleet Registry, 1848

| Ship Type | Number Registered | Average Tonnage |
|---|---|---|
| Barks | 5 | 329 |
| Brigs | 93 | 229 |
| Schooners | 548 | 131 |
| Sloops/Scows | 128 | 43 |
| Steamships (Paddle) | 95 | 409 |
| Steamships (Propeller) | 45 | 321 |

*Source:* Mansfield, *History of the Great Lakes,* 439, citing U.S. Bureau of Navigation data.

The earliest lake steamships were little more than small sailing ships equipped with engines. The first steamship in the U.S. lake fleet was the *Walk-in-the-Water* of 1818—a 150-foot side-wheeler with a capacity of only 338 tons and two masts, the foremast rigged with a square sail. On the oceans commercial ship owners continued to rig their steamships with sail well into the century because of the impossibility of obtaining fuel on long voyages, but the extensive forests along the lakes meant steamship crews could anchor almost anywhere and send crews ashore to chop wood.[14]

Although builders quickly gained enough confidence in the reliability of their engines to do away with sails and many sailing ships were converted to steam, the reverse also occurred. The operating and economic performance of many steamers as late as the 1860s, especially after the railroads began providing competition, caused them to be converted back to sail. That was the fate of the Chicago-built steamer *James Allen* in 1840 and the steamer *Comet* twenty-nine years later.[15]

By the 1850s the side-wheeler was beginning to lose out to the propellers. There were twice as many side-wheelers as propellers on the lakes in 1848; by 1860 they were outnumbered 197 to 138 by propellers. The shipping demands of the Civil War offered something of a reprieve, but the ratio of side-wheelers in the fleet continued its decline after hostilities ended.

Although many of the largest side-wheel steamers were broken up and their engines transferred to smaller ships, they continued to be built in diminishing numbers for specialized excursion markets into the twentieth century. The *Seeandbee*, a corruption of the abbreviation of the initials of its owner, the Cleveland and Buffalo Transit Company, was a four-stack, side-wheeled, 500-foot-long passenger liner launched in 1912 for service on Lake Erie. In 1924 the Detroit and Cleveland Navigation Company had built the *Greater Buffalo*, a 519-foot side-wheeler. Both vessels were requisitioned by the navy and converted to training carriers during World War II.[16]

## Screw Propellers

Although screw propeller development dates from at least 1775, it was the Swedish engineer John Ericsson, the designer and builder of the ironclad warship *Monitor* during the Civil War, who in 1836 patented the screw propeller in England, from which the continuous development of the device can be traced. After being unable to convince the British navy to adopt it, he immigrated to the United States in 1839 and began to demonstrate the device to the public.

The U.S. Navy ultimately adopted the propeller for its ill-fated warship *Princeton* (1844), but not until some entrepreneurs in upstate New York had acquired from Ericsson the rights to use the invention on the Great Lakes. The 138-ton *Vandalia*, launched in 1841, was the first operational ship in the world to use the Ericsson screw for propulsion. A second vessel followed in 1842 and seven in 1843, including the 262-ton *Independence*, built in Chicago.[17]

Early propellers were unable to deliver the speed of side-wheels for passenger service but were considerably more efficient in freight service because of their smaller engines and mechanical apparatus. On side-wheelers both the paddle-wheels and the apparatus needed to transfer the power from the engines to them were bulky and made it difficult to moor ships with their hulls flush with the dock for efficient loading.

The earliest steamships used an A-frame to transfer power from the engine to the side-wheels, but that was soon supplanted by a device called a "walking beam," which reduced vibrations and gave a

The Goodrich line's pride and joy was the steel steamer *Virginia*, but it was built for day crossings of Lake Michigan with insufficient overnight berths for transfer to the weeklong excursion cruise market when the railroads and automobiles took away most of the cross-lake passenger market. (Great Lakes Historical Society, Vermilion, Ohio)

By the turn of the century the design of Great Lakes bulk freighters was fairly standard—a pilothouse forward, cargo space amidships, and the engine room at the stern. The *J. B. Ford,* built in 1904 and shown here in 1998, ended her long career as a floating cement warehouse on the Calumet River on Chicago's south side.

smoother ride. It looked somewhat like a giant teeter-totter and was so large it consumed a considerable amount of space that otherwise could be occupied by passengers or freight. Other ships used swinging connecting rods that gave the apparatus the look of a lame man on crutches, and still others used horizontal engines on the main deck, concealed by the cabin.

The screw propeller did away with all of that by placing the drive shafts deep in the hull below the waterline, and it didn't take naval architects long to move the engine to the stern, concentrating the power plant in a single small compartment and reducing the length of the drive shafts considerably. With the side-wheels gone, hulls could be widened to nearly the full width of locks, further increasing cargo capacity. The propeller had the added advantage of being less vulnerable to damage during docking or by ice—a major consideration on the lakes when metal hulls were developed and the shipping season was lengthened into winter.

However, Great Lakes ship owners were a pragmatic lot, so the great gains in cargo space made possible by the screw propeller meant the early propellers were relatively small in size and consigned to freight service. The average tonnage of propellers on the lakes as late as 1860 was only two-thirds that of side-wheelers.[18]

The *Independence,* built in Chicago in 1843, was designed as a sailing ship with a single propeller to drive her into headwinds. Her operators early in her existence must have discovered the advantages of steam and the screw propeller, because in her first year *Independence* made a Chicago-Buffalo round trip in seventeen days, an improbability under canvas when the average round trip took closer to a month. In 1846, the ship was hauled overland around the rapids on the Saint Mary's River to finish her career as the first propeller on Lake Superior, where she was wrecked in 1853.[19]

Typical of the early propeller ships was the 273-ton *Hercules,* a packet built in Buffalo in 1843. She was 137 feet long and equipped with fourteen staterooms and space for an additional forty-six berths. Her 15-ton engine fit in an area of 6 square feet. Most important, the engine could run on ten cords of wood a day, in contrast to the fifty required by the big side-wheelers of the time. The ship cost $20,000 to build.[20]

Chicago's Goodrich Line was probably as good an example as any of the dilemma facing ship operators of which type of ship to buy. The packet line began operations in 1856 with a leased side-wheeler and in its nearly six years of operation before the Civil War acquired two ships powered by paddle wheels and five by propellers, one of which was converted to a side-wheeler. Goodrich even experimented with side-mounted propellers on the *Sunbeam,* albeit unsuccessfully. Between the end of the Civil War and his death in 1885, Albert E. Goodrich bought thirteen side wheelers, ten of them new, but only five propellers. However, of the four new hulls ordered in the final years of his life three were propellers and two of them were built of iron.[21]

## Iron ships

Iron ships were the next quantum leap in technology on the lakes; iron, and later steel, hulls permitted lighter and larger ships than could be built of wood. They

By the 1970s, Great Lakes shipbuilders, because of the development of bow thrusters for steering in port, adopted the practice used on the oceans and put the pilothouse atop a tall superstructure at the stern of the vessel. The 634-foot *Buffalo,* owned by American Steamship Company, was built in 1978 and is capable of carrying more than 23,000 tons of ore, stone, or coal. (American Steamship Company)

136

**Above:** Shipping companies on the Great Lakes early in the twentieth century developed vessels capable of unloading themselves to serve ports without elaborate facilities. The *Gilbert* is shown along the Chicago River ca. 1925 unloading sand for the construction of Wacker Drive. (Great Lakes Historical Society, Vermilion, Ohio)

**Right:** Early self-unloaders used a gantry-mounted clam shovel to move bulk commodities like sand from the hold to a conveyor belt extended over the side of the ship to the dock. (Great Lakes Historical Society, Vermilion, Ohio)

were also less vulnerable to damage from ice and, absent the corrupting influences of salt water and marine organisms, were extremely long-lived. It was not unusual for Great Lakes hulls to last seventy years; in fact, iron and steel hulls proved to be more vulnerable to technological obsolescence than any corrosive effects of lake water.

America's first iron ship on the lakes, the wrought-iron, paddle-wheel frigate *Michigan* launched in Erie, Pennsylvania, in 1843 weighed about half of a wooden warship of similar dimensions and, later renamed *Wolverine,* remained in service for eighty years in various capacities, including a stint as a training ship at the Great Lakes Naval Training Center north of Chicago during World War I.[22]

The first iron hulls appeared on pleasure craft in the United Kingdom as early as 1777, but they were not practical on commercial vessels until foundries within a decade developed the capability of forging iron plates. Even then the first iron-hulled steamer, the *Aaron Mahby,* was not built until 1822, followed in three years by the first iron-hulled American ship, the *Codorus,* on the Susquehanna River. The first iron barge appeared in 1829 on the Lehigh River, and by 1840 there were more than a hundred of them in service on various rivers.[23]

Iron was slow to be adopted on the Great Lakes, and the first iron ships were built by the government. The *Alert* was launched in Buffalo in early 1843 as a government topographical survey vessel, and by the end of the next year the government added to its freshwater fleet the iron warships *Michigan* on the Upper Lakes and *Jefferson,* a propeller, on Lake Ontario. The first iron merchant on the lakes, the Canadian *Richelieu,* began its career in 1845, but no U.S. commercial builder was willing to take a chance on iron until 1861 when Buffalo's Anchor Line ordered the 650-ton *Merchant.*[24]

The inertia was the result of a number of factors. Despite the advantages of iron in ship construction, which included

lighter weights; sturdier hulls that resisted hogging, or sagging at the bow and stern; and the ability to subdivide hulls with bulkheads for safety—wooden bulkheads leaked—ship owners also initially considered iron to be too brittle, and wood was still a plentiful alternative. Early problems with iron hulls in salt water, where fouling by barnacles reduced their speed and efficiency until antifouling paints were developed, undoubtedly contributed to the inertia by Great Lakes ship owners to embrace the new technology, even though fouling was not a problem in fresh water.[25]

However, the principal drawback, especially on the Great Lakes, was their cost. Although the warship *Michigan* had been built for $152,478, or slightly less than half the cost of the wooden sloop of war *Cumberland* ($320,000) launched at about the same time, foundries could not match the price of conventional shipyards for wooden merchant hulls until the Midwest's supplies of cheap timber began to dwindle and mass production reduced the unit cost of iron and steel. The relative infancy of the iron industry in the United States also kept costs high—40 to 100 percent greater than in the United Kingdom. The 190-foot iron *Merchant* cost the Anchor Line $60,000 to build in 1861, but Chicago's Goodrich paid only $19,000 to have the 170-foot wooden propeller *Union* built a year earlier.[26]

The conversion to iron hulls began after the Civil War and permitted progressively larger steamships, offsetting their inherently higher operating costs due to larger crews (relative to schooners) by permitting a great increase in cargo capacity. Beginning in 1871, the 1,200-tonners *Alaska, Japan, China,* and *India* were launched for the Lake Erie-Chicago market at a time when the average burden of a sailing ship on the Great Lakes was only 156 tons. But by 1880 there still were only twenty U.S.-owned iron hulls on the lakes out of a total merchant fleet of 3,127.[27]

However, it wasn't long before the maritime industry concluded that the larger hulls made possible by iron and steel meant the Great Lakes fleet could operate with fewer ships. Chicago, which had more than 13,000 ships visit its two river ports annually in the early 1880s carrying a combined total of 4.5 to 4.8 million tons of cargo, by 1898 was visited by only 7,624 ships, but collectively they carried 5.3 million tons.

The rapid growth of the iron and steel industry in and around Chicago in the last half of the nineteenth century and its increased appetite for ore, limestone, and coal helped create a market for larger vessels because the industry had to stockpile raw materials in sufficient quantities to last through the winter when the lakes were closed to shipping. Coal imports to Chicago increased from just over 1 million tons in 1871 to almost 6 million tons in 1885, and iron and steel production in the city more than doubled in the decade after 1870 to 7.3 million tons from 3.65 million tons. By 1880 Illinois was the fourth-largest steel-producing state. In 1897 lake receipts included 1.8 million tons of iron ore and 1.3 million tons of coal.[28]

The merchant marine responded by putting into production a new design of bulk carrier unique to the Great Lakes. The *R. J. Hackett* was built in 1869 with a small pilothouse near the bow, the engine at the stern, and a single cargo hold amidships for easier loading—the characteristic profile of Great Lakes ships through most of the twentieth century. The *Onoko,* a larger steel version of the bulk carrier, with a hold for 3,000 tons of ore appeared in 1882.

Within six years Alexander McDougal in West Superior, Wisconsin, was producing a strange-looking fleet of ore carriers called "whalebacks" that were characterized by hulls rounded on the top (though flat on the bottom), turrets fore and aft for the pilot and engines, and a pig-snout prow. One of the last ones built in 1898 had a capacity of 8,000 tons. The only passenger whaleback built was the *Christopher Columbus,* which operated out of Chicago.[29]

The 1,500-ton *Columbus* was built for the 1893 Columbian Exposition to ferry visitors from downtown Chicago to the fair in Jackson Park on the south side and in 1898 was acquired by Chicago's Goodrich Transportation Company for the Chicago-Milwaukee run. A. W. Goodrich, the son of the founder, had crossed the Atlantic on steel ships and was convinced they were the future of the merchant marine. In 1891, the twenty-five-year-old Goodrich bought the 1,500-ton, steel, twin-screw *Virginia,* which is a good example of the longevity of Great Lakes-built vessels. It was requisitioned by the navy for World War I and after the hostilities was returned to merchant duty, renamed *Avalon,* and sailed between Los Angeles and Catalina Island until the 1950s.[30]

In the closing years of the century steel bulk carriers were being built that exceeded 400 feet in length, and 500-footers were on the drawing boards. The great size was made possible not only by steam and steel but the big corporations with the financial wherewithal to buy such ships. The corporate fleets of the railroads and steel industry ultimately came to dominate the merchant marine on the lakes. The owner-masters like August and Hermann Schuenemann by 1899 has been supplanted by lawyers like Elbert Gary, who ran U.S. Steel Corporation. The company in the early twentieth century owned the largest American-flag fleet, known as the Pittsburgh fleet, with seventy-eight steamships and twenty-seven schooners and barges. Other fleets operated under names now familiar only to maritime buffs—Gilcrest (sixty-nine vessels), Mitchell (nineteen), Cleveland-Cliffs (twelve), Hawgood (eleven), and Pickands Mather (eleven).[31]

## Mechanical Loading and Unloading

Perhaps the least-known technological component of the shipping revolution in the nineteenth century was the mechanical loading and unloading systems, which permitted the quick transfer of tons of cargo to and from ships. The steam elevator, as it was originally known, was developed in the 1840s for the grain trade, and by the end of the century had evolved into machinery for handling other commodities in bulk. George H. Hulett designed ore unloaders—giant clamshell jaws that could devour ore from a hold in 10-ton gulps. Before that, crews of longshoremen used shovels to fill buckets with ore. One man could shovel 10 tons a day.[32]

For most of the first half of the nineteenth century, on the rivers, lakes, and oceans the only practical way to move grain was by individual sacks that could be carried by a man from dock to deck. Frequent transfers between canal boat, steamboat, and steamship on the long journey from farm to market required a huge investment in labor at each transfer point. Since ownership in the first half of the nineteenth century remained with the original shipper until sold at the point of destination, farmers or local merchants who purchased the crop often had to ride along with their harvests to make sure it wasn't manhandled or pilfered.[33]

The steam engine changed that system very abruptly at midcentury. Railroads reached far inland from the navigable rivers and lakes and began to bring the enormous harvests of the prairies to the cities served by cheap water transportation. It was difficult for stevedores in the river cities to manually handle much of an increase in bagged grain, but in Great Lakes ports like Chicago technology very quickly offered a solution.

Joseph Dart in Buffalo in 1842 put into operation the first steam-powered grain elevator, and within six years the idea had spread westward to Chicago. Dart's invention was simply a multistory warehouse built on the bank of a river feeding the Great Lakes; on the land side wagons or railroad cars could be unloaded onto a steam-engine-driven conveyor that carried the grain to the top of the building. After being weighed and sorted into the proper bins, the grain was dumped down a chute by gravity into the hold of a waiting ship.

A single Illinois Central Railroad elevator could simultaneously unload twelve railroad cars, and by 1857 the twelve big elevators in Chicago combined had the capacity to process 500,000 bushels every ten hours—a quarter of the volume Saint Louis moved over its levee to and from steamboats in all of 1854. The resulting efficiencies meant Chicago could transfer grain at a cost of half a cent a bushel versus five cents in Saint Louis.[34]

However, the railroads, the newest steam technology to arrive on the scene, were a mixed blessing to the maritime industry despite the traffic they fed to the ports. It wasn't long after their arrival that they began to take away traffic from the steamboats, canals, and ships that had dominated trade in the Midwest for the first half of the century.

# *Chapter Eleven* Sails or Rails?

Chicago's strength as a port was as a transfer point between its extensive canal, lake, and railroad systems. The Hennepin Canal sternwheel towboat *Harold Grant* is shown being unloaded onto raiload gondolas along the Sanitary and Ship Canal in Chicago. (Illinois Department of Natural Resources)

• The arrival of the iron horse at midcentury had an even more dramatic effect on Middle America than the steamboat had decades earlier, or the motor vehicle would have fifty years later. It freed transportation and, as a result, development, from the geographical constraints of the waterways and imposed a discipline of time on the transportation system that had been lacking when vessels had to wait for fair winds or cargoes to sail.

The steamboats and ships that paddled the meandering watercourses were no match for the rails, which were laid in nearly straight lines between cities. Neither gale, nor ice, nor low water stopped the iron horse. Within a few years of its arrival, Chicagoans were setting their watches to conform to the departure of trains, not the rising of the sun.

In the 1850s a healthy percentage of steamboat and sailing ship masters were at least part owners of their vessels, and those individuals and partnerships were not equipped to compete against the rail corporations and their professional managers who conducted predatory price wars and ran their trains on tight schedules. A steamboat left the levee when it had enough of a load to make a profit, whether it took until the next day or next week; trains left every morning precisely at 9 A.M., although arrival times, especially for manifest freight trains, were somewhat erratic.

In fact, timely service was so important that the railroads met in Chicago in 1881 and adopted the four-zone standard time system, and the rest of the nation was forced to accept it. Before that, every city set its own time. Railroads, which could build spurs leading right into a factory, were also less dependent upon horse drayage for pickup and delivery of shipments than were ships.[1]

Within a few years of their arrival, and certainly by the opening of the Civil War, the railroads had taken away most of the passenger and lucrative package freight business from the waterways. Within a few decades they have driven the river steamboat operators to the verge of ruin; the colorful steamboats of Mark Twain were gone, and the surviving traffic, mainly coal on the Ohio River, was hauled in strings of barges. Many canals were closed or living on borrowed time. Great Lakes shipping survived on a diet of bulk commodities—grain, ore, and minerals—on which it could be price-competitive. Surprisingly, several small steamship lines on Lake Michigan were able to exist into the twentieth century on a cross-lake trade in passengers, fruit, and packages until motor trucks put them out of business.

Chicago, more than any city in the United States and certainly more than any city in Middle America, benefited from the iron horse. Chicago at first attracted railroads as an extension of its Great Lakes shipping routes; then railroads began to arrive for the same reasons the city was a nexus of Indian trails: anyone traveling from east to west had to detour around the southern end of Lake Michigan. Within a few years Chicago's railroad plant reached a critical mass; any railroad wanting to be competitive had to build a line to Chicago to get connections to other railroads there. The city, which in the second half of the nineteenth century became the site of the densest concentration of railroad tracks on earth, became the place where all American railroads met but none passed.[2]

It was also a place in which the railroads developed a synergy with the waterways. An eastbound bushel of wheat to feed New York or Europe was transferred from boxcar to ship in Chicago, and westbound timber to build Omaha or Denver had to pass by ship to the Chicago railhead before continuing its journey across the plains by train. The existence of a relatively healthy canal and lake shipping industry also kept railroad freight rates lower than they probably would have been otherwise. Since the shipper determined the routing of his goods, low rates attracted traffic.[3]

The city had thirty thousand inhabitants when the railroads arrived and more than a million and a half by the end of the century. Its dual role as a lake and river (canal) port was greatly expanded as a rail center. The railroads not only interdicted Saint Louis-bound traffic on the Mississippi River but went beyond. Chicago's commercial sphere of influence, which extended perhaps 70 to 100 miles inland before the arrival of the iron horse, within a decade stretched to Minnesota, Wisconsin, Iowa, Indiana, and even Missouri. By the end of the century it stretched 1,000 miles across the Great Plains to the foothills of the Rocky Mountains as cattle moved east in stock cars and, after a brief stop in Chicago's abattoirs, continued their journey to New York and Philadelphia as carcasses in refrigerated cars.

## The Arrival of the Iron Horse

America's first common-carrier railroad began in 1828 in Baltimore, and for the next twenty years, railroads were built westward, finally arriving in Chicago in 1852 to meet some western lines. The Illinois Canal Commission in 1833 took a serious look at substituting a railroad for the canal it intended to build, but Joseph Duncan, an ardent canal supporter, was elected governor in 1834 and nothing came of the idea.[4]

Three years later, Illinois was awash in railroad schemes, none of them coming within 100 miles of Chicago, which was getting the canal as its reward in the political compromise that resulted in the state's $9.5 million Internal Improvement Act of 1837. Besides the canal, the act called for the building of no less than eight state-subsidized railroads crisscrossing Illinois, but only one 59-mile section, from Springfield to Meredosia on the Illinois River, was completed before the financial panic of 1837, subsequent depression, and failure of the state's credit put an end to the scheme. By 1842 the Meredosia railroad was not producing enough revenue to cover operating expenses and was reduced to using mules to pull its trains after its single locomotive wore out.[5]

When Illinois got a real railroad in 1848, it was financed to a great extent by northern Illinois farmers and merchants far from the Illinois and Michigan Canal who were trying to get their grain to the holds of ships docked along the Chicago River. Chicago merchants, apparently satisfied with the city's role as a lake and impending canal port, accounted for only $20,000, or 8 percent, of the original 1847 stock subscription. Despite the lack of local support, the Galena & Chicago Union Rail Road was an immediate financial success and in a few years had plenty of competition.[6]

The Galena Rail Road organizers in 1847 also looked to the East and acquired the dormant Indiana charter of the Buffalo & Mississippi Railroad in order to extend their line through Indiana to meet the eastern railroads then being built across Michigan. But they were unable to raise sufficient funds to build in both directions and abandoned the Indiana venture after the Michigan Central announced its intention to extend its line to Chicago.[7]

The Michigan Central had Boston capital behind it. The state of Michigan had built a 143-mile railroad west from Detroit to Kalamazoo before running out of money in 1846 and selling the line to the Boston financier John W. Brooks for $2 million. He brought his colleague John Murray Forbes into the deal, and Forbes was the driving force behind the further extension of the Michigan Central in 1848 to the eastern shore of Lake Michigan, 218 miles from Detroit.[8]

Once the intention of a rival line to proceed to Chicago became obvious, Forbes realized he could not compete by relying on lake steamers for the final 90 miles of the journey across Lake Michigan, and his associates began negotiating access to Chicago. His railroad reached the Indiana state line in 1850 just ahead of the rival Michigan Southern (later known as the Lake Shore), and both railroads quickly obtained dormant charters to get to the Illinois state line; in 1852 they got trackage rights into Chicago over two Illinois railroads.[9]

The two Michigan lines' connections to railroads farther east abruptly gave Chicago a rail link to New York, and the railroad stampede from the east was on, as railroads based in New York's rival ports of Philadelphia and Baltimore built or subsidized lines to the Windy City. Eastern financiers, like Forbes, also began acquiring control of the railroads being built west, north, and south from Chicago and providing the deep pockets that paid for their extensions deeper into the interior.[10]

Chicago, which didn't have a single railroad when the I & M Canal opened in April 1848, within six years was the terminal for ten of them, stretching for 3,000 miles in every direction. By 1856, those railroads were operating fifty-eight passenger trains and thirty-eight freights a day to and from Chicago. By 1889, six million freight cars passed through Chicago, pushed and pulled by three hundred switch engines and another hundred locomotives assigned to interline transfers. There were slightly more than 30,000 miles of railroads in the United States in 1860, and despite very little growth during the Civil War the nation's railroad plant had more than doubled to 70,600 miles by the end of 1873. By then, some railroad executives were warning that too many lines had been built.[11]

Vessel height on the Sanitary and Ship Canal, shown above before its completion in 1900, has always been dictated by the Sante Fe Railroad bridge at Lemont, built in 1899 (David R. Phillips Collection). Towboats operating between Lemont and Chicago often have pilot houses that can be raised for better visibility along the canal and then lowered to clear the bridge, shown in a contemporary view at left.

By 1870 the railroads had become sufficiently dominant over the inland grain and passenger trade that Illinois became the first state in the Union to impose economic control over them when the granger movement got a provision in the state's new constitution empowering the state to regulate warehouses—but only in Chicago—and to enact legislation to protect "producers, shippers, and receivers" of grain. The next year the legislature complied with the constitutional mandate and created the Board of Railroad and Warehouse Commissioners, setting limits on passenger fares, establishing maximum rates for grain storage, and decreeing that freight rates be based on distance. In *Munn v. Illinois* the U.S. Supreme Court ruled that grain elevators in the past twenty years had become an almost monopolistic business in the Midwest and could be regulated in the public interest.[12]

The routing of the first railroads to Chicago established the order of battle with the waterways. Three of the ten arrived from the east; the others fanned out to the north, west, and south. Two of the eastern railroads connected with New York, and the other with Philadelphia. Five of the western lines reached and ultimately crossed the Mississippi River. The Chicago and Rock Island was built parallel to and as a competitor of the I & M Canal. The Chicago, Alton & St. Louis was parallel to the Illinois River. The route of the Illinois Central was parallel to (though not adjacent to) the Mississippi. The later arrivals after the Civil War were for the most part railroads that were intended to go elsewhere but wound up being diverted to Chicago to be able to compete for traffic.

Cincinnati, once the dominant river city and the nation's largest meatpacker, by 1861 was connected to Chicago by a 276-mile chain of railroads built end to end through Indiana. Before the end of the century three additional lines were built so that Cincinnati's primary rail connection became Chicago, which long before had passed Cincinnati as the nation's major meatpacking center. The railroads also helped transform Chicago into the world's largest and most efficient grain market, surpassing Saint Louis. By 1856, the efficiencies, to which the railroads, Chicago's twelve grain elevators, and the relatively large hold capacities of Great Lakes ships all contributed, enabled wheat to be handled at a cost amounting to only a tenth of that of the Saint Louis steamboat levy.[13]

Although much of Chicago's traffic was agricultural, manufacturing and wholesale goods in the second half of the nineteenth century became increasingly important industries because of the transportation system. The industrialization of the city began as early as 1845: a significant factor in Cyrus McCormick's decision to relocate his mechanical harvester manufacturing operation from Virginia to Chicago in 1845—in addition to being closer to the developing agricultural markets—was the availability of transportation.[14]

## The Railroad Advantage

Even in the 1850s, when trains were relatively primitive, the railroads had some substantial advantages over the rivers, canals, and lakes that enabled them to capture the passenger market once dominated by the waterways. Although express passenger trains at that time rarely averaged above 30 miles an hour, canal boats could travel only as fast as a man could walk, and stagecoaches, although they could attain a speed of 10 miles an hour, averaged considerably less. The biggest and best steamboats on an express run could make 10 miles an hour upstream and 15 or 16 miles an hour downstream; the average for smaller vessels was lower.[15]

A steamship on the Great Lakes in the 1850s might average 5 miles an hour with stops for fuel and in ports along the route. In 1839 a Buffalo-Chicago round trip by lake steamer with several stops en route took sixteen days, an average speed of just over 4 miles an hour. Within a few years that average had been increased to 5.3 miles an hour, although delays caused by bad weather could make shambles of sailing schedules.[16]

Railroads also benefited from having more direct routes. A trip between Chicago and Detroit is 283 miles by rail but more than 600 by lake around the northern tip of Michigan. A river steamboat journey from Pittsburgh to Saint Louis was 1,164 miles, but when the two cities were finally linked by railroad after 1857, the distance was cut nearly in half to 612 miles. The water route between Chicago and Moline, Illinois, in the nineteenth century was 607 miles; the railroad cut it to only 165. The railroads lopped nearly 500 miles off the Chicago–New York water route and about 560 miles off the Chicago-New Orleans canal-river route.

One of the first customers to abandon the waterways in favor of railroads was the U.S. Post Office. Irregular service in the 1850s cost steamboats the federal mail contracts, which contained penalties for nonperformance. An attempt by the steamboat industry and its allies in Congress to mandate a mail service by steamboat between Cairo and New Orleans in 1852 was opposed by the postmaster general in 1857, who described it as inferior to such service by "a well managed" railroad.[17]

Merchandise was the next category of freight to shift from water to rail. Chicago Board of Trade documents indicate that in 1852 Chicago's lone railroad, operating that full year, hauled considerably more meat and merchandise (package freight) than the I & M Canal, but less grain, lumber, and iron. The railroad handled 36 million pounds of merchandise to and from the city, opposed to 14.8 million pounds on the canal. Seven years later Chicago's three western railroads (Galena; Chicago & Rock Island; and Chicago, Burlington & Quincy) handled almost 231 million tons of merchandise, but the canal just over 1 million.[18]

The loss of merchandise traffic was less dramatic on the lakes. In 1859 the three eastern railroads (Michigan Central; Lake

Getting rail and highway systems over Chicago's many waterways required a variety of bridges: bascule, lift, and cantilever bridges shown spanning the Calumet River.

Chicago had become the nation's largest railroad center before the Civil War. The impact of the railroads on the city is shown in this 1925 aerial photo from Eighteenth Street facing north toward the Loop (top). Construction had already started on a project to straighten the south branch of the Chicago River by removing the bend. (Chicago Maritime Society)

Shore; and Pittsburgh, Ft. Wayne & Chicago) combined hauled 188 million pounds of merchandise to and from the city—80 percent of it westbound to Chicago. The city's lake port that year handled about 85 million pounds of merchandise—about half of what the railroads carried—but still dominated the grain, lumber, and iron trade. Lumber hookers hauled almost 300 million board feet of lumber to Chicago that year; the eastern railroads slightly more than 6 million feet.[19]

## Rail versus Canals

Nineteenth-century canals and turnpikes, unless they were adjacent, generally did not compete; however, when canals were built alongside existing roads, they captured most of the freight business at the expense of the wagons but were too slow to make a dent in the stagecoach passenger trade. The railroads in turn had a devastating effect on freight wagons and both highway and canal passenger traffic but were somewhat less successful in capturing the canals' bulk freight business, which was more sensitive to price than time. The draymen and stagecoach operators who survived did so by transforming themselves into local feeders for the railroads.[20]

The earliest railroads in the 1830s also had difficulty competing for capital with the publicly funded canals. The Baltimore & Ohio Railroad in its first six years of operation could raise only enough capital to extend its lines for 81 miles. New York tolerated the building of seven independent railroads end to end along the length of its Erie Canal, principally to feed traffic to the canal and provide transit during the winter months when it was closed. But the

railroads very early captured the canal's passenger traffic and by 1882 had made such a dent in its freight traffic that the state abolished tolls. In Indiana the ill-advised, 458-mile Wabash and Erie Canal connecting Toledo and Evansville was completed in 1856 and put out of business by competition from the New Albany & Salem and the Lake Erie, Wabash & St. Louis (Wabash) railroads by 1874.[21]

The Illinois and Michigan Canal stood up somewhat better to competition from the Rock Island & La Salle (later Chicago & Rock Island) Railroad. The railroad was chartered in 1847, as the name implies, by a group of men from western Illinois as an extension of the canal to connect its terminal at La Salle with the Mississippi River at Rock Island. But Joseph E. Sheffield, a New Haven investor who was its principal backer, insisted in 1851 that the line go all the way to Chicago. He prevailed and construction on the Rock Island began in the spring of 1852 in Chicago and was completed the following year to La Salle along the entire length of the I & M Canal and to a large extent on the canal right of way. The railroad was extended to the Mississippi the following year.[22]

Although the railroad was supposed to compensate the I & M for use of its land by providing a subsidy for any lost freight, it used a loophole in the law to renege. The economic effect was immediate, and the canal's patronage declined by 25,996 passengers in 1852 when the railroad started running trains on the 40-mile route between Joliet and Chicago. Speed and reliability were the main factors: a canal packet took more than a day to make the trip that a train could cover in three hours. The canal also was vulnerable to periods of

The south branch of the Chicago River ca. 1930 after the straightening project. The area south of the Loop and east of the river (left) was still dominated by railroad yards until redeveloped in the 1980s. The yards west of the river are for the Chicago and Alton freight terminal and Union Station visible at the top left of the photograph. (Chicago Maritime Society)

**Table 11.1** Traffic on the I & M Canal and Rock Island Railroad

| Commodity | 1859 | | 1871 | |
|---|---|---|---|---|
| | Railroad | Canal | Railroad | Canal |
| Grain (bu.) | 1,330,254 | 2,876,529 | 15,462,537 | 6,758,637 |
| Lumber (ft.) | 15,489,750 | 64,824,186 | 43,086,800 | 37,484,127 |
| Merchandise (lb.) | 40,832,722 | 1,073,821 | 159,101,310 | 964,383 |
| Iron | 13,938,460 | 638,413 | — | 2,055,098 |

Source: Chicago Board of Trade, *Second Annual Statement* (Chicago, 1859), 83–104, and *Fourteenth Annual Report* (Chicago, 1871), 86–109.

low water on the Illinois River, its principal connection to the west, that made navigation impossible for months at a time. In 1853 almost all passenger traffic moved to the railroad after it reached La Salle, and high-value package freight began to make the switch soon thereafter.[23]

Chicago Board of Trade reports from the period document the competition between the two modes between 1859 and 1871. Of the four largest commodities handled on the route in 1859—grain, lumber, merchandise, and iron—the railroad handled almost all of the merchandise freight in both directions and twice as much iron, mainly westbound, as the canal. The I & M carried four times as much lumber, primarily westbound, and twice as much grain, mostly headed east, as the Rock Island. By the end of 1871 the canal still carried more lumber and had eclipsed the railroad in iron, though in diminished quantities, but the railroad carried substantially more merchandise and grain and had developed a sizeable traffic in animal products—hides, wool, livestock, meat, lard, and butter—which was negligible on the canal (table 11.1).

For a time the canal was able to hold on to and even increase its bulk traffic—grain, stone, coal, and lumber. As late as the 1866 shipping season, the I & M Canal hauled nearly twice as much grain to Chicago as the Rock Island. Faced with a competitor that had the flexibility to build rail spurs to serve industries on the very banks of the I & M, the canal commissioners took several steps to remain competitive, including deepening the waterway between Chicago and Lockport and enlarging the locks at the Chicago River, enabling bigger vessels to negotiate that section, but no farther west.[24]

For a time the two enterprises even engaged in a rate war. The canal commissioners lowered rates from time to time to compete but were unable to come up with anything like the 1879 agreement between the Rock Island and Michigan Southern to allow the through-routing of their freight cars over both lines to save the cost of transferring grain between cars in Chicago. Eventually the railroad rate wars common in the late 1800s decimated canal traffic, resulting in the diversion of 80 percent of the grain traffic to eastern ports to the railroads by 1876.[25]

The long, slow decline coinciding with similar problems on the rivers began after 1882. Traffic on the Illinois and Michigan Canal peaked at just over 1 million tons in 1880, compared to about 20 million tons handled by all the western rivers at that time. After the Sanitary and Ship Canal opened in 1900, replacing the eastern section of the I & M Canal between Chicago and Joliet, traffic on the surviving western section fell below 400,000 tons. It was closed in the 1930s after the federal government completed a system

the 1880s began to haul fresh berries from Louisiana to Chicago out of season. Within a few years it was hauling trainloads of bananas as part of a 2,000-mile sea-land route from Central America to Chicago.[31]

## The Great Lakes

The situation on the Great Lakes after the railroads arrived was somewhat different. Although long-distance passenger and package freight traffic shifted from water to rail before the Civil War, a few local steamship lines were able to maintain cross-lake service in passengers and freight on Lake Michigan until well into the twentieth century.

The western railroads interchanged considerable traffic with lake ships through most of the last half of the nineteenth century, and the eastern railroads were forced to form their own steamship lines to compete, at least until the federal government banned such practice in the Panama Canal Act in the early 1900s. Before the end of the century a number of small Midwest railroads operated a ferry service for their trains across Lake Michigan in an effort to bypass what was becoming a railroad bottleneck in Chicago.

Bulk cargo, more cheaply served by ships than trains, for the most part stayed on the lakes, and Chicago became a center of riverside grain elevators and lumber yards before the Civil War. Chicago's westbound lumber trade more than tripled to 984.7 million board feet between 1858 and 1871, as did eastbound grain. By 1871 the city handled nearly 57.5 million bushels of wheat, corn, oats, rye, and barley.

Four western railroads—the Chicago and North Western; Illinois Central; Rock Island; and Chicago, Burlington and Quincy—by 1872 accounted for the lion's share of all eastbound corn and wheat arriving in Chicago: 69 percent of it continued its trip east by ship. The railroad historian Albro Martin opined that the cost of settlement of the Illinois prairie could not be justified until an inexpensive form of transportation such as the railroad was devised.[32]

Flour was another matter. Probably because it was not easily transferred between the different modes of transportation and was vulnerable to contamination by moisture, the railroads captured a majority of that commodity after the Civil War. By 1872, only 13 percent of the flour traffic moved east on the lakes; the eastern railroads had 77 percent of trade, and the western lines 6 percent.[33]

Animal products were a new market developed by the railroads after the introduction of stock cars to haul livestock to Chicago and refrigerator cars to take their carcasses to markets in the East. Although some salted pork, hides, and lard moved east on ships before the arrival of the railroads, by 1871 Chicago's eastern railroads hauled 74,000 tons of fresh and cured meat out of the city, contrasted to only about 77 tons on lake ships.[34]

The iron and steel industry that developed in Chicago in the second half of the nineteenth century was one that benefited from the synergy between the lake and railroad transportation systems. The industry consisted principally of importers and distributors before Eber B. Ward in 1857 established the Chicago Rolling Mill to reroll iron bars into rail. The discovery of deposits of iron ore on the shores of Lake Superior in the 1850s, the availability of cheap water transportation for both ore and coal, and the expanding market for steel rail combined to create the city's steel industry. By 1875, the city was consuming 1.6 million tons of coal annually, much of it for steel production, and more than 793,000 tons of iron ore. By 1880, Illinois ranked fourth in the nation in iron and steel production with almost 418,000 tons, and the city had more than six hundred companies, employing seventeen thousand persons in that industry.[35]

## Passenger and Freight

The Great Lakes basin had developed to a point in the 1830s that large paddle-wheel steamships were being built to serve a commercial passenger market that just over three decades earlier had been adequately handled by canoes. The 473-ton commercial steamer *Michigan* built in 1833 was 156 feet long and had a passenger capacity of nearly five hundred, but within four years it was surpassed by the $120,000 *Illinois*—800 tons and 205 feet long—built specifically for the Buffalo-Chicago route. Like most side-wheel steamships of the day, the Illinois had private passenger cabins at $20 per trip, including meals, and deck space for cargo and steerage passengers, who were charged half as much as for first class. In seven round trips in the first three years of the vessel's existence the *Illinois* carried an average of about sixty passengers per five-day leg and earned about $5,000 per round trip—about a third attributable to freight.[36]

Within a few years six to eight steamships were assigned to the Buffalo-Chicago route, and by 1850, at the height of the passenger steamship era (1830–1860) on the Great Lakes, there were two daily departures on the route from each city. The circuitous route, slow average speeds, and high cost of paddle-wheel steamships were their undoing. The faster railroads began to take away the passenger traffic after 1850, and the propeller-powered steamships, which had larger cargo capacities, could haul freight more cheaply.[37]

As is often the case in times of rapid technological change, the steamship industry was slow to realize its vulnerability. The 2,002-ton *Western World*, which by some accounts was as opulent as anything on the oceans when she was completed in 1855, lasted just three years before being tied up by her owners for lack of traffic. The same fate claimed the *Buffalo, Plymouth,* and *Mississippi*—all tied to the dock a considerable time before the Civil War disrupted commercial passenger traffic. When passenger service revived somewhat after the war, it was to a great extent controlled by fleets of railroad-owned vessels.[38]

As early as 1852 the New York & Erie Railroad (Erie) put together the Union Steamboat Company and began operating as many as fourteen package freight and passenger steamers from various Great Lakes ports, including Chicago. Within three years a competitor had emerged in the form of Commodore Cornelius Vanderbilt's Western Transit Company. During the Civil War it operated ten combination passenger-freighters between Buffalo and Chicago, including the opulent 1,850-ton *Queen of the West*.[39]

Vanderbilt's rival, the Pennsylvania Railroad, in 1867 started up the Anchor Line between Duluth, Chicago, and Buffalo. Within a few years the Lehigh Valley; Delaware, Lackawanna & Western; Central of Vermont; Great Western; Grand Trunk Western; and Great Northern railroads also had fleets on the lakes. The end to the railroad-owned shipping lines came in 1915 after Congress banned cross-ownership in the Panama Canal Act, and they were sold to the Great Lakes Transit Corporation. It continued to operate a shrinking fleet until World War II.[40]

Several smaller Midwest railroads in the late nineteenth century built fleets of specialized ships to carry their rail cars across Lake Michigan to avoid the Chicago bottleneck. Although the first railroad car ferry dates from 1857 in Buffalo, that type of vessel did not reach Lake Michigan for thirty years. A subsidiary, jointly owned by three railroads with lines to the Straits of Mackinac at the northern end of Lake Michigan, in 1887 ordered and put into service the *St. Ignace,* an icebreaking wooden ferry fitted with railroad tracks to haul freight cars across the straits. Five years later the Toledo, Ann Arbor & North Michigan (Ann Arbor) designed and built a somewhat more substantial icebreaking vessel with four tracks capable of holding twenty-four rail cars on Lake Michigan

The synergy between rail and water in Chicago involved such commodities as grain, coal, and steel. A collier is being loaded from the stern forward (note the bow riding higher) at a rail transfer yard on the Calumet River. The power plant to the right has a dock for coal barges, and an ore boat sits in a dry dock at the bottom. The three ships are of the configuration typical of lakers during the first seven decades of the twentieth century—pilothouse forward and engine room astern, separated by a long cargo hold amidships. (Great Lakes Historical Society, Vermilion, Ohio)

crossings. The *Ann Arbor No. 1,* as the vessel was called, was the direct predecessor of the fleets of car ferries that plied the lakes until 1983.[41]

By 1897 the Flint & Pere Marquette Railroad had its namesake *Pere Marquette* car ferry in service between Ludington, Michigan, and Manitowoc, Wisconsin, and Grand Trunk Railway later started car ferry service between Milwaukee and Grand Haven and Muskegon in Michigan. The services at least in the beginning were considered successful because trains were relatively short and would fit nicely on a single ferry: the *Ann Arbor* in the early 1900s was hauling twenty-six thousand cars a year cross the lake and claiming to make a profit on it.

However, by the 1920s trains had grown to such a length that six voyages taking two or three days were required to get a single long freight train across the lake. The last surviving car ferry line, which was operated by the Chesapeake & Ohio Railroad and in 1963 acquired the Baltimore & Ohio (successor to the Pere Marquette) and its substantial rail terminal in Chicago, began a program of "controlled withdrawal" from the lakes, completed in 1983.[42]

By 1900 the railroads had effectively monopolized land transport and had captured so much traffic off the waterways that the federal government began to regulate them, not only by means of such agencies as the Interstate Commerce Commission (ICC) but special legislation. The ICC, created in 1887 but not given the powers necessary for effective regulation until after the turn of the century, was intended to control such things as rates and service, but by World War I the federal government was forced to temporarily nationalize not only the railroads—to clear up a massive wartime traffic jam along the East Coast—but the remnants of the riverboat industry as well. The latter had sunk to such a state that it was no longer capable of contributing to a war effort, and Washington was forced to rebuild it almost from scratch.

By then, the canal age was history, and Chicago's canals were little more than sewage ditches with little traffic to justify their existence as navigable waterways. For more than a generation Chicagoans associated the terms "San" and, later, "Cal-Sag" with stench, just as "Bubbly Creek" and the (I & M) "Canal" had wrinkled the noses of their parents and grandparents years earlier.

It was in that context that federal, state, and local government in the twentieth century embarked on another canal building program in Chicago.

# Part Three

## The Twentieth Century

# *Chapter Twelve* The San, Cal-Sag, and Hennepin

• The survival and growth of Chicago's canals in the twentieth century long after the canal age had ended and most of them elsewhere in the country had been abandoned was not so much the result of any desire to revive inland navigation—although that was a factor—as it was an attempt to solve the city's sanitation problem. Chicago was built on a low-lying marsh that caused all sorts of drainage problems, which ultimately forced the city to raise its streets and jack up its buildings in the 1850s and 1860s.

However, that failed to solve the growing problem of what to do with all the sewage, which was becoming a public health concern; epidemics associated with poor sanitation were common in the nineteenth century. The growth of the stockyards on the south side after 1865 compounded with animal waste and offal what had already become a serious problem caused by sewage and the toxic byproducts of an industrializing city. Chicago, which had a population of less than thirty thousand in 1850 within twenty years had grown to a city of nearly three hundred thousand (table 12.1). The Chicago River in 1870 was not a place a prudent person would swim: effluent from the stockyards bubbled downriver to mix with industrial pollution, untreated human waste, and

The Sanitary and Ship Canal was built in the 1890s to correct Chicago's severe sewage problems and prevent pollution of the lake. The Water Reclamation District, as the Metropolitan Sanitary District is now known, maintains a plant at the junction of the canal and Cal-Sag Channel to aerate water by pumping it over artificial waterfalls. The lighthouse in the background is at the junction of the two canals.

whatever the crews of the ships choking the river might throw overboard.

So, as canals elsewhere became passé after the arrival of the railroads, Chicago, the nation's railroad capital, increasingly turned to them as a way to solve its sanitation problem. Other Great Lakes cities simply flushed their sewage into the same lake from which they drew drinking water, but Chicago decided to send its effluent down the river to the west. To do that it resurrected the dual-service canal.

**Table 12.1** Chicago Population

| Year | Population |
|------|------------|
| 1830 | 40–50* |
| 1840 | 4,417 |
| 1850 | 29,963 |
| 1860 | 109,260 |
| 1870 | 298,977 |
| 1880 | 503,185 |
| 1890 | 1,099,850 |
| 1900 | 1,698,575 |
| 1910 | 2,185,283 |
| 1920 | 3,212,000 |
| 1930 | 3,367,438 |
| 1940 | 3,369,608 |
| 1950 | 3,620,962 |
| 1960 | 3,550,404 |
| 1970 | 3,369,367 |
| 1980 | 3,005,072 |
| 1990 | 2,783,728 |
| 1998 | 2,800,000* |

* estimate   *Source:* U.S. Census Bureau.

They were not a local invention; Italy's Naviglio Grande, an irrigation canal completed in 1458 to serve Milan and the Po River valley, by the end of that century had been improved by Leonardo da Vinci with the addition of locks to permit navigation. Four centuries later in America, major canal projects such as the Tennessee-Tombigbee Waterway were often justified to the taxpayers as dual-service canals with both commercial and recreational uses.

The reason for Chicago's canals was a little more urgent than pleasure boating. The city had an ample water supply from Lake Michigan and a navigation canal but was forced to dig a new canal and reverse the flow of the Chicago River to flush its sewage downstream to the Mississippi River. The resulting Sanitary and Ship Canal was made large enough to handle barges and replaced the obsolete Illinois and Michigan Canal. When growth overtaxed the San, the city dug the Calumet-Sag Channel between the Calumet River and Lemont to provide additional capacity for both sewage and, eventually, barges.[1]

As railroads increased their domination of inland transport in the second half of the nineteenth century, single-use navigation canals proved vulnerable to that competition and the resulting changes in trade patterns. Some canals were obsolete before they opened, including the 75-mile Hennepin Canal, built between 1890 and 1907 as a shortcut across northern Illinois to connect the Great Lakes and Upper Mississippi River. It never carried more than a fraction of the traffic that had been predicted and was abandoned in midcentury.

Within another fifty years, as the twenty-first century dawned, technology had once again resulted in major changes in Chicago's transportation picture. The railroads were no longer dominant, having lost much of their market to motor trucks, airplanes, pipelines, and automobiles. However, the surviving canals, although they had lost market share, had resumed the role they had comfortable held in the 1880s—as the freight ways of bulk commodities.

The trade patterns that had dominated Chicago's maritime economy for most of the city's existence once again had changed. The massive federal rebuilding of the inland river system in the first half of the century resulted in a shift in the movement of many commodities from an east-west axis through New York to a north-south axis down the Mississippi to New Orleans. As the century closed, the Sanitary and Ship and the Cal-Sag combined were handling more freight traffic than the city's lake ports.[2]

### The Hennepin Canal

The Illinois and Michigan Canal had stimulated the settlement and development of northeastern Illinois beginning in the 1830s, and it wasn't long before the residents of the northwestern quadrant of the state began to agitate for an east-west canal. At the time steamboat traffic on the Upper Mississippi was the dominant form of transportation in the area. A trip to Chicago required a long, bumpy ride in a

stagecoach, and goods bound for New York by ship first had to be sent by steamboat to New Orleans or hauled by wagon overland to Chicago. As early as 1834, some residents of the area met in Hennepin on the Illinois River to discuss the possibility of a canal from there to Rock Island on the Mississippi.[3]

The opening of the I & M Canal in 1848 between Chicago and La Salle on the Illinois River made it possible to ship goods by water between Rock Island and Chicago, but only by means of a circuitous, 607-mile route down the Mississippi to Grafton, up the Illinois River to La Salle, and by the I & M Canal the remaining 97 miles to Chicago. Its proponents argued that the proposed western canal would cut that trip to 188 miles, and in 1864, 1866, 1874, 1879, and 1881 held conventions in such places as Davenport, Iowa, Rock Island, Geneseo, and Ottawa to lobby for the project. The 1881 Davenport

Chicago's canals are often used as parking lots for vessels as shown in this 1999 photograph of three fishing tugs tied up along the Sanitary and Ship Canal at Lemont. The tugs are of typical Great Lakes configuration with stern doors for playing out and retrieving nets.

The canal towboat *Kiowa,* which is distinguishable by its hydraulic pilothouse in the raised position, pushes two barges heavily laden with stone east on the Sanitary and Ship Canal at Lemont.

convention resulted in the appointment of a Hennepin Canal Commission, which met in Chicago to promote the idea to various Midwest organizations and the Buffalo, New York, Board of Trade.

The campaign quickly became a turf war with New York supporting its economic satrapy in Chicago in favor of the canal and Saint Louis, which was still concerned about the rise of Chicago as a rival, in opposition. When the New York Board of Trade in 1881 had introduced in Congress a bill appropriating $1 million for the canal project, Saint Louis interests got the amount reduced to $30,000—just enough for a survey of the route. The battle continued for most of the rest of the decade, and by the time Congress in 1890 appropriated $500,000 to get construction started the canal was taking on the aura of a pork barrel project.

Its principal shepherd in Washington not surprisingly was Representative Thomas Henderson, a Republican and Civil War veteran from Princeton, Illinois, whose district the canal would traverse. Henderson was an ally in Congress of Joseph G. Cannon, a Republican from Danville, who would later gain fame as one of the most powerful speakers of the U.S. House of Representatives (1903–1911).

The plan they induced Congress to fund was to dig a canal from the conflu-

ence of the Rock and Mississippi Rivers in Rock Island to the bend where the Illinois River turns to the east at Bureau. The theory was that a riverboat could travel the 75.2 miles by canal from Rock Island to Bureau, then up the Illinois River for 11 miles to La Salle. The final 97 miles to Chicago would be by the western section of the I & M Canal and new Sanitary and Ship Canal, then in the planning stages.

By 1890, when construction started on the Hennepin, traffic on the I & M Canal and Illinois River was already in decline largely because of competition from the railroads that crisscrossed northern Illinois at intervals of 7 to 10 miles. The Hennepin Canal was built parallel to and in some cases within sight of the Chicago & Rock Island Railroad (later Chicago, Rock Island & Pacific), which had absorbed much of the I & M Canal's traffic and had been serving the Hennepin's territory for forty years. The canal's builders had to bridge the Rock Island main line no less than three times, as well as four branch lines of the Chicago, Burlington & Quincy; one of the Rock Island & Peoria; and one of the Chicago & North Western railroads.[4]

Despite all the competition, Congress continued to provide the $7,319,563.39 necessary for the Corps of Engineers to complete the project, including nine aqueducts, sixty-seven highway bridges, nine railroad bridges, and a 29.3-mile feeder canal to the Rock River in Rock Falls to water the main canal and avoid pumping stations. The 10-mile eastern section was the most difficult, requiring ten locks for the canal to ascend from the Illinois River valley and three aqueducts just to cross meandering Bureau Creek. The descent to the Mississippi was more gradual. From an engineering standpoint the canal's principal interest was the experimental use of concrete in the place of cut stone for locks and bridge abutments at Milan, a material that proved so successful it was adopted by the United States for construction of the Panama Canal (1904–1914) a few years later.[5]

The Hennepin Canal finally opened for business in 1907 under the name Illinois and Mississippi Canal, but traffic was disappointing from the start, and the kind of development boom that hit Chicago in the 1830s after the I & M was proposed never happened along the Hennepin. In fact, the townships on the Hennepin's banks in Bureau County declined in population between the 1900 and 1920 censuses. Traffic on the canal averaged only about 10,000 tons annually in its first twenty-five years of existence and peaked in 1933 at 30,161 tons; the I & M in its heyday in the 1880s carried between 742,074 and 1,011,287 tons annually.[6]

By 1950 the Hennepin had deteriorated to the point that water levels were insufficient to sustain anything but the lightest loads, and the Corps of Engineers operated the waterway two days a week or by appointment for commercial users. The last major shipper, International Harvester Company, sent steel products between its plants on the Calumet River and in Rock Island during World War II, but that market died when the war ended. The Illinois and Mississippi Canal was closed in 1951 and deeded to Illinois in 1970 as a state park under its original name of Hennepin.

## Barge Technology

By the end of the nineteenth century canals had become the victim not only of the railroads but the conversion on the rivers from steamboats to barges and towboats. Although the Great Lakes merchant marine as early as the 1840s developed mechanical systems like the steam elevator for handling bulk cargoes, the riverboat industry was slower to change. The river steamboats continued to be loaded manually by gangs of laborers, and because the canals exchanged a considerable amount of traffic with the steamboats, they were vulnerable to the same inefficient system.

The solution to bulk cargo handling that appeared on the rivers, first in the coal trade and much later for other bulk

Lockport remains, as it was in the 1850s, a busy canal port. The Garvey Marine towboat *Chris White* is shown with its pilothouse raised sitting next to a tow of parked and empty barges.

The *Chris White* with pilothouse lowered.

The typical river and canal barge is 195 feet long, 35 feet wide, has a draft of 9 feet, and can carry 1,500 tons of cargo. This one shown on blocks at a Sanitary and Ship Canal repair yard has squared ends to fit against other barges in a tow. Cables secure the barges to each other.

because of the 4-foot-8-inch draft limitation were restricted to loads of slightly less than 100 tons, although they had a capacity of 150 tons in deeper water.[7]

Once steam power replaced mules on the I & M, canal boats were typically towed like barges to their destinations, often onto Lake Michigan and down the Illinois and Mississippi Rivers to avoid the expensive task of having to transfer cargo to another vessel. That proved to be a temporary solution, however. The I & M, as the nineteenth century drew to a close, had become something of an obsolescing bottleneck; it was only half as deep as necessary to handle the big new barges, and its locks at 102 feet long and 19 feet wide were too small for what would become the standard barge size—175 feet long and 26 feet wide.

The solution obvious from as early as the 1850s was to enlarge the I & M. Ellis S. Chesbrough, Chicago's chief engineer, had recommended digging a larger canal for sanitation as well as navigation as early as 1858, although nothing was done until the Civil War proved the canal was inadequate for gunboats and large transports. However, a bill introduced in Congress in 1862 to widen and deepen the eastern section of the canal as well as the Des Plaines and Illinois Rivers channels ran afoul of opposition from rival states and was defeated. The Corps of Engineers in 1867 recommended extending the Illinois River all the way to Chicago by using the route of the Des Plaines and I & M Canal.[8] In 1871 the city and state finally acted, primarily to ameliorate the growing sanitation problem, by spending $3.3 million to widen the section between Chicago and Lockport to 120 feet, deepening it to 6 feet, and merging the two 102-by-19-foot locks at Chicago into a single lock 220 feet long and 20 feet wide. Pumps lifted the polluted water from the Chicago River's south branch into the canal. The project did nothing for the section of the I & M canal west of Joliet, however. By that time, it was obvious that improvements to the

commodities, was the barge, a floating box that permitted mechanical loading and unloading. The largest river steamboats by the 1880s could carry 2,000 tons of cargo on 6 feet of water, although on the northern rivers, like the Illinois, the steamboats were considerably smaller. Just after the Civil War, grain barges on the Mississippi could carry 650 tons, but by the 1880s they had grown in size and capacity to 1,600 tons. By lashing barges together a single tow was capable of carrying 10,000 tons. On the other hand, canal barges on the Illinois and Michigan and Hennepin waterways

Illinois and Des Plaines Rivers to permit steamboat navigation as far north as Joliet—although it provided a somewhat more circuitous route than the western section of the I & M canal between Joliet and LaSalle—made more sense than rebuilding the entire canal.[9]

In 1882 the Corps of Engineers, as part of its study of the feasibility of the Hennepin Canal, looked at the possibility of widening the I & M to 80 feet and dredging it to a depth of 7 feet. The locks would have been 170 feet long and 30 feet wide. However, the officer in charge of the study concluded that making the Illinois River navigable between La Salle and Chicago made more sense. A few years later, another corps officer concluded that there were only two practical canal routes out of Chicago and cutting a new canal between the Calumet and Des Plaines Rivers (the Cal-Sag route) made more sense than widening the I & M.

## The Sanitary and Ship Canal

It was the issue of pollution that finally forced Chicago to act and build the dual-use canal suggested by Chesbrough in 1858. He had been sent by the Board of Sewerage Commissioners in 1856 to study sanitation systems used in larger European cities and concluded that Chicago was better off sending its sewage by canal down the Mississippi than allowing it to flow into Lake Michigan. Sporadic outbreaks of cholera were a serious problem in Chicago in the 1800s, and the stench from sewage and stockyards offal dumped into the river was a constant source of complaints.[10]

Pumping Chicago River sewage into the I & M canal was only a temporary solution, which became obvious when thirty days of rain in 1879 caused a backup of the Des Plaines River into the Chicago River, flushing the city's sewage into the lake from which it obtained its drinking water. An 11 1/2-inch rainfall in August 1885 again caused the Des Plaines River to back up, polluting Lake Michigan with

Chicago River effluent when the canal pumps at Bridgeport couldn't keep up with the flood. The Corps of Engineers had already concluded that its interest was restricted to navigation, which required an 8-foot-deep channel, but a sanitation canal would require a 14-foot-deep channel to be low enough to allow Lake Michigan water to flush the sewage downstream to the southwest by gravity without any boost from pumps.[11]

By 1877, complaints over the stench from suburban Joliet and downriver caused Dr. John Rauch, the secretary of the State Board of Health, to look into the issue and conclude that lake water should be used to flush the slow-moving canal. Chicago in 1884 spent $251,000 on new pumps, but that solution lasted for only two years when the lake water level began one of its cyclic drops and the new pumps couldn't divert enough water to flush the canal. Periodic outbreaks of cholera and typhoid fever, including one in 1890, gave the problem greater urgency.

In 1886 the City Council, as the lake water level began to fall, authorized the creation of a Drainage and Water Supply Commission but did not provide any funds. Finally, a bill was introduced in the state legislature in Springfield in 1886 to create a metropolitan sanitary district in Cook County with the power to build and operate a sewage and ship canal and to levy taxes to pay for it. The 1889 law that resulted after a long series of public hearings was unique in that for the first time it created a regional government encompassing both the city and its suburbs—jurisdictions that usually jealously guarded their independence from each other. However, the sanitation problem had become so severe that the combined electorate in a referendum on November 5, 1889, overwhelmingly approved the new agency by a vote of 70,958 to 242.

Construction on the new canal began two years later during a period of labor unrest and was interrupted in 1893 by a strike in Lemont by two thousand quarry and canal workers seeking higher pay. Although overshadowed by the Haymarket incident on May 4, 1886, in which a bomb was thrown into a group of policemen at a labor rally, killing eight persons and wounding fifty-nine, and the Pullman strike of 1894, the canal strike erupted in violence when, according to one account, workers—many of whom had been drinking in the thirty-eight saloons in town—took to the streets and encountered strikebreakers. Two strikers were killed and several wounded in the ensuing melee. However, John Peter Altgeld, Illinois's progressive governor, who pardoned some of the Haymarket participants, personally investigated the Lemont incident after sending in the state militia to restore order and placed the blame on the strikebreakers and contractors.[12]

Despite the strike, improved mining techniques and machinery not available when the I & M canal was built more than half a century earlier enabled workers to complete its replacement in less than eight years. As in the case of the Hennepin Canal, some of the canal-building technology employed a few years later on the Panama Canal was honed during construction of the Sanitary and Ship Canal.

Its opening on January 2, 1900, was rather abrupt: the Sanitary District trustees at dawn that day, without even notifying the governor or scheduling the usual inaugural ceremony, rushed demolition of the dam near Damen Avenue in Chicago separating the Chicago River from the new canal out of fear that Saint Louis intended to go to court, seeking an injunction to prevent the flushing of sewage down-

Barges can be docked and unloaded almost anywhere along the rivers and canals and unloaded with backhoes.

stream to the Mississippi and polluting that city's water supply. The trustees first tried unsuccessfully to dynamite the dam but, when that failed, set it afire. Ultimately they were forced to call in a dredge, and it completed the job by noon. Saint Louis ultimately took Chicago to court but lost the case when a report by scientists concluded that the sewage was sufficiently diluted to render it harmless by the time it reached Joliet.[13]

Chicago also faced a legal challenge from neighboring states over the diversion of Lake Michigan water because the canal effectively reversed the flow of the Chicago River. The river for thousands of years had emptied into Lake Michigan and eventually into the Saint Lawrence River, but the canal reversed the flow, and the Chicago River in 1900 effectively became a canal for Great Lakes water bound for the Gulf of Mexico. Although the U.S. War Department on May 8, 1889, authorized Chicago to divert downstream as much as 10,000 cubic feet of lake water, the diversion issue ultimately wound up in federal court when other Great Lakes states challenged it as a threat to lake levels. The U.S. Supreme Court in 1934 placed a limit of 1,500 cubic feet per second on the amount that could be diverted, in addition to amounts Chicago pumped for domestic reasons, such as drinking water. After more legal wrangling, the courts set 3,200 cubic feet per second as the maximum allowable diversion from all sources, and a lock built in 1838–1939 effectively closed off the mouth of the Chicago River from the lake to control the diversion.[14]

The opening of the Sanitary and Ship Canal also rendered superfluous the eastern section of the I & M Canal, although its right of way proved valuable, first for use as railroad spurs and later as an access road for maintenance vehicles for the railroad lines flanking it. Finally, the Chicago and Cook County in the 1960s used the right of way to build the Stevenson Expressway to the southwest suburbs.

A collateral project undertaken in 1926

to eliminate the eastward bend in the south branch of the Chicago River south of the Loop had nothing to do with navigation, although it did make it easier for towboats to negotiate that section of the waterway. The river was straightened to improve street access to the Loop from the south side.[15] The 28-mile Sanitary and Ship Canal was as large as a medium-sized river—21 feet deep and 160 feet wide—but as a navigable river it went nowhere. The problem was that it connected on the west with both the Des Plaines-Illinois Rivers system, which was not navigable above La Salle, and the obsolete western section of the Illinois and Michigan Canal between La Salle and Lockport. That section of the I & M by the early 1900s had deteriorated in some locations to the point it could barely handle vessels with a draft of 2 feet, or half its design capacity. Experiments in 1926 showed that barges with an 18-inch draft could still negotiate the canal with a specially designed towboat, but they could carry only 20 tons of cargo apiece.[16]

## The Illinois Waterway

Although General J. H. Wilson of the U.S. Corps of Engineers as early as 1867 had recommended extending the Illinois River (via the Des Plaines and I & M) all the way to Chicago by means of locks and dams and a canal around the river's rapids at Marseilles, by the 1880s his agency had become distracted by proposals to build the Hennepin Canal. The 1882 corps study by Major W. H. H. Benyuard again recommended making the Illinois and Des Plaines Rivers navigable to Lockport instead of expanding the I & M Canal, which the state had just ceded to the federal government.[17]

The theory was to effectively convert the two rivers into a continuous navigable waterway—in effect, a canal between La Salle and Lockport. The southernmost 80 percent of the proposed waterway between La Salle and Grafton, where it joins the Mississippi, was somewhat less of a problem for navigation than the northernmost 60 miles between La Salle and Lockport. There was a gradual drop of only 21 feet in the southern 231 miles, but in the north the rivers fell 99 feet in just 60 miles. An 1835 survey by the state found seventy-one shoals over which water was only 2 to 3 feet in depth. Although the head of navigation, or the farthest point up the river that vessels can travel, was La Salle, extended periods of low water made that destination tenuous to all but the smallest steamboats.[18]

With little prospect for federal money for the Illinois River because Congress was committed to improving the Ohio River and had just financed the Hennepin Canal, the state in 1908 committed to a $20 million bond issue to build a navigable channel from La Salle to Lockport. Congress two years later voted to begin a $66 million project to build fifty-four locks and dams and to provide a 9-foot navigation channel on the Ohio between Pittsburgh and Cairo, Illinois. That was the beginning of the federal campaign to transform the western rivers to handle barge traffic instead of steamboats.[19]

Illinois's plan for the river that bears its name was to build what is known as a "slack-water system"—a series of dams to back up water into "pools" deep enough for barges and towboats to navigate and locks to enable them to get around the dams. The dams effectively transformed the Des Plaines–Illinois waterway into a series of steps beginning at Lockport and descending 34 feet at Brandon Road 5 miles downriver, another 22 feet at Dresden 15 miles farther downstream, 15 feet at Marseilles about 26 miles downriver, and 19 feet at Starved Rock (Utica) another 14 miles to the west. Two other dams farther downriver were scheduled to be replaced with larger locks. All the locks were designed at 600 feet long and 110 feet wide to simultaneously handle a towboat and as many as eight barges collectively carrying 12,000 tons of cargo and give the waterway a uniform traffic capacity from the Mississippi to Lake Michigan.[20]

The state didn't have much better luck building what became known as the Illinois Waterway than it had with the I & M Canal more than half a century earlier. Construction didn't get underway until 1921, and by 1930, when the Great Depression was playing havoc with state finances, Illinois ran out of money with the project about three-fourths complete. At that point the federal government, which had completed the massive Ohio River project a year earlier, took over the Illinois Waterway and finished it in 1933. The first commercial cargo—two barges with 250 tons of freight consigned to twenty-five different shippers and pushed by the twin screw, diesel towboat *Turnbull* arrived in Chicago via the waterway on March 13, 1933.[21]

Because of the depression and because the barge industry was still rebuilding after nearly being driven to extinction by the railroads a quarter century earlier, traffic on the Illinois Waterway was slow to develop. However, within a year tonnage on the waterway exceeded what the I & M had carried in its best year (slightly more than 1 million tons in 1882). Traffic on the new waterway hit 1.7 million tons in 1935 and 3 million tons in 1940. The biggest growth occurred after World War II, to a large extent because of the export grain trade; traffic hit nearly 45.8 million tons in 1970, two-thirds of it farm and food products and slightly less than half of it originating or terminating in Chicago. Traffic peaked in 1975 at nearly 60 million tons, although in the final twenty-five years of the century the waterway handled traffic in the range of 40 to 50 million tons.[22]

The effect of the Illinois Waterway on Chicago's canal traffic was dramatic. Traffic on the Sanitary and Ship Canal increased from 482,096 tons in 1933 to more than 5.3 million tons at the onset of World War II in 1941. But the largest increases followed the war—from nearly 5.2 million tons in 1946 to almost 16.5 million tons in 1955 and 24.4 million tons in 1970 (table 12.2).[23]

**Table 12.2** Chicago Canal Traffic, 1996 (in thousands of tons)

| Commodity | Inbound | Outbound | Through | Intra | Total |
|---|---|---|---|---|---|
| Coal | 4090 | 211 | 2122 | 6 | 6429 |
| Petroleum | 1780 | 105 | 1700 | 296 | 3827 |
| Chemicals | 1054 | 125 | 678 | 85 | 1942 |
| Crude oils | 1360 | 1007 | 2046 | 280 | 4693 |
| Soil, sand, gravel | 810 | 775 | 680 | 280 | 2545 |
| Metals, ores, scrap | 3 | 232 | 682 | 0 | 917 |
| Manufactured goods | 868 | 7 | 1826 | 0 | 2701 |
| Agricultural products | 323 | 844 | 53 | 0 | 869 |
| **Total** | | | | | **20,493*** |

*Minor categories of traffic excluded from enumeration but included in total.

Source: U.S. Army Corps of Engineers, *Waterborne Commerce of the United States*, part 3, *Waterways and Harbors, Great Lakes, Port of Chicago*, 86–88.

## The Calumet-Sag Channel

The final link in Chicago's canal system was the Calumet-Sag, built in the first quarter of the century for sewage and expanded after World War II to handle barge traffic, which was becoming necessary to serve Chicago's south side Calumet port. Calumet had passed the Chicago River in commercial traffic in 1906 and in the ensuing decades became the city's principal lake port, although it had no connection to the Illinois River. Through cargo between the lake and inland rivers had to be transferred between ship and barge at the dwindling number of facilities along the Chicago River just outside the city's downtown area or be shipped back up the lake by barge from Calumet to the Chicago River to reach the Sanitary and Ship Canal.

The Cal-Sag Channel was dug by the Metropolitan Sanitary District, beginning in 1911 and completed in 1922, as a second sewage and drainage canal along the line of an old feeder canal to bring Lake Michigan water to the I & M. Its secondary purpose was navigation. The channel was built west from the Little Calumet River tributary at Blue Island to connect with the Sanitary and Ship Canal at a junction just east of Lemont, although that connection was not completed until 1933. But with a width of only 60 feet and a lock at Blue Island only 50 feet long it proved woefully inadequate for the increased shipping demands at Calumet. Despite the fact that its builders included several wider passing basins along the 16-mile route, as a practical matter the canal could be used only by tows the width of a single barge.

Despite its limitations traffic on the canal, which had been designed with a navigation capacity of 1 million tons a year, increased from 21,149 tons in 1933 to more than 1.1 million tons in 1944. After the war traffic quadrupled to nearly 4.6 million tons annually, however.

The completion of the Illinois Waterway and heavy World War II traffic finally convinced the federal government that the Cal-Sag was hopelessly inadequate, and Congress in the 1946 Rivers and Harbors Act approved its widening. By then it was obvious that the Cal-Sag, not the Sanitary and Ship, would be the major Great Lakes–Gulf route. The growth of downtown Chicago, especially the area north of the Chicago River, following the war and

Bridges over canals, like this one over a lock near Sheffield on the Hennepin Canal, were often operated by the boat crews.

the concomitant jump in automotive traffic made it increasingly difficult for commercial shippers to use the Chicago River because of the public outcry over frequent raising of the bascule bridges. Motorists had been willing to endure the delays because of wartime exigencies; in fact, delays caused by bridge closings was a convenient excuse for downtown workers late to work or meetings. Once peace returned, the public was not so forgiving.[24]

The Cal-Sag widening was delayed by several years because of the lack of local interest, but the Illinois legislature in 1951 created the Chicago Regional Port District to handle the development of the Calumet area, and the new agency's first biennial report in 1953 contained a comprehensive

plan for the development of the Calumet port. At the time both Canada and the United States were beginning to develop an interest in building the Saint Lawrence Seaway, which held the prospect of increased international maritime traffic to Chicago. However, the Cal-Sag widening did not begin until 1955, when construction on the seaway was already underway.[25]

The $200 million project, which included the widening of the Cal-Sag to 225 feet for 16.2 miles from Lemont to the Little Calumet, the replacement or removal of seventeen railroad bridges, and the construction of the 1,000-foot-long and 110-foot wide Thomas J. O'Brien locks in the Calumet River, was finally completed in

1965. Traffic increased from 4.9 million tons in 1964 to more than 6 million tons in 1970, and in 1994—excluding the double counting of tows using the section of the Sanitary and Ship Canal between Lemont and Lockport to get between the Cal-Sag and the Des Plaines River—the Cal-Sag carried more traffic than the Sanitary and Ship Canal for the first time in their existence. In 1996, Cal-Sag traffic was 12.6 million tons, in contrast to 7.6 million tons on the Sanitary and Ship Canal.[26]

Traffic on Chicago's canals in the twentieth century, more so than in the nineteenth, was dependent upon the success of the rivers that served as their connections for barge traffic. The barge industry, which had been in its death throes in 1900, by midcentury had been resuscitated and by the opening of the twenty-first century was relatively healthy. That remarkable renaissance, although it has been overshadowed by the building of the airways and interstate highway system, was the result of one of the most successful public works programs in history conducted by the United States government.

The I & M Canal in the 1830s and 1840s was dug largely by hand, but by the time its replacement, the Sanitary and Ship Canal, was dug in 1895 mechanical equipment like steam shovels and conveyor belts made the job easier and faster. (Lewis University, Canal and Regional History Collection)

# *Chapter Thirteen* The River Renaissance

The width of the Lower Mississippi River south of Saint Louis permits much larger tows than are possible on the constricted channels serving Chicago. This tow has thirty-five barges, although tows as large as forty-eight barges are not uncommon.

• For much of the twentieth century the riverboat, railroad, and motor truck industries and their lobbyists were engaged in a running debate over the issue of government subsidies—who got more to the detriment of whom. Over the years federal land grants helped build some canals and railroads, public money was used to improve waterways with such things as locks and dams and lighthouses, cities bought stock in railroads to assist in their capitalization, the depression-era Reconstruction

Finance Corporation became a lender of last resort for the railroads, and government built the highway system without which there would be no interstate motor trucks.

So when southern politicians dipped into the pork barrel for $2 billion to fund the Tennessee-Tombigbee Waterway connecting those two rivers in Alabama and creating a navigation channel from Tennessee to the Gulf of Mexico, the railroad industry unsuccessfully lobbied against it and the Louisville & Nashville Railroad (now CSX) fought a seven-year legal battle, also unsuccessful, to stop it. The railroads also were unable to prevent construction of Locks and Dam 26 on the Mississippi River near Alton, Illinois, and the Saint Lawrence Seaway. On the other hand, the waterway and trucking associations unsuccessfully objected to assorted provisions in a succession of federal laws after 1969 that culminated in the Staggers Act of 1980 deregulating the railroad industry.[1]

The account of the fight between transportation modes and environmental groups over government subsidies and regulations would by itself fill a book, a very large volume indeed. The controversy over Army Corps of Engineers Major Charles L. Hall's futile 1928 report that the construction of locks and dams on the Upper Mississippi River above Saint Louis was economically unsound was dwarfed late in the century by the controversy over corps economist Donald C. Sweeney's report that the proposed $1 billion expansion of five of those locks on the Upper Mississippi and two on the Illinois (La Grange and Peoria) was not financially justified by the traffic on the rivers. Various environmental organizations entered the controversy in 2000 after Sweeney claimed publicly that some of his superiors modified his unfavorable comments to justify the project. The Army Inspector General's office late that year, after investigating the allegations, found that there were indications the Corpse of Engineers was biased in favor of the project and that some ranking officers had modified data to justfy the project.[2]

However, the practical effect of all the subsidy programs on maritime Chicago and other river cities during the twentieth century was to revive a moribund industry, the riverboats, to the point where it could compete with railroads and, to a lesser extent, motor trucks. The renaissance of the rivers is an example of a very deliberate and successful federal transportation pol-

icy that under the guise of national defense—the same excuse used to justify the interstate highways program—was used to rebuild a transportation industry. In the case of the interstate highways, the government built the roads and left their use to private industry. The waterways in 1917 not only needed rebuilding but the government had to come in and run the barges on them.[3]

The western rivers by 1900 needed a massive investment in dams and locks to create a navigation channel to carry barges and tows large enough to be competitive with the railroads. Low water at certain times of the year resulted in virtual embargoes on river traffic in the steamboat era. The railroads had been financed largely by private capital, but what was left of the steamboat and barge industry in 1900 was still largely a mom-and-pop operation without access to the kind of money needed to rebuild the rivers. The Ohio River and its tributaries alone needed a system of fifty-six locks and dams; the Upper Mississippi River between Saint Louis and Saint Paul needed twenty-five, and the Illinois River needed eight. The federal government was the only agency with pockets deep enough to undertake such an enterprise.

It was only a few years into the thirty-year project when World War I intervened and caused what was probably the nation's most serious transportation crisis. Hauling masses of wartime materiel to the East Coast resulted in a monumental traffic snarl on the railroads, causing the federal government to nationalize the rail system for the first and only time in history. The mess not only resulted in the birth of the nation's intercity trucking industry and highway program, but it caused Washington to create almost from scratch a federally owned barge line because most of the riverboat companies had already gone out of business. Before Federal Barge Line was finally sold back to private industry after World War II, it had been instrumental in modernizing the rivers with steel barges,

Rebuilding locks on rivers is a major undertaking and requires shutting down the river to traffic for months. The Illinois River was "closed" for two months in 1995 to enable the Army Corps of Engineers to rebuild locks at Lockport, Joliet, Morris, and Marseilles, the last of which is shown after it had been drained and while new gates were being installed.

diesel power, and propeller-driven towboats. The reprivatized river industry, by the end of the twentieth century, was relatively stable and combined with the Great Lakes handled about 14.2 percent of the nation's freight, measured in ton-miles.[4]

## Steamboat and Railroad Monopolies

In the 1850s, when the iron horse first appeared on the scene, the steamboats had a monopoly on transportation in much of the Midwest and were decidedly arrogant about the interloper. The steamboat industry considered the rivers to be its own freeway system and any rail or highway bridges as hazards to navigation, which

some certainly were. When the Chicago & Rock Island Railroad built the first bridge over the Mississippi in 1855, steamboat interests indignantly, but unsuccessfully, fought it as just such a hazard.

The U.S. Supreme Court had ruled in the 1852 Wheeling Bridge case that a highway bridge authorized by Virginia over the Ohio River was an obstruction to navigation and ordered it modified. Congress six months later nullified the Supreme Court decision with a statute declaring the bridge legal and no hazard to navigation, and when the case wound up before the court the second time, the law was declared valid because Congress had the power to regulate interstate commerce.[5]

Even before the court had issued its second ruling, the attempt by the Rock Island Railroad to bridge the Mississippi River between its western terminal and Davenport, Iowa, became an issue that pitted the steamboat industry and Saint Louis against the railroads and Chicago. When Secretary of War Jefferson Davis refused the railroad permission to use some federal land on an island in midriver for its bridge, the railroad in 1855 got a favorable court decision in Chicago, overturning his ruling. The resulting bridge then became an issue with the steamboat industry when after several minor accidents the steamboat *Effie Afton* on May 6, 1856, rammed the structure, causing a fire that rendered the bridge unusable and destroyed the vessel.

John S. Hurd, the steamboat owner and operator, with the backing of his colleagues in that industry and the Saint Louis Chamber of Commerce claimed that the currents had carried the *Effie Afton* into the bridge pilings; on the other hand, the railroad claimed that the steamboat pilot had deliberately rammed the bridge. Hurd sued the railroad for creating an obstruction to navigation, and in a case tried in Chicago, Abraham Lincoln defended the Rock Island. According to railroad industry legend, Lincoln obtained a hung jury after visiting the bridge to personally check on the currents with the help of a boy.[6]

However, the principal issue in the trial was whether railroads could bridge a navigable river. Perhaps the most prescient, but overlooked, thing said at the trial was by Lincoln during his closing argument as quoted by the press: From September 8, 1856, to August 8, 1857—an eleven-month period preceding the trial—more than 12,500 freight cars and 74,000 passengers had passed over the rebuilt bridge on trains. Clearly the railroads and the east-west trade axis they served were quickly supplanting the north-south axis served by the steamboats.[7]

Within a decade the tables had turned and the railroads were accused of being arrogant monopolists controlling the grain trade from the local railway station to the

The Illinois River lock at Marseilles was rebuilt and had new miter gates installed in 1995.

A two-barge tow proceeds upstream through the Lockport locks in 1997. The barges are covered because they are carrying grain. Less vulnerable commodities, like stone and coal, ride in open barges. (Michael Brown)

giant elevators in Chicago and the ships that carried the harvest east. There was a public outcry to regulate them, culminating in 1887 when Congress created the Interstate Commerce Commission, conceding that because railroads crossed state lines they were a federal problem. But by the time the new agency studied the problem, began issuing effective rules and tariffs after passage of the Hepburn Act in 1906, and survived the inevitable court challenges, the railroads had effectively put the steamboats out of business.[8]

The Illinois Central Railroad, which in 1859 hauled 2.5 million bushels of grain, by 1871 handled nearly 18.5 million bushels, most of it to Chicago. It was one of five railroads in the Midwest that so effectively dominated the grain trade that they became known collectively in the industry as the "granger roads." The in-

crease in size of locomotives, trains, and freight cars was a major factor in their success. The typical 1830s train of fifteen to twenty cars had by the 1850s grown to thirty cars and just before the turn of the century averaged about fifty cars. The earliest freight cars had a capacity of only 10 tons; by the 1870s they had doubled in capacity, and in the early 1900s they doubled again to 40 tons—the maximum size practical for wooden cars. Therefore, the average freight train of 1840 could probably have handled 150 tons of freight, whereas its successor in the early 1900s had a capacity of 2,000 tons.[9]

By way of contrast, a three-boat tow on the Upper Illinois River and I & M Canal could handle only about 400 to 450 tons, although big barge tows on the larger rivers might have been able to handle 10,000 tons at times of high water. By

1855, the average barge on the Ohio River handled more than 7,500 bushels of coal, as that fuel was measured in those days, or slightly less than 300 tons, and by the 1880s barges with a capacity of more than 700 tons were common. A single tow on the Mississippi in 1878 set a record of thirty-two barges collectively carrying 22,300 tons of coal, but that was successively eclipsed until 1907 when the giant 1,479-ton stern-wheeled towboat *Sprague* took a sixty-barge tow with a cargo of 67,307 tons of coal down the Mississippi.[10]

The *Sprague's* record occurred as the towboat industry was in decline, however. The June 1914 journal of one steamboat captain indicates that on a three-week journey from Pittsburgh to Saint Paul he did not pass another river tow except for a few operated by some local sand and gravel dealers. His towboat, the *Joe Fowler,* which drew only 4 feet of water, struck bottom several times on the Upper Ohio River and ran aground at Shawneetown, Illinois. It took all night to free the steamboat.[11]

Corps of Engineers studies showed that traffic on the Ohio River, where the coal originated, had declined from 9 million tons in 1905 to an all-time low of only 4.6 million tons in 1917. The situation was worse on the Illinois River; traffic on the I & M Canal, which usually accounted for roughly half of the total traffic on the river, declined from a high of more than a million tons in 1882 to less than 100,000 tons in 1901, although traffic increased after the Sanitary and Ship Canal opened.[12]

## The Government Steps In

President Theodore Roosevelt had become alarmed as early as 1901 by the deterioration of the river steamboat and barge industry and urged Congress to improve the waterways to make the United States competitive internationally. Roosevelt, who at the same time urged the United States to take over the faltering French project to build the Panama Canal, was concerned about the implications of a declining waterway system, especially the Ohio River, for national defense.[13]

Even as the last steamboats were being laid up for lack of traffic, the new railroad monopoly, which had expanded from 35,000 miles of track in 1865 and would reach its maximum size of 254,000 miles in 1916, was showing symptoms of trouble. The railroads were already under attack by the progressive politicians of the day for such things as the collusive practices of the robber barons and predatory pricing when in 1899 a car famine occurred as 1,000 freight cars were stranded in the congested port of New York awaiting loading or unloading and a larger number sat in New Jersey. The New York port by then accounted for 41.6 percent of the nation's freight traffic, including a third of its exports and 60 percent of its imports. By then, some railroad main lines were already operating at capacity.[14]

There was no competition for the railroads in the first two decades of the twentieth century, except for the Great Lakes and coastal shipping. The lack of hard roads meant the automobile was strictly a local conveyance; in fact, tire kickers in the early years of the century often took the train to shop in the showrooms of auto manufacturing centers like Chicago and shipped their purchase home on the train. The motor truck of the time, which often consisted of little more than a motorized buggy with the rear seat removed for cargo space, was developing as a local delivery vehicle, hauling freight from the docks and local railroad freight terminals to warehouses, stores, and customers. Intercity trucking, like the automobile, had to await the building of the hard-road system by the states and federal government after World War I.[15]

High inflation and newly imposed federal regulations that capped freight rates combined to create a financial crisis in the railroad industry even before World War I. By the fall of 1915 some 40,000 miles of railroad, or one-sixth of the U.S. rail system, were already under court supervision or awaiting receivership. When the United States entered the war in 1917, the sudden surge in military traffic to East Coast ports, combined with the lack of available ocean shipping because of losses to German submarines, quickly caused a massive rail traffic jam on the East Coast. At one time there was a shortage of as many as 158,000 cars as thousands of freight cars sat loaded on sidings, spurs, and yards, awaiting unloading.

On August 29, 1916, Congress, in an army appropriation law commonly called the Federal Possession and Control Act, gave the president the power to take control of any transportation system in the United States should an emergency require it. President Woodrow Wilson issued the proclamation on December 26, 1917, nationalizing the railroads under a new agency called the United States Railroad Administration and appointing William G. McAdoo, his son-in-law and secretary of the treasury, as its director general.[16]

Early in 1918 McAdoo was also given control of the inland waterways. The 1916 Control Act had set up a Council of National Defense to study both the railroads and waterways, and after Wilson nationalized the waterways, its findings were turned over to McAdoo. Since the steamboat and barge industry was almost extinct, the last major line having failed in 1910, McAdoo was forced to commandeer whatever barges and towboats he could find, many of nineteenth-century vintage, and call pilots out of retirement to operate them. The new federally owned barge company operated principally on waterways needed to get materiel to port—the New York Barge Canal, the enlarged successor to the Erie Canal; the Lower Mississippi River between Saint Louis and New Orleans; and the Black Warrior and Tombigbee Rivers in Alabama.[17]

The hastily acquired fleet of only five towboats and twenty-eight barges, purchased in part from the Kansas City Missouri River Navigation Company and in part leased from the Army Corps of Engi-

neers, didn't make its first sailing until September 28, 1918, from Saint Louis. Warrior River service didn't begin with a single towboat, two self-propelled barges, and ten coal barges until December of that year, after the war had ended. Despite the armistice the Railroad Administration in early 1919 ordered nine modern towboats, sixty standard barges, and four self-propelled barges for its new barge line, which by then had become known as the Mississippi-Warrior Service after the two principal rivers on which it operated.[18]

The railroads were returned to private control after the war, but not the waterways. Federal officials were concerned the new enterprise could not survive on its own, so the Transportation Act of 1920, which returned the railroads to the control of their corporations, transferred control of the Mississippi-Warrior Service from the Railroad Administration to the War Department to put together a peacetime demonstration of a common-carrier barge line. The 1924 Inland Waterways Corporation Act created the government-owned Federal Barge Line to take over Mississippi-Warrior. Congress bought the first $5 million in shares to get the new corporation started, although the law had provisions for the eventual sale of the company to private interests should the opportunity arise. The law made the Federal Barge Line subject to the same regulations as other common carriers and, to prevent predation of its traffic by railroads, required the Interstate Commerce Commission (ICC) to set joint barge-rail rates for shippers using railroads as river feeders or distributors.

## Renaissance on the Rivers

Despite some encouraging signs after World War I, the survival of the barge industry and the new federal carrier was anything but assured. Washington had to cover its barge line's deficits for several years, introduce new equipment to modernize an industry mired in nineteenth-century technology, and rebuild the water-

River towboats in the late 1800s were powered by steam and propelled by stern-wheels, but modern towboats are diesel-powered and driven by propellers. Note the shallow draft and channel in the stern into which the propellers are recessed to protect them from damage on the bottom of shallow rivers.

way system to handle larger and more efficient tows. Objections by private operators on the New York Barge Canal and the Ohio River forced the government line to withdraw from those potentially lucrative markets. Then three major corporations formed their own in-house barge lines—Carnegie Steel, Jones and Laughlin Steel, and Standard Oil of Baton Rouge. In 1927—because Federal Barge didn't have sufficient capital to expand onto the Upper Mississippi, although it did begin providing service on the Lower Illinois River—the Minneapolis Real Estate Board organized the Mississippi Barge Line to provide service to that metropolitan area. The Federal Barge Line added service all the way to Chicago in 1933 after the locks and dams on the Upper Illinois River were completed.[19]

Wartime exigencies got the modernization of the waterways fleet underway almost before the ink was dry on Wilson's proclamation federalizing the system. The Railroad Administration's order for new vessels included forty barges made of steel for the Mississippi River service, although it also included twenty wooden coal barges for the Warrior operation. A wooden barge had an effective life cycle of five years, but a steel barge could continue in active service four to six times that long. The agency also ordered for the Warrior four steel, self-propelled cargo barges similar to the most modern equipment in operation on European rivers. Each could carry 1,600 tons of freight.

The biggest innovation was the six steel, twin-screw, tunnel-type towboats, each capable of generating 1,800 horsepower. Three similar, but somewhat smaller, towboats were bought for the Mississippi. The term "tunnel" refers to the channels on the underside of the hull in which the screw propellers are recessed to protect them from damage in shallow water. The tunnels also permit somewhat larger propellers, providing more thrust, than would be possible if they were instead suspended below the hull and thus vulnerable to shoals.[20]

Despite the adoption of the screw propeller on the Great Lakes, beginning in the 1840s, however, the river towboats continued to favor paddlewheels until the middle of the twentieth century, or until the problem of protecting screw propellers from damage in the shallow rivers could be solved. Side-wheels were originally favored on steamboats because they gave the craft maneuverability, but as barge tows became common it was more efficient to have a single large paddle wheel at the stern of the towboat. Propellers were not entirely successful, especially on downstream flanking operations and in reversing power, until improved reduction gears and better rudders were introduced during World War II.[21]

The development of larger diesel engines that made their use possible on the railroads in the 1930s also resulted in their adaption to the waterways at about the same time, although the dieselization of both industries didn't occur until after World War II. The typical towboat at the beginning of the century was a sternwheeler powered by a reciprocating steam engine with an appetite for fuel that required at least one coal barge to be lashed to the boat to avoid refueling stops. The conversion to oil as a fuel got rid of the coal barge and gave the towboats a somewhat longer range, but the quantum leap in efficiency occurred in the 1930s with the introduction of the diesel engine. A towboat could double its horsepower by conversion from steam to diesel, and its owners could reduce the size of engine-room crews because such tasks as water tending, stoking, and oiling were unnecessary. The stern-wheel steamer *Joseph B. Williams,* the most powerful towboat afloat in 1898, had a crew of sixty-seven; by 1928 the *John W. Weeks* could operate with a crew of twenty; and the diesel propeller *Crescent City,* when it was launched in 1958, could be operated with a crew of only eleven. Diesels also had the advantage of being easier to start than steam engines and were not vulnerable to the threat of explosions.[22]

## Slackwater

Despite all the federal aid and new technology, the revival of the waterways was a slow process, which took the first half of the twentieth century. The Great Depression put a damper on both traffic and investment in the 1930s, but so did the lack of adequate shipping channels to handle the larger barges and tows. The plan gradually adopted by the Corps of Engineers was to create a 25,000-mile system of navigable rivers, including the so-called Great Lakes–Gulf connection between Chicago and New Orleans, that would have a minimum, standard, 9-foot deep navigation channel year-round. Shoals in the western rivers usually develop in late summer and early fall when rainfall is slight and last until the snowmelt in February, causing levels to rise.

Since the middle of the nineteenth century the Corps of Engineers had been urging slack-water systems of locks and dams rather than canals or other techniques to maintain river navigation channels. The effect is rather like deep garden steps climbing a slight slope, only in the case of the Ohio River the "steps," or navigation pools created by the dams, were strung out over 974 miles and descended 420 feet in elevation between Pittsburgh and Cairo, Illinois.[23] The Upper Mississippi between Minneapolis and Cairo falls 355 feet over a distance of 832 miles and required twenty-seven dams to create the necessary slack-water system. The 291-mile Illinois–Des Plaines River between the end of the Sanitary and Ship Canal in Lockport and the Mississippi River, fell by 110 feet in elevation, requiring six lock-dam combinations.[24]

As on canals, on rivers the size of the locks, not just the depth of the navigation channel, determines shipping capacity. The Corps set the national standard for locks on the western rivers at 110 feet wide and 600 feet long, a dimension sufficient to permit a towboat and eight standard (195-by-35) barges to use it in one operation. Larger locks and double locks to permit simultaneous two-way traffic were added later at critical bottlenecks like Locks and Dam 26 at Alton, Illinois. The political compromise resulting from four years of controversy over that dam ended in 1979 when Congress approved construction of the $470 million project and,

as a sop to the railroad industry, complaining over taxpayer subsidies to the waterways, imposed for the first time a user fee in the form of a tax on marine diesel fuel to help pay for it.[25]

After the Ohio River dam system was completed in 1929, Washington quickly turned its attention to finishing the Illinois Waterway to complete the Great Lakes–Gulf connection in 1933 and building a slack-water system on the Upper Mississippi north of Saint Louis, a task completed in 1939. Although the Upper Mississippi, which wanders for 554 miles along Illinois's western border, has been somewhat neglected in maritime literature, it had a substantial increase in traffic in the final decades of the twentieth century—a jump of 25.5 million tons, or 155 percent, in the twenty-five years between 1970 and 1995. By 1995 it accounted for 41.9 million tons of freight or half again as much as handled by Chicago's ports. About 61 percent of the Illinois traffic on the Mississippi that year was food, grain, and coal (table 13.1).[26]

World War II both ended the depression and caused an increase in river traffic when the Great Lakes shipyards were pressed into service to build small auxiliaries and warships that were then sailed through Chicago down the Illinois Waterway and Mississippi River to the Gulf. However, a major expansion of the river barge industry didn't occur until after the war when the oil, steel, and coal industries began to look to barges to save transportation costs. By then barge rates were about half of what railroads charged. As private investment poured into the barge and towboat market, the railroad industry renewed its lobbying for Washington to both sell the Federal Barge Line and to impose a user fee on the waterways users to defray some of their costs. The line was finally sold by the government in 1953 to a subsidiary of Saint Louis Ship and Steel Company for $9 million, plus $2.7 million in liabilities, or about a third of the amount

**Table 13.1**  Illinois Barge Traffic by Waterway, 1970–1995 (in millions of tons)*

| Waterway | 1970 | 1975 | 1980 | 1985 | 1990 | 1995 | Change, 1970–1995 | Percent Change |
|---|---|---|---|---|---|---|---|---|
| Illinois | 45.76 | 59.98 | 50.92 | 43.08 | 48.14 | 48.84 | +3.1 | +6.73% |
| Mississippi | 16.40 | 23.24 | 23.75 | 32.03 | 33.94 | 41.92 | +25.5 | +155.6% |
| Ohio | 8.19 | 7.22 | 11.89 | 13.60 | 22.89 | 26.71 | +18.5 | +226.2% |
| Total** | 70.35 | 90.64 | 88.61 | 91.64 | 108.15 | 118.45 | +48.1 | +68.4% |

*Figures are rounded.

**Kaskaskia River omitted from breakdown but included in totals.

*Source:* Illinois Department of Transportation, *Illinois Waterborne Commerce Statistics, 1970–1995* (Chicago, 1997),  29, 31.

the federal government had invested in the project since 1920.[27]

Limited by the size of the locks, barges had reached their optimum size in the 1930s, so the major postwar innovations in the industry came in the form of towboats. The *Hoover,* at 2,000 horsepower, was the most powerful towboat on the rivers when she was launched in 1931, but the *Illinois,* built as a stern-wheeler in 1921, developed 2,400 horsepower after she was converted to tunnel propellers in the 1930s. After the war dieselization produced the powerful twins *United States* and *America* in 1958—the first towboats with four propellers and engines developing 9,000 horsepower. However, by 1974 they were eclipsed by towboats developing 10,500 horsepower.[28]

As a practical matter the largest towboats were consigned to the Lower Mississippi where they could push forty-eight-barge tows without having to contend with locks. The average tow on the Illinois and Upper Mississippi Rivers was more like fifteen barges. The limitations of the Illinois Waterway and Chicago canal system for all intents and purposes restricted towboats to 2,000 horsepower or less and the optimum tow to six, although as many as eight could be accommodated with some juggling. The large number of low bridges over the canal also resulted in the develop-

ment of rather squat, hybrid towboats with pilothouses capable of being raised hydraulically for better visibility between bridges. Chicago shipyards also used all sorts of innovative techniques to build bigger vessels to stay competitive in the river market: the Calumet Shipyard and Dry Dock Company built in 1949 the *A. M. Thompson,* a 3,000-horsepower diesel towboat, for service on the Lower Mississippi. The problem of negotiating the low bridges over the Calumet-Sag was solved by building the vessel in sections and attaching the upper superstructure in Lockport.[29]

For shippers of bulk quantities of dry cargo, the economics of barges were compelling. The industry, which in 1940 accounted for less than 4 percent of the nation's freight transportation market (as measured in ton miles), by 1976 had captured more than 12 percent—a quarter of it being coal and a fifth of it petroleum products and chemicals. The waterway industry's principal rival after 1950, as it had been for a century, was the railroads. But the heavily regulated rail industry in the second half of the century had become the weak link, albeit still an important one, in the nation's transportation system, and the newly revived barge industry was quick to capitalize on every opportunity.

For one thing, by 1976 the average

barge carried 1,200 tons of cargo, in contrast to 61 tons by the average rail car; for another, more powerful towboats meant that between 1955 and 1976 the capacity of the average tow increased from 1,990 tons to 4,100 tons, a factor that gave the industry an average cost per ton mile of a fifth of that of the railroads. By the 1970s, the railroads by developing unit trains, or

trains dedicated to a single commodity that operated as units between two terminals, were able to offer rates only about 50 percent higher than those charged on the waterways. The advantage held by water was somewhat less in the Chicago metropolitan area because locks and canal widths restricted the size of tows.[30]

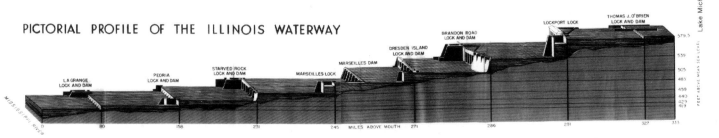

PICTORIAL PROFILE OF THE ILLINOIS WATERWAY

The Illinois River and canals leading to Lake Michigan at Chicago in the 1920s and 1930s were rebuilt into a 333-mile-long navigable waterway by means of eight locks and dams. The diagram shows the elevation ships have to climb from the Mississippi River at Grafton, Illinois, 410 feet above sea level, to Chicago at 579.5 feet. (U.S. Army Corps of Engineers)

# *Chapter Fourteen* Decline of the Great Lakes

The Chicago Ship Building Company's (later American Ship Building) yards near the mouth of the Calumet River were a busy place in the early 1900s, but they closed for lack of business in the early 1980s. (Great Lakes Historical Society, Vermilion, Ohio)

• Competition from other transportation modes, which nearly caused the demise of the riverboat by the beginning of the twentieth century, was slower to make itself felt on the Great Lakes because the bulk freight on which the merchant marine depended couldn't travel as efficiently or as cheaply by rail, highway, or pipeline. Even some passenger and package freight traffic survived into the twentieth century because the railroads couldn't bridge the lakes as they had the rivers. But the lakes' merchant marine, which had been the dominant transportation system in the Upper Midwest as late as 1850, by World War I was suffering from an excess of competition from new transportation systems.

Although the railroads were the domi-nant mode of land transport by 1860, within seventy years pipelines, motor trucks, buses, automobiles, and airplanes all claimed a share of their markets. As the century progressed, America's Inland Seas, as the lakes are often called, began to be considered by the public to be less of a transportation artery—although they still carried considerable commerce—and more of a recreational resource. The yacht replaced the schooner and packet on the lakes.

Over the nearly two centuries between the building of Fort Dearborn and the beginning of the twenty-first century, passenger traffic on the lakes went through no less than three metamorphoses: In the first thirty years of commercial commerce (1830–1860), paddle-wheel steamships were the primary way to travel across the Upper Midwest, and after that (1860–1920) packet steamers still provided travelers and tourists with local transportation between places like Chicago and Milwaukee and the western Michigan shore. Early in the twentieth century big excursion ships, almost as luxurious as anything afloat on the oceans, appeared and offered weeklong cruises the length and breadth of the lakes.

Freight was the main business of the merchant marine from the beginning, and as the cities of Cleveland, Detroit, and Chicago industrialized, it was the plodding freighters that brought them coal to run their blast furnaces and power plants, cement to build their homes and offices, and steel to construct their railroads. When the great forests were finally exhausted, putting an end to the huge timber trade on Lake Michigan, farmers planted orchards on the cleared land and shipped peaches, apples, and berries across the lake to Chicago. Sometime after the Civil War, Great Lakes freighters began to grow in size to handle the millions of tons of ore and coal being consumed by the steel industry, and in the 1970s leviathan vessels—1,000 feet long and with machinery that enabled them to unload themselves—appeared on the lakes.

The lakes' merchant marine survived the depression in the American steel industry in the 1980s that sent scores of ships to the scrap yard, as well as the failure of the Saint Lawrence Seaway to live up to its promoters' expectations and flood the Midwest with international shipping. It also survived the container revolution in the ocean shipping industry that sent container ships to ports like Savannah, Georgia, instead of Chicago, because the Saint Lawrence Seaway locks were built too small.

In the early decades of the twentieth century, as many as 350 U.S. and Canadian companies operated nearly 2,000 vessels on the lakes, and as late as 1938 the twenty-one largest U.S. companies combined had a fleet of 308 ships with a capacity of 2.6 million tons—79 of them owned by the Pittsburgh Steamship Company, a subsidiary of U.S. Steel. However, at the end of the century the fleet of the four large surviving U.S. companies had shrunk to 44 vessels, although combined their capacity still was almost 1.7 million tons. The survivors were Oglebay Norton Marine Services Company, 12 ships; Interlake Steamship Company, 11 vessels; USS Great Lakes Fleet, 11 ships; and American Steamship Company, 10 ships.[1]

## The Coming of the Giants

The trend toward increasingly larger ships that began in the 1880s with the widespread use of steel in maritime construction continued into the twentieth century, culminating in the 1970s with the introduction of the "thousand-footers," as they are known in the industry. That was the practical limitation on ship size on the Upper Great Lakes because the Poe Locks at Sault Sainte Marie connecting Lakes Superior and Huron were 1,100 feet long. The thousand-footers, which exceeded in length the largest battleship in World War II, the 863-foot *Yamato,* were landlocked in that they could not leave the Upper Lakes without being disassembled.[2]

The prototypes of the lakes' bulk carrier are considered by many maritime historians to be the *R. J. Hackett* and *Forest City,* both 213-foot-long vessels of 922 tons built in Cleveland in 1869 at a time when the main cargo vessel on the lakes was still the schooner with an average gross registered tonnage of slightly less than 160. The schooner *Rouse Simmons* built in 1868 was registered at 205 tons, but since gross register tonnage is a measurement of volume of the inside of the hull, not the weight of its cargo, she would have had an interior hull capacity of 20,500 cubic feet—theoretically enabling her to haul about 300 tons of coal or 370 tons of corn—or about a sixth of the cargo capacity of the *Hackett.*[3]

Before the end of the century, the Great Lakes shipyards were building vessels

The Chicago-owned *American Republic,* shown being loaded near Sandusky, Ohio, is typical of the configuration of Great Lakes ships built after 1970 in that the superstructure containing the bridge and crew quarters has been raised and moved to the stern and the vessel is capable of unloading itself by means of the cantilever conveyor near the stern of the 623-foot ship. (Michael Brown)

more than twice the length and four times the cargo capacity of the *Hackett.* In 1895 the Chicago Shipbuilding Company built the lakes' first 400-footer, the *Victory.* The standard-design bulk freighter *E. M. Ford* launched in 1898 was 428 feet long and could carry 7,000 tons of cargo.[4]

The controlling factors of ship size, then as now, were the locks. On the Upper Lakes ships could get no larger than the locks at Sault Sainte Marie, Michigan—the Soo, as the waterway is commonly known. Vessels engaged in international traffic were smaller because the locks on both the Welland Canal connecting Lakes Erie and Ontario and the canals on the Saint Lawrence River farther east restricted their size.

The state of Michigan completed schooner-size, 350-by-70-foot locks at the Soo in 1855 and enlarged them to 515 by 80 feet in 1870 for the iron ore trade. However, that traffic increased so quickly with the growth of the steel industry that by 1888 it was the largest commodity handled on the Great Lakes and the Soo locks were among the busiest in the world. Canada in 1895 completed a 900-by-60-foot lock on its side of the border, and the United States responded the following year by completing the Poe lock at 800 feet long, 100 feet wide, and a depth of 22 feet.[5]

The bigger locks and steel construction techniques for ships quickly resulted in an increase in the size of ore boats to more

than 500 feet after the turn of the century. The *Augustus B. Wolvin,* when built in 1904 in Lorain, Ohio, using a revolutionary system of arched plate girders to increase hull length to 560 feet and cargo capacity to more than 10,000 tons of ore, became the largest vessel on the lakes. Only nine years earlier, the largest ship on the lakes, the Chicago-built *Victory,* had a capacity of 5,200 tons of ore in her 400-foot hull. However, the *Wolvin*'s new girder design was so successful that Chicago Shipbuilding was promptly commissioned to build the 569-foot steamers *Elbert H. Gary* and *William E. Corey,* and in 1906 the company built five 600-footers for the Pittsburgh Steamship Company, the largest operator on the lakes.[6]

The increases in ship size were accompanied by improved systems to load and unload them. Such things as tipples, dockside silos, and grain elevators permitted relatively quick loading; indeed, even a 600-foot ship could have its holds filled with coal, ore, or grain in two hours, but unloading took five times as long. The solution to that imbalance arrived in 1908 when the first self-unloading ship was launched. The technique required installation of a conveyor belt at the bottom of the cargo hold attached to a second conveyor belt mounted on a cantilever boom that could be swung over the side of the ship for unloading. The device proved so efficient, especially at smaller docks, that within thirty years of their development sixty-five ships on the lakes had been built with or converted to self-unloading machinery.[7]

Seven-hundred-foot vessels capable of handling nearly 30,000 tons of ore or coal appeared on the lakes after World War II. The ill-fated *Edmund Fitzgerald,* when it was launched in 1958 at 729 feet and with a capacity of 27,500 tons, was not even the largest vessel on the lakes. But when the *Fitzgerald* went down in a storm on Lake Superior in 1975, there were already more than a dozen thousand-footers in service, under construction, or on order. The first was the *Stewart J. Cort* launched in 1972, followed the next year by the *Presque Isle.*[8]

The completion of the new 1,100-foot Poe locks at Sault Sainte Marie in 1968 and the passage of the U.S. Maritime Act of 1970, in which Congress declared the Great Lakes to be the nation's fourth seacoast, making low-interest loans available to shipbuilders there, brought about a dramatic increase in ship size to 1,000 feet and cargo loads approaching 70,000 tons. The federal subsidies also resulted in a spurt of shipbuilding—thirty-one new American hulls between 1970 and the end of 1981, in addition to thirty-two new Canadian ships not affected by the U.S. program—in which almost all Great Lakes operators modernized their fleets and retired older vessels.[9]

## Tug Barges

Even while the major steamship companies were building larger ships to get greater efficiency out of their fleets, a new class of hermaphroditic vessel was developed to dramatically cut ship operating costs by reducing crew size. Tug barges, as their name implies, came about after marine engineers developed a mechanism to enable a tugboat to lock itself to the stern of a giant barge—actually an unpowered ship hull notched in the stern to receive the bow of the tug. The first attempt at such a vessel on the Great Lakes was the leviathan *Presque Isle,* a $35 million thousand-footer built in 1973 by Litton Industries for lease to the U.S. Steel Corporation.[10]

Chicago has been visited by many strange ships on the lakes, including two captured German U-boats, one from each of the world wars. The World War I *U-C-97* was sunk by the gunboat *Wilmette* for target practice in the lake in 1921, but the *U-505* (shown), captured on the high seas in World War II, was sailed to Chicago and dragged overland to become a permanent exhibit at the Museum of Science and Industry. (Chicago Maritime Society)

Meigs Field was built on Northerly Island in the lake after World War II to give Chicago a small downtown airport. The yacht basin to the west is Burnham Harbor, one of many projects that in the last half of the twentieth century converted Chicago's lakefront from maritime commerce to recreational uses. (Chicago Maritime Society)

However, the *Presque Isle* tug's rather rigid connection to its barge, a design known by marine architects as an "integrated tug barge," failed to achieve the efficiency in crew size its owners had expected. An improved mechanism that allowed the tug to unlock itself and abandon the barge in a matter of seconds in an emergency—the "articulated tug barge"—showed up on the lakes less than a decade later when Dow Chemical Company and Hannah Marine Corporation, a tug and barge operator based along the Sanitary and Ship Canal in the Chicago suburb of Lemont, put in service the tank barge *E-63*, a 407-foot vessel with a capacity for 60,000 barrels of chemicals, and the 3,200-horsepower tug *Mark Hannah*. The new articulated tug barge system used a set of hydraulic pins on either ride of the bow of the tug to lock it into channels in the notched stern of the barge.[11]

Then an Amoco Corporation subsidiary

in 1982 replaced some of its obsolescing ocean and Great Lakes tankers with tug barges, including the 414-foot barge *Great Lakes* that the articulated tug *Michigan* pushed to and from the company's Whiting refinery just south of Chicago, carrying 70,000 barrels of gasoline or diesel fuel per trip. The tug barge, which had a crew of nine, replaced the tanker *Red Crown* and her crew of twenty-five and permitted the company to reduce daily operating costs by $2,000 per vessel per day. A tug barge cost about $10,000 a day to operate.[12]

Despite the immediate success of the *Mark Hannah-E-63*, which was able to operate with a crew of only twelve, in contrast to the twenty-eight men who would be required on a self-propelled ship of comparable size, the new articulated systems were slow to catch on. The recession in the early 1980s and depressed steel industry upon which the Great Lakes merchant marine depended were certainly factors, as was the federally subsidized replacement of much of the Great Lakes fleet in the 1970s and early 1980s that exhausted the capital resources of many ship owners at a time when the new technology was just coming on line. However, by the end of the century the only new or rebuilt hulls introduced on the lakes were tug barges, a number of which were converted standard ship hulls from which the engines had been removed.[13]

The *Integrity,* a 460-foot cement barge capable of carrying 17,600 tons of that commodity and pushed by the tug *Jacklyn M.,* was built in 1996 for the LaFarge Corporation—the first new hull built on the Great Lakes since 1982. However, the last two tug barges to enter service on the lakes were both conversions from older steamships, including the *Pathfinder,* converted from the hull of the 1953-vintage steamship *J. L. Mauthe* in 1998, and the *PM-41,* converted later that year from the hull of the 398-foot car ferry *City of Midland 41,* originally built in 1940.[14]

## The Cross-Lake Packets

The railroads put the big passenger steamships out of business on the Great Lakes before the Civil War, but they did not totally kill its passenger traffic as smaller lines cropped up to cater to local markets ill served by the railroads. For much of the second half of the nineteenth century and the first decade of the twentieth a healthy packet and passenger trade existed across Lake Michigan handled by a number of local companies that subsisted to a large extent on the traffic in fresh fruit grown in western Michigan and sold in the burgeoning markets in Chicago and Milwaukee. The Lake Michigan packets also carried whatever package freight was available, cross-lake passengers, and, as the century dragged on, a fair number of tourists and people on excursions.[15]

Because the ports on both sides of the lake were little more than shallow river mouths, the vessels they used were smaller and lighter than the bulk freighters that came to dominate the lakes before the end of the nineteenth century. The packet typically had a series of gangways, or doors, in the hull just above the waterline to allow passengers and containers of freight to be loaded and unloaded; on the other hand, the bulk freighter had solid sides and was loaded from the top by simply dumping the cargo, like iron ore or coal, into open holds that were then sealed with hatch covers before sailing.

The Chicago streetcar subway tunnel beneath La Salle Street on the Chicago River restricted ship drafts to 16 or 17 feet and forced the cross-lake packets to crowd up to docks east of La Salle Street and along the South Water Street (now Wacker Drive) market. After Navy Pier was built, their docks were shifted there. The ill-fated *Eastland*—265-by-38-by-19.5 feet and rated at 1,961 gross tons—was probably the most famous Lake Michigan packet built, though not the largest or most successful.

The biggest of the packet lines, Goodrich Transit Company, operated out of Chicago, but traffic on the cross-lake routes became heavy enough for competition to develop soon. Rivals such as the Graham and Morton Transportation Company operated from Benton Harbor, Michigan, and the Indiana Transportation Company from Michigan City, Indiana. The market had grown to such an extent that by the end of the nineteenth century smaller cities on the eastern shore of the lake also formed shipping companies: the Holland and Chicago Transportation Company operating from Holland, Michigan, and the Saint Joseph–Chicago Steamship Company—the owner of the *Eastland* at the time of the disaster—based in Saint Joseph both provided competition for Goodrich and Graham and Morton.

Although there were earlier unsuccessful attempts, the packet lines began as a single enterprise in 1842 to connect with Chicago the Michigan Central Railroad then being built toward Saint Joseph, Michigan, from Detroit. Samuel Ward and his nephew, Eber Brock Ward, operated a few small paddle-wheelers to handle the cross-lake mail contract, but after the Michigan Central and Lake Shore and Michigan Southern Railroads reached Chicago in 1852, the Wards sold out to one of their captains.[16]

Albert E. Goodrich left the Ward line after its sale, moved to Chicago, and with another former Ward employee chartered the Wards' 165-foot side-wheeler *Huron* and entered the cross-lake business in 1856. The following year he bought the vessel outright from the Wards for $16,000. It was an inauspicious beginning: the *Huron* didn't steam on a regular schedule but only when and where traffic dictated. Passengers rode in the open on deck but could take refuge in the freight cabin during storms. However, the vessel made Goodrich enough money to enable him in 1860 to buy for $32,000 the new side-wheeler *Comet*.[17]

The company was able to survive not only a precipitous, albeit temporary, decline in passenger traffic following the *Lady Elgin* disaster on another line in 1860, but the loss of its *Sunbeam* in a storm on Lake Superior in 1863 with only one survivor among the 30 persons aboard and the fire that destroyed its *Seabird* and killed 102 aboard in Lake Michigan in 1868. At the time of Goodrich's death at age fifty-nine in 1885, the Goodrich Transportation Company was the largest locally owned operator on Lake Michigan with seven ships. The fruit traffic from Michigan to Chicago was continuing to expand, as it would do until refrigerated railroad cars began to make a dent in the market after 1890 and excursion passenger traffic from Chicago to Michigan was increasing.[18]

The last decade of the nineteenth century and first decade of the twentieth were the golden age of the cross-lake packets. Goodrich's son and successor in 1891 bought the steel, twin-screw-propeller, 1,985-ton *Virginia*; acquired the 4,000-passenger whaleback *Christopher Columbus* for the heavily traveled Chicago-Milwau-

kee excursion route; and in 1909 paid $387,272 to have built the 6,626-ton steel steamship *Alabama* with capacity for 2,500 tons of cargo and 2,000 passengers. The *Columbus* was a hapax legomenon—a one-of-a-kind passenger steamer built on an ore boat hull—but the *Alabama* launched a flurry of steel ship building by the packet lines just as two competitors appeared on the horizon and the government began to impose more stringent safety regulations on the industry in the aftermath of the *Titanic* disaster.[19]

Refrigerated railway freight cars made some dent in the fruit market, but the development in the decade of World War I of the motor truck as a vehicle capable of providing interstate transportation instead of simply handling local deliveries and the touring car doomed the Lake Michigan packet industry. Trucks took away the fruit trade, and autos diverted enough of the passenger traffic to undermine that cross-lake trade, but perhaps the hardest blow to the industry was the *Titanic* disaster, which resulted in the passage of Wisconsin Senator Robert M. La Follette's Seaman's Act in 1912. The law, for example, effectively reduced the rated passenger capacity of the Goodrich Lines whaleback *Christopher Columbus* in daytime excursion service from 4,000 passengers to 2,200 and made it difficult to hire crews of part-timers on a seasonal basis. Traffic was heaviest in the summer and fall and almost nonexistent in the cold months, when most of the ships were laid up for the season.[20]

Albert W. Goodrich, the founder's son, saw the handwriting on the wall and in 1920 sold his interest in the family-owned line to a group of investors in Manitowoc, Wisconsin, where he kept his fleet in the winter. By 1924 the line was running a deficit, and as was typical in declining industries, the new owners engineered mergers as a solution to the problem of declining traffic and excess capacity. The Goodrich line that year gobbled up its competition, including Graham and Morton, saddling it with excessive debt in a

declining market. Although as late as 1928 the line operated twelve steamers in regular service between twenty-two ports on both sides of Lake Michigan, when traffic fell in 1930 due to the depression, the line was forced to file for bankruptcy and ultimately was liquidated.[21]

## The Excursion Lines

As packet traffic on the Great Lakes began to fade, shipping companies began to look to the passenger excursion trade for survival, offering ocean-style cruises lasting as long as a week. However, success in the business was to a large extent dependent upon the size and configuration of the ships. Some of the largest vessels, like the Cleveland and Buffalo Transit Company's *Seeandbee,* were diverted to the growing excursion trade that by the 1920s included weeklong cruises from Chicago's Navy Pier, traversing the length of Lakes

Michigan, Huron, and Erie. But because of their configuration for day trips the cross-lake packets were doomed. Goodrich's *Christopher Columbus,* despite its large capacity, had little in the way of overnight accommodations and remained consigned to the Chicago-Milwaukee day excursion market for which it was designed, and the company flagship *Alabama,* despite being rated to carry 2,000 passengers, had sleeping accommodations for less than 300. The *Eastland* was rated for 2,800 day passengers but had sleeping accommodations for only 300, excluding 150 bunks in steerage that would hardly appeal to well-heeled tourists out for a cruise on the lakes. On the other hand, the *Seeandbee,* a 6,381-ton side-wheeler launched in 1912, had berths for 1,220, although her day-trip capacity was 6,000 (table 14.1).[22]

Robert C. Davis, Goodrich's general passenger agent in Chicago, discerned the potential of the cruise market even as the

The last cross-lake passenger vessel in service on Lake Michigan as the twentieth century closed was the 410-foot car ferry *Badger* shown operating between Ludington, Michigan, and Manitowoc, Wisconsin, in 1998. It was originally built as an icebreaking railroad car ferry and converted for auto and truck use in 1992.

**Table 14.1** Lake Michigan Passenger Ships
(Dimensions in feet except for tonnage and passenger capacity)

| Ship | Year Built | Length | Width | Draft | Tonnage | Overnight Passenger Capacity* |
|---|---|---|---|---|---|---|
| *Seeandbee* | 1912 | 500 | 98 | 14.0 | 6,381 | 1,220 |
| *Alabama* | 1910 | 271 | 44 | 15.2 | 1,684 | 296 |
| *South American* | 1914 | 290 | 47 | 16.6 | 1,427 | 510 |
| *Eastland* | 1903 | 265 | 38 | 19.5 | 1,961 | 200** |

*Capacities are for overnight or longer cruises. Daytime excursion capacities were considerably higher, up to 6,000 on the *Seeandbee*. The passenger capacity of ships also varied over the years because of federal safety regulations.

**The *Eastland* was not designed for and rarely, if ever, was used in the cruise market. The passenger capacity estimate is based on sleeping accommodations, excluding 150 bunks each for male and female steerage passengers. The initial rated passenger capacity (in excursion service) was 2,800 in 1903, but that was reduced to 2,000 in 1913 after the *Titanic* disaster and was increased to 2,500 in 1915 just before the *Eastland* capsized.

*Sources:* Fred Whitlark, "Seeandbee Remembered," 2–15; Elliott, *Red Stacks Over the Horizon,* 180–182; Richard H. Braun, "The Georgian Bay Line," *Inland Seas,* 54:3 (Fall 1998): 183; Hilton, *Eastland,* 21, 50, 239.

*Alabama* was on the way, and in 1912 broke away to form his own steamship line and raised the $500,000 necessary to build a ship exclusively for that market. The Chicago, Duluth and Georgian Bay Transit Company's 450-passenger *North American* was in service by June of the following year. Service was so successful that the company ordered a sister ship, the 510-passenger *South American,* later in 1913. The Georgian Bay Line, as it was popularly known, survived its owner's death in 1916 and near bankruptcy during World War I to operate cruises from Navy Pier in Chicago—the dominant cruise market on the Great Lakes—to Lakes Superior, Huron, and Erie as far east as Buffalo. As the cruise market improved somewhat in the waning days of the depression, the company in 1939 chartered the idle *Alabama* to handle the Chicago-Duluth and later the Chicago-Mackinac run, although the ship proved uneconomic on those runs.[23]

The Great Depression took its toll on the cruise business, as did World War II. The Georgian Bay Line in 1939 reported a loss of $60,066 and the next year posted a profit of only $8,996.50 on revenues of $743,288. The cruise ships *Seeandbee* and *Greater Buffalo* were requisitioned by the navy in 1942 and converted by American Ship Building into aircraft carriers for training duty on Lake Michigan. Both were scrapped after the war.[24]

The disastrous fire that killed 188 persons aboard the Canada Steamship Lines' excursion ship *Noronic* at its pier in Toronto in 1949 was the death knell for the rest of the excursion trade. The surviving vessels were unable to meet the more stringent fire safety regulations imposed after the disaster, and the companies that owned them did not have the financial wherewithal to build new and safer vessels. The Georgian Bay Line, which sold its *North American* in 1963, announced four years later it was selling the *South American* for $111,111 because it was unable to afford to have its superstructure rebuilt and could not find a replacement. The company then dissolved.[25]

## Chicago Reenters the Shipping Business

At the end of the twentieth century, except for a cross-lake ferry service between Ludington, Michigan, and Manitowoc, Wisconsin, operated by the former railroad car ferry *Badger* and occasional annual visits by German and French ships, the Great

Lakes cruise business was essentially dead. What emerged in Chicago a few years after the Georgian Bay Line's demise left the city without a flag on the lakes was a succession of acquisitions of shipping companies—some far removed from Chicago—by Chicago corporations. The real-estate millionaire Sam Zell began acquiring companies that specialized in maritime cruises under the American flag, but not on the lakes.

Provisions of the U.S. Passenger Vessel Act, intended to save the U.S. Merchant Marine by forbidding foreign-flag carriers from operating between U.S. ports, effectively prevented non-American vessels from commerce between any two U.S. ports without stopping at some foreign port in between. The law requires that the ships qualifying for domestic trade not only be manned by Yankee crews but be built in the United States and be owned by U.S. citizens.[26]

Zell was able to use the foreign exclusion provisions of the law in the last decade of the twentieth century to build the nation's largest American passenger ship operation. He first, in 1980–1984, acquired controlling interest in the then publicly held Delta Queen Steamboat Company in New Orleans, a riverboat cruise operator. A few years later he created American Classic Voyages Company as a holding company based in Chicago, and in 1993 it acquired American Hawaii Cruises, which, as the name implies, runs

Navy Pier, built in 1916 for cross-lake packets, by the 1990s had been converted to a recreation and convention center, although it was still used for infrequent calls by oceangoing cruise liners such the German Hapag-Lloyd line's *Christopher Columbus,* shown docked in 1998 on its annual Great Lakes junket.

The decline of Great Lakes shipping has idled many harbor tugs. These Hannah Marine tugs await business on the Calumet River in 1999.

**Opposite page:**
Tug-barges—unpowered ship hulls with a notch in the stern for a tugboat—began appearing in numbers on the Lakes beginning in the 1980s. Here the tug *Mark Hannah* pushes the barge *E-63* through the ice in the Straits of Mackinac. (Hannah Marine)

recreational voyages in the waters around those islands. After obtaining an exemption from the built-in-America provisions of the Passenger Vessel Act with the promise it would build a ship later, the company acquired from the Holland American Line the 1,212-passenger cruise ship *Nieuw Amsterdam,* renamed her *Patriot,* and put her into service in Hawaii, where the company effectively had a monopoly on the market.[27]

As the cruise market continued to expand in the prosperous 1990s and despite losses on its operations in three of the last five years of the century, American Classic Voyages then launched an ambitious expansion program. First, on March 9, 1999, the company placed orders for delivery in 2003 and 2004 of two 1,900-passenger cruise liners at $470 million apiece for the Hawaiian venture. Then, to revive the moribund coastal cruise market on the West Coast between San Francisco and Alaska and on the East Coast between Florida and Halifax, Nova Scotia, American Classic Voyages ordered the first two of five planned $35 million, 226-passenger

coastal cruise vessels for delivery early in the twenty-first century. The design of the ships approximated that of vessels used by the defunct Fall River Line between 1847 and 1937, and at 300 feet long they would be capable of traversing the Saint Lawrence Seaway into the Great Lakes.[28]

Zell's wasn't the only Chicago-area business enterprise to gain control of a shipping company far removed from the shore of Lake Michigan. The Northern Illinois Gas Company (now Nicor) was one of a number of regulated utilities that decided to diversify to improve its seasonal revenue stream, in Nicor's case concentrated in the winter heating season. The company in 1982 got Tropical Shipping Company, a Caribbean line, as part of its acquisition of a Florida holding company. Although other subsidiaries acquired in the diversification program were eventually cast adrift, Tropical Shipping performed so well financially that Nicor kept it. At the end of the century the line owned thirteen container ships serving twenty-three ports, mainly in Florida and the Caribbean, and had announced a $40

Chicago Ship Building
employees posed with some
of their construction
machinery in 1915. (Great
Lakes Historical Society,
Vermilion, Ohio)

million plan to build two more ships.[29]

The Panama Canal Act prohibited railroads from owning maritime companies,
but rail equipment suppliers were not covered—a loophole that enabled Chicago's
GATX Corporation, a rail-car leasing company, in 1973 to buy American Steamship
Company. It was one the largest ship operators on the Great Lakes in terms of cargo
capacity and one of the four survivors at
the end of the twentieth century of what a
hundred years earlier had been hundreds
of shipping companies. GATX, originally
known as Atlantic Seaboard Dispatch, had
been founded in 1898 in the Chicago
stockyards by Max Epstein to broker the
sale of used railway cars but quickly ex-

panded into the leasing of them. The leasing business proved so profitable that by
the end of World War II the company
owned 54,447 railroad freight cars, including 37,342 tank cars; however, the general
financial malaise of the railroad industry
in the 1960s and 1970s caused GATX, like
other railway supply companies, to diversify into other transportation ventures.[30]

American Steamship, which had been
founded in 1904 as Boland and Cornelius
by its two ship-owning partners, had been
quick to embrace the new technology that
became available to the merchant marine
in the twentieth century, including in the
1930s self-unloading equipment to enable
ships to serve small ports without elaborate

dock facilities, in the 1960s bow thrusters to enable pilots to maneuver their ships in port without the use of tugs, and in the 1990s global satellite positioning systems to steer ships. However, in 1969 on the eve of its acquisition by GATX the company was saddled with an aging fleet.[31]

Its most immediate problem in 1969 was the modernization of American Steamship's fleet of thirty-three vessels. Using low-interest loans made available after 1970 by the federal Maritime Administration, American Steamship promptly ordered ten new hulls delivered between 1973 and 1981. The company's $250 million building program was somewhat unusual in that American Steamship resisted putting all its money in the 1,000-foot vessels then coming into popularity and ordered a range of ships from the 635-foot *Sam Laud,* launched in 1975 with a capacity of more than 17,000 tons of coal, to the 1,000-foot *Belle River* (later renamed *Walter J. McCarthy Jr.*), launched in 1977 and capable of hauling nearly 68,500 tons.[32]

The variety of new vessels, all self-unloaders, enabled American Steamship to reduce the size of its fleet from twenty-nine vessels with a collective annual oper-ating capacity of 35 million tons in 1969 to eleven ships with a capacity of 26 million tons by 1984 in time to weather the depression in the steel industry in the 1980s and reduced lake traffic thereafter. More important, the new fleet had an annual average capacity of 2.89 million tons per year per ship, that is, more than double the old fleet's annual capacity of 1.21 million tons. Steel still accounted for slightly less than half (46%) of the company's revenues as late as 1997, followed by raw materials for the construction industry (24%) and coal (23%).[33]

Even as the Great Lakes fleet shrank in size in the second half of the twentieth century, new companies came into existence to fill niches the big ships abandoned, ignored, or could no longer efficiently serve. James A. Hannah Sr. concluded in 1948 that tank barges were a more efficient way than tank trucks to move liquid cargo, especially petrochemicals, around the Chicago area. Hannah Inland Waterways, as the family-owned company was called, expanded over the years as a local barge and tug operator and in 1972 expanded into the Great Lakes and later the Gulf.

The GATX-owned *Indiana Harbor* is one of the 1,000-foot-long leviathans that appeared on the Great Lakes beginning in the 1970s. It is capable of carrying 78,000 tons of cargo. (American Steamship Company)

The *Consumers Power* is typical of the design of Great Lakes ships in the middle of the twentieth century. It was a self-unloader but had its pilothouse at the bow and engine room and crew quarters at the stern—the profile for bulk steamers since the 1880s.

However, the company is probably best known for its 1981 decision to put the first articulated tug barges in operation on the Great Lakes—the *Mark Hannah* and *E-63*. By the year 2000, the company had two such tug barges in operation in its fleet of eleven tugs and eight liquid-cargo barges. The second tug barge operation was the tug *Susan W. Hannah* and the 440-foot cement barge *Medusa Conquest*.[34]

The shrinkage of the merchant marine was not the biggest disappointment to promoters of the maritime industry in the Great Lakes in the twentieth century, however. The failure to develop international traffic on a scale that promoters of the Saint Lawrence Seaway had hoped would rejuvenate lake ports was a setback, as was the failure of those ports, Chicago especially, to capitalize on the container revolution that swept the world shipping industry after 1955. The railroads captured that transcontinental traffic because the Seaway was built too small.

# *Chapter Fifteen* Chicago's Lost Opportunities

• Chicago, one of the world's busiest ports in 1870 in terms of ship traffic, one hundred years later wasn't even the busiest on the Great Lakes, despite its use by a variety of lakers, saltwater vessels from Europe, and barge traffic off the Mississippi River. Great concrete grain elevators stood idle on the banks of its rivers, rusting and abandoned shipyards were posted with signs warning trespassers to stay away, and vacant tracts sat where steel mills had once belched smoke.

The Chicago River by the end of the century had been transformed into what was essentially a recreational waterway in a canyon of steel and glass office towers. The closing of the ship turning basin at the mouth of the river in 1999 and the conversion of industries along the Ogden Slip from industrial to commercial and residential uses a few years earlier were a belated recognition of the changes in the role of the river that had been occurring since the beginning of the century. The city in the 1990s also converted Navy Pier from a maritime white elephant into a recreational and exhibition center also serving a variety of tour boats.

On the south side, the Calumet River late in the century had undergone a devolution from the break-point entrepôt it had been for a hundred years to a waterway in some ways resembling the city's ancient portage. Instead of flotillas of canoes the Cal carried strings of barges pushed by diesel towboats bound from the Gulf Coast

By the 1990s Chicago's grain elevators, like these on Lake Calumet, stood idle. Most grain moved by barge down the Mississippi River or by rail to the Gulf.

Ships, like the one whose masts can be seen at right, were often sunk at shore to help build seawalls, as in this 1924 scene on the lakefront at Washington Street. The gunboat *Wilmette,* which was converted in 1918 from the hull of the ill-fated *Eastland,* can be seen docked in the background near some Illinois Central Railroad freight cars. (Chicago Maritime Society)

through Chicago to places like Burns Harbor, Indiana, and Milwaukee.

Traffic patterns had changed once again: shippers moved their grain by rail or barge to avoid the expensive switching charges at Chicago's port, and the shrunken steel industry's output was easily handled by its newer mills along the south shore of the lake in Indiana. By 1984, the river port of Saint Louis once again surpassed Chicago in the tonnage of water shipments—a position it had not been in since the steamboat era more than a century earlier.[1]

The opening of the Saint Lawrence Seaway in 1959 resulted in a spurt of international saltwater traffic for a decade, but the high seaway tolls and the trend toward increasingly larger ships on the ocean favored the Atlantic ports over those that, like Chicago, were limited to vessels small enough to navigate the Seaway canals. Increased containerization of maritime freight in the last half of the century and the domination of that traffic by the railroads hurt Chicago's port. The city's efforts

to meet the competition were invariably too little, too late.

The building of the Municipal Pier (later renamed Navy Pier) in the second decade of the century to serve lake packets occurred just as motor trucks appeared and were beginning to capture that cross-lake traffic. The construction of an intermodal center at the mouth of the Calumet River in the second half of the century occurred after the railroads had mobilized to capture the containerized freight market from both the Seaway and Panama Canal.

In 1871, at the height of the city's popularity as a port, traffic was dominated by grain and timber. The lumber business was dead by the end of the century and had been replaced by steel; grain traffic held on until the 1990s, but with diminishing importance. As late as 1990 Chicago exported 595,000 tons of grain, or only 5.1 percent of the city's lake commerce, although shipments were still at half the levels they had been in 1871. Within four years that traffic was gone too.

The new maritime commerce, as the twentieth century was closing, consisted of four categories of commodities. By 1997 bulk dry cargo—such things as wood, minerals, iron, and scrap—accounted at 7.9 million tons for almost a third of the city's maritime commerce. Coal, petroleum products, and manufactured products—cement, paper, and steel—each at more than 4.5 million tons accounted for slightly less than a fifth of the total. The only other major commodity, chemical products, accounted for about 7.8 percent.[2]

On the other hand, foreign traffic had been negligible in 1871, but by 1996 it accounted for about 15 percent, and two thirds of the foreign traffic was to and from Canada. The bulk of the overseas traffic of only 1.4 million tons was finished steel products. Most of the Canadian trade was in dry bulk cargo (table 15.1).[3]

## The Shipyards

In the second half of the twentieth century, Chicago's once thriving shipyards became a casualty of the declining size of lake fleets and the city's somewhat restricted facilities that would not allow them to compete in construction of the thousand-foot bottoms then in vogue. All but the smallest towboats had to be built in sections that were assembled downriver, where low bridges over the canal were not a problem.

The first Chicago-built ship dates from 1838 and the first dry dock from a decade later. By the 1850s several yards were flourishing building primarily schooners and steam propellers. The large iron and steel steamships that appeared toward the end of the nineteenth century were more than a single entrepreneur and a handful of shipwrights could handle technologically or financially, so their businesses increasingly evolved into larger and larger enterprises until the Chicago Shipbuilding Company was organized in 1889 with a capitalization of $350,000 and a 21-acre yard along the Calumet River. The com-

pany's first ships two years later were the 2,432-ton steel freighters Marina and Masoba, and by 1898 the company had thirty-four vessels in service and three on the stocks.

### Table 15.1
### Chicago Waterborne Commerce, 1997
(in thousands of tons)

| Commodity | Foreign Tonnage | Domestic Tonnage |
|---|---|---|
| Coal | 284 | 4,563 |
| Petroleum products | 445 | 4,103 |
| Chemicals | 109 | 1,843 |
| Bulk dry cargo* | 1,719 | 6,235 |
| Manufactured products** | 1,144 | 3,444 |
| Food and grain | 139 | 780 |
| Machinery | 19 | 36 |
| **Total** | **3,859** | **21,004** |

*includes wood, minerals, iron, and scrap.
**includes cement, paper, and steel.
Note: Data are rounded.
Source: U.S. Army Corps of Engineer, Waterborne Commerce of the United States: Part 3, Waterways and Harbors, Great Lakes, Port of Chicago (1997), 11–12.

In the early 1900s, the company merged with several other Great Lakes yards to become the American Shipbuilding Company, which for many years was the dominant builder on the lakes. It was the company picked by the navy during World War II to convert two side-wheel passenger steamers, the Seeandbee and Greater Buffalo, into the aircraft carriers Wolverine (Seeandbee) and Sable (Greater Buffalo) to train combat pilots. The company's yard on the Calumet River was too small for such a project and the conversions were done in Buffalo.

The most spectacular project completed by American Shipbuilding's Chicago yards was another conversion. The Marine Robin had been originally built in 1945 as a 591-foot freighter for ocean service but in 1952

**Above:** The mouth of the Chicago River in the 1920s was still a busy port, as can be seen from the assorted ships docked along its warehouses and the railroad yards. However, some ships were already using the new Municipal (later, Navy) Pier. (David R. Phillips Collection)

**Right:** By 1938, when the locks (center) were under construction at the mouth of the river to comply with federal court orders limiting the diversion of lake water to the Chicago River, Chicago's downtown harbor was almost devoid of commercial traffic. (David R. Phillips Collection)

In 1993, when this aerial shot was taken, the Chicago River and its north branch were essentially recreational waterways, and most of the superstructure on deserted Navy Pier (top) had been razed. (David R. Phillips Collection)

By 1998 Navy Pier had been resurrected, but as a convention and amusement center and dock for all manner of excursion boats.

was sold to a the M. A. Hanna Company of Cleveland, which wanted to stretch her and convert her to a self-unloading Great Lakes ore boat. Too large for the Saint Lawrence and Welland Canals, the ship was cut into three sections in Baltimore and later had a 123-foot center section added. A new bow was built in Pascagoula, Mississippi, and the by then two sections of the ship were towed up the Mississippi and Illinois Rivers to Chicago, where they were welded together to transform the *Marine Robin* into the 714-foot *Joseph H. Thompson*. In 1991 the *Thompson* was shortened by 53 feet and converted into a giant barge.[4]

Although at least three other shipyards

were in operation in Chicago after World War II, the only major one was the Calumet Shipyard and Dry Dock Company, a business founded in 1927 by the family of James A. Rogan when he and three partners bought the twenty-year-old Kraft Shipyard, a yacht builder. Calumet was possibly the only shipyard on the Great Lakes that because of Chicago's unique location was able to specialize in building river barges and towboats, although it occasionally built lake tugs and small vessels for the government. It was the yard that in 1949 built the towboat *A. M. Thompson* in sections.[5]

Although many of Chicago's shipyards survived the depression of the 1930s only to prosper during World War II and the years after when the Great Lakes fleet was rebuilt, they were unable to survive to the end of the century when the freshwater merchant marine began to shrink. American Shipbuilding, plagued by years of losses, called it quits in 1981. Its Chicago yard was simply too small to compete for construction or maintenance even with the company's other Great Lakes yards. In the postwar years American Shipbuilding had employed as many as three hundred persons but had only fifty on the payroll when it shut down.[6]

## The Death of the Downtown Port

The development of Chicago's ports in the twentieth century was influenced by the master plan that the architect Daniel Burnham put together, beginning in 1907. It envisioned the creation of lakefront parks except at the mouths of the two rivers, where industry would be concentrated. The Chicago Harbor Commission, appointed in 1908, was so swayed by the

plan that when its own report was published in 1909 it recommended the building of large piers at the mouth of the Chicago River, widening of the Calumet River, creating an inland harbor at Lake Calumet, the elimination of obstructions on both rivers, and the replacement of bridges that impaired river traffic.[7]

As a result of the report, the city designated both the Chicago and Calumet Rivers as harbors and began planning the first of two giant 3,000-foot-long piers flanking the mouth of the Chicago River. The Municipal Pier (Navy Pier) was completed in 1916 and was designed to accommodate both passengers and package freight. But shifting traffic patterns obviated the need for the twin pier to the south before it could be built, and Navy Pier never fulfilled its promise.[8]

Although the pier handled considerable interlake passenger traffic into the 1920s, when as many as twelve passenger ships would be simultaneously docked there, it was obsolete for freight traffic almost from the day it opened. There was

The Chicago River in 1998 was a canyon walled by skyscrapers and functioned mainly as avenue for pleasure craft.

Ships, like the *William E. Corey* shown going down the ways at Chicago Ship Building Company in 1905, were launched sideways because of the limited clearances and width of the the Calumet River. (Library of Congress)

insufficient highway or rail access to handle cargo from large freighters, and the pier was designed to handle side-loading ships typical of the cross-lake packets. It did not have sufficient open dock space for the cranes necessary for vertical loading and unloading from the holds of deep-draft freighters.[9]

The pier's opening also coincided with the development of heavy-duty motor trucks just before World War I and the start of the nation's hard-road building program just after the war. Motor trucks by 1913 had developed into substantial vehicles. That year Charles Jeffrey, who assembled

Rambler passenger cars in his plant in suburban Kenosha, Wisconsin, built for the army the first of his four-wheel-drive Quad trucks with a 2-ton cargo capacity. By the end of the decade the development of pneumatic tires and the building of hard roads enabled the emerging cartage industry to pick up some of the cross-lake traffic. In 1921, the Benton Harbor–Chicago Motor Truck Service was advertising a thrice-weekly schedule between Berrien County, Michigan, and Chicago.[10]

Navy Pier was used as a navy training center during World War II and afterward, between 1946 and 1965, served as the University of Illinois's Chicago campus for returning veterans. However, by 1955, with the prospect that the proposed Saint Lawrence Seaway would greatly increase international traffic, the city made plans to use it to serve oceangoing vessels. That did not prove satisfactory, and after the pier remained vacant for most of the 1970s and 1980s, the city began to look at plans to convert it into anything from a shopping plaza to a gambling casino. Most of the superstructure was demolished, and finally, in 1995, it reopened as a recreation and convention center that, among other things, offered tourist and excursion boat rides as well as a dock for occasional calls by the German Hapag-Lloyd Tours line's *Christopher Columbus* during its Great Lakes cruises.[11]

The Chicago River, once one of the busiest stretches of water on earth, suffered a similar decline as maritime traffic gradually began to gravitate to the Calumet River after 1880, and although the downtown harbor a decade later was still handling 7 million tons of freight annually, the decline became pronounced as the twentieth century progressed. By 1980, downtown port traffic had dwindled to only about half a million tons a year—the bulk of it barge traffic in transit between Lake Michigan and the Sanitary and Ship Canal—and traffic on the north branch of the river had declined to 2.6 million tons. Land along the main branch of the river simply became too valuable for factories or warehouses and was redeveloped as office towers and high-rise apartment buildings.

The last major shipper on the main stem of the river, the *Chicago Tribune,* moved its newsprint warehouse to the north branch in the 1980s, converted to railroad transportation, and in early 1984 sold its eight-ship lake fleet to Group Degagnes, a Canadian shipping company. The last steamship to use the river on a regular schedule for deliveries most likely was the *Medusa Challenger,* a 538-foot cement carrier of 1906 vintage, and probably the last large vessel in the twentieth cen-

tury to regularly use the Chicago River was the chemical tug barge *E-63* on its lonely trips between the lake and the Sanitary and Ship Canal.[12]

The elimination of the turning basin at the mouth of the Chicago River in 1999 over the objection of the maritime industry effectively put an end to the Chicago River's use by lake ships. A wall cutting off the basin from the river was erected as a result of 1967 and 1980 U.S. Supreme Court consent decrees in a lawsuit by Wisconsin against Illinois for diverting excessive quantities of Lake Michigan water down the Chicago River and Sanitary and Ship Canal. The decree required any excess diversion to be pumped back into the lake.[13]

## Calumet

By 1900 the facilities at Calumet accounted for 3.5 million tons of shipping—about 2.5 million tons of it iron ore—and it became obvious to city officials that they had better include it in any maritime plans. The 500- and 600-foot ships then coming on line were too large for the Chicago River, and the steel industry that had ordered those giant ore boats and colliers had already moved to the Calumet area. The Calumet River in the first seven decades of the nineteenth century emptied into Lake Michigan by means of a succession of sloughs through which a channel had to be cut, beginning in 1870, to make it navigable to ships.[14]

The Chicago Harbor Commission in its 1909 report adopted Burnham's suggestion that the Calumet area be left as a port and recommended several improvements that unquestionably would establish the area as the city's principal port, including the widening of the Calumet River, elimination of the restrictive bridges there, and the creation of a harbor in Lake Calumet a few miles inland. Two years later the city council accepted the report and designated Calumet as a harbor, then did nothing for half a century. The Harbor Commission's recommendations were followed in 1920 by a report to the City Council Committee on Harbors, Wharves, and Bridges ratifying the earlier recommendation about turning Lake Calumet into a port—a belated recognition by the city that the Calumet area was by then handling more than 20 million tons of traffic annually, much of it diverted from downtown.[15]

The only practical way to deepen Lake Calumet to make it navigable was by dredging; the 2,300-acre lake was only four feet deep. As early as 1925 the New York, Chicago & Saint Louis Railroad (Nickel Plate Road) proposed to develop the lake but the matter never made it through the City Council. Congress in 1933 authorized $400,000 for the dredging of the lake to a depth of 21 feet and building a 3,200-foot-long ship basin at the south end of the lake to serve a proposed rail-highway-water transfer terminal. The dredging was completed in 1939, but the terminal proposal languished.[16]

In fact, although the city had acquired title to the lake in 1921, nothing was done about terminals there until 1953 when a state agency, the Chicago Regional Port District, was created to get something started. By then a number of postwar waterway projects that would benefit Chicago put increased pressure on the city to expand its harbor. Because of problems in moving wartime traffic between the Great Lakes and the Mississippi River, the Corps of Engineers widened the Cal-Sag Channel—the waterway that was the final link in the Gulf Coast–Great Lakes connection proposed many years earlier. The other major project was the Saint Lawrence Seaway which, its promoters said, would turn the Great Lakes cities into ocean ports.[17]

The inadequacy of the locks on the Saint Lawrence River meant that the industrial Great Lakes' principal water connection to the ocean during World War II was Chicago's rivers and canals. Great Lakes shipyards built 119 warships, including 28 submarines alone by the Manitowoc Shipbuilding Company; 264 landing ships; 129 oceangoing freighters or tankers; and many smaller craft: most of the larger vessels were sent through the Chicago river and canal system. The Saint Lawrence locks around the Lachine Rapids above Montreal at the time could handle vessels no larger than 270 feet. That bottleneck, which meant that neither the United States nor Canada could use their Great Lakes shipyards to their fullest capacity in the two world wars, was the impetus behind the building of the Saint Lawrence Seaway in the 1950s.[18]

## Overseas Trade

Almost from its inception as a port, Chicago envisioned itself as a potential international maritime trading center, a dream that was not realized until after the Seaway opened, and even then overseas traffic was never on the scale envisioned by some of the project's promoters. Although canals around the Saint Lawrence rapids date from 1783, they couldn't accommodate anything much larger than a *bateau*. The completion of the Welland Canal around Niagara Falls in 1825–1829 and of the Beauharnois and Lachine Canals in 1842–1848 around the rapids on the Saint Lawrence River for the first time permitted ship access from the Great Lakes to the Atlantic, but nothing longer than 100 feet and drawing more than 9 feet of water. That was good enough for the brigantine *Eureka* to sail from Cleveland for San Francisco in 1849 with a load of gold seekers.

Although there were Canadian sailings earlier, the first vessel to make the trip from Chicago to Europe was the *Dean Richmond,* which sailed July 14, 1856, with a load of wheat; after a stop in Milwaukee to top off its hold, it arrived in Liverpool on September 29. The *Madeira Pet* made the reverse trip between April 24 and July 14 the next year. However, international sailings were insignificant compared to domestic traffic. Only fifteen voyages between the Great Lakes and Europe occurred in 1858, and in 1860 there were only thirty-nine. Even during the

Civil War the size of the Canadian locks prevented the navy from transferring the warship *Michigan* to blockade duty on the East Coast.[19]

World War I caused the first major transfer of vessels between the lakes and the Atlantic. Great Lakes shipyards built small vessels for the war and shipped many of them through Chicago and down the Mississippi River. By then the Saint Lawrence and Welland locks had been enlarged to a length of 270 feet, a width of 45 feet, and a depth of 14 feet. The Canadian government requisitioned some of its lakers for wartime service, causing some companies in that British Commonwealth dominion to charter small tramp steamers from neutral Scandanavian countries for intralake service.[20]

More or less continuous overseas service to Chicago dates from 1931, when the *Anna,* a small Norwegian steamer, arrived in Chicago with a load of wire. Two years later the Norwegian Fjell Line began scheduled, or liner, service, as it is known in the trade, followed by the rival Oranje Line in 1937. Both discontinued service during World War II but resumed in 1946 and were followed in the next few years, despite shortages of suitable hulls because of wartime losses, by several other European lines interested in establishing a presence in the market in anticipation of the opening of the Seaway. As a result, overseas traffic in the Great Lakes increased from 100,000 tons in 1948 to 758,549 tons in 1955, with cement, wood pulp, and liquor and wine accounting for the largest categories of imports, and animal feed and hides being the most important exports. By 1959, after the Seaway opened, Chicago alone handled more than a million tons of overseas trade, nearly a quarter of it corn.[21]

Even before the opening of the Seaway there were 130 ships on the Great Lakes involved in overseas trade on a regular basis, but they were small by ocean standards—typically with a capacity of 2,600 tons of cargo on the oceans but only 1,600 tons on the lakes because of the shallow canals and harbors. Larger oceangoing ships, including the ubiquitous C-2 class, which included 2,580 mass-produced Liberty ships and 130 kindred vessels, were too large for the Saint Lawrence locks, however. Steaming time between Chicago and Europe took twenty-two to twenty-three days, about half of that just to get to Montreal, but that was a considerable improvement over the seventy-seven to eighty-one days required by the voyages a century earlier.[22]

Despite opposition from the railroads and some states with Atlantic ports, fearing a potential loss of traffic, the United States and Canada between 1954 and 1959 proceeded with the $1.7 billion Seaway project, about $470 million of which involved navigation and the balance hydroelectric power generation. Congress also approved, as part of the project to bring international traffic to the Great Lakes, an additional $256.9 million for the Corps of Engineers to deepen connecting channels in the lakes to 27 feet. The older Saint Lawrence locks were replaced with new ones 730 feet long, 75 feet wide, and capable of handling vessels with a 25 1/2-foot draft—the standard used when the Welland Canal around Niagara Falls was rebuilt in the 1930s.

Some speculative statistics produced during the debate over the Seaway indicated that Chicago would become the world's largest city, and the New York Port Authority projected that New York would lose 3.5 million tons of shipping a year in shipping to Chicago, costing the city 200,000 jobs. The U.S. government had projected that as many as eighteen to twenty-six oceangoing ships would be assigned to the lakes, providing as many as eleven to sixteen overseas sailings a month. On the other hand, the Lake Carriers Association, a trade group of lakes ship owners based in Cleveland, was dubious of the value of the Seaway to the U.S.-flag merchant marine because American ships and crews were too expensive to compete.[23]

## The Seaway

The effect of Seaway traffic on Chicago was immediate and dramatic; unfortunately, it was also short-lived. The city, which in 1957 reopened Navy Pier to international traffic in anticipation of a boom, reached its postwar peak of about 32 million tons of ship traffic in 1965 before beginning a long decline. The boom was more obvious at Calumet, which handled 31 million tons of ship traffic, than to downtown Chicago, including Navy Pier, with only about 902,000 tons. However, by 1990 Calumet River ship traffic had fallen to a third of its 1965 level—to less than 9 million tons, and Great Lakes traffic on Lake Calumet over the same span had declined from more than 2 million tons to 1.3 million.[24]

Barge traffic on Chicago's canals fared somewhat better in the final quarter of the twentieth century, although it also suffered a decline after 1974 but was able to recover in the 1990s. Lake ships, primarily because of the strength of the steel industry and the Seaway's boost to international shipping, accounted for more than half the port activity in Chicago as late as 1973. However, by 1995 the canals accounted for about two-thirds of the traffic.[25]

As it became obvious within a few years of its opening, the Seaway had been designed to 1940s standards that were rapidly changing in the second half of the century. Unfortunately the construction of the Seaway coincided with a substantial increase in the size of saltwater ships and the aggressive movement of railroads into the containerized freight business. Total Seaway traffic peaked at 57.4 million tons in 1977 but in the 1990s had declined below 40 million tons annually. In 1999, the Seaway carried a total of 36.4 million metric tons (2,204 pounds per metric ton), about 11.4 million tons of which was overseas trade.[26]

There were a number of reasons why the Seaway did not live up to some of the more optimistic projections of its proponents and turn the ports of the Great Lakes into international trade centers. For one thing, the 1,800-mile length of the Seaway route from Chicago to the mouth of the Saint Lawrence worked against it, especially since the rival Chicago–New Orleans barge route was only about 1,500 miles and the railroad route to New York was only about 900 miles. It was no coincidence that in 1998 foreign shipments of 67.6 million tons at New Orleans and 55.6 million tons at New York each dwarfed the foreign maritime trade at all U.S. Great Lakes ports combined—11.7 million tons.[27]

A study by the U.S. Maritime Administration for Lykes Lines, a New Orleans–based steamship company that once had liner service to the Great Lakes, illustrated the problem. The study concluded that Lykes could generate six times as much revenue on the route between the United States and Egypt by using the port of Norfolk, Virginia, instead of Great Lakes ports. Norfolk had the advantage of a year-round steaming season, a shorter route, and faster turnaround times for ships because Norfolk's port was considerably larger than anything on the lakes. A United States–Egypt round trip was forty days from Norfolk, but sixty days from the Great Lakes. The study concluded that ships to and from Norfolk also could carry heavier loads because they were not restricted by the relatively shallow depth of the Seaway. On the ocean, a Lykes ship could be fully loaded with 16,000 tons to a draft of 32 feet, but to clear the Seaway locks the same ship could be loaded with roughly 10,000 tons to a draft of only 26 feet.[28]

The relatively modest levels of international traffic produced by the Seaway were a major disappointment to Chicago's maritime industry. Although overseas shipments through the Seaway declined from 16,997,472 tons in 1970 to 11,480,796 tons in 1988, in the twenty-five years after 1970 Chicago lost almost two-thirds of its overseas traffic, for the most part grain exports. The decline dropped the city from first to fourth among Great Lakes ports in overseas trade, behind Duluth-Superior, Toledo, and Detroit.

The largest use of the Seaway in the last quarter of the century was by domestic Canadian shipping. Intra-Canadian traffic accounted for about 46 percent of Seaway tonnage in 1991, Canada–United States trade 35 percent, and overseas shipping 19 percent. Three years later, overseas shipping accounted for only 18 percent of the traffic on the U.S. side of the lakes. Domestic U.S. shipping through the Seaway was negligible.[29]

The falloff also coincided with a similar decline in domestic traffic due to the steel industry's financial troubles and closure of local mills. Annual traffic between Chicago and other American Great Lakes ports declined from 19.7 million tons to 3.9 million tons between 1970 and 1988. Coal declined by almost 6 million tons annually, iron ore by 7 million tons, and limestone by 1 million tons. Grain exports fell by 2 million tons, and by 1988 Chicago's giant grain elevators with a combined capacity of 79 million bushels were operating at a fraction of their capacity (table 15.2).[30]

Once the federal government rebuilt the nation's barge industry and completed the lock system in the 1930s, it became cheaper to ship grain by river to New Orleans for transfer to ocean ships than through the Seaway to Montreal for transloading. A study by the Chicago Board of Trade in the early 1990s indicated the Chicago–New Orleans–Rotterdam route cost about $11.35 per ton as compared to $22.50 through the Seaway. High railroad reciprocal switching charges in Chicago for individual shippers were also a problem, although unit train rates were negotiable.[31]

The quest of Great Lakes ports for international traffic has not been without environmental consequences. Such fish as the sea lamprey, rainbow smelt, and alewife all invaded the Great Lakes long before the opening of the Saint Lawrence Seaway. Perhaps the most notorious of the invaders was the sea lamprey, a parasitic fish native to the North Atlantic Ocean, which entered the Great Lakes in the late nine-

teenth century and along with overfishing was blamed for the decimation of local fish populations.

### Table 15.2
#### Port of Chicago Tonnage*
(in millions of short tons)

| Year | Tonnage |
|------|---------|
| 1950 | 31.72 |
| 1955 | 38.97 |
| 1960 | 38.81 |
| 1965 | 45.97 |
| 1970 | 48.25 |
| 1975 | 42.59 |
| 1980 | 32.99 |
| 1985 | 22.61 |
| 1990 | 22.54 |
| 1995 | 25.33 |
| 1996 | 27.89 |
| 1997 | 24.87 |

*Includes both branches of the Chicago River and its main stem, Calumet River and Lake Calumet, Sanitary and Ship Canal, and Cal-Sag Channel.

Source: U.S. Army Corps of Engineer, *Waterborne Commerce of the United States: Part 3, Waterways and Harbors, Great Lakes, Port of Chicago* (1950–1997).

In the late twentieth century the zebra mussel, a mollusk that infests and clogs water intakes, and round goby both invaded the lakes. The goby is a pugnacious fish that aggressively competes for food with native species and even devours their roe and fry. Maritime commerce probably contributed significantly to the introduction of both species through ship ballast tanks and to the rapid spread of the zebra mussel after its discovery near Detroit in 1988. The mollusks frequently attach themselves to barge and recreational boat hulls, a characteristic that caused their spread down the Illinois Waterway to the Mississippi River system.

## The Container Revolution

Even before the changing trade economics began to undermine the steel and grain-based maritime traffic in Chicago, the city's port had become embroiled in a struggle for a share of the then emerging intermodal freight business. As it turned out, container freight was Chicago's last hope to remain a major player in international maritime trade. Early experiments in hauling motor truck trailers on railroad trains date from the 1920s and using locked shipping containers for package freight on ships dates from the 1930s, but maritime historians generally date the first container ship from 1956, when Malcolm Maclean, the founder of Sea-Land Services, converted a 532-foot tanker, the *Ideal X*, into a vessel capable of handling 58 containers.

Before then, freighters used cranes maneuvering netlike slings containing cargo to and from holds; the slings were loaded by gangs of longshoremen by hand or forklift trucks. Despite quantum leaps in efficiency, which included faster loading and unloading, cutting costly port time, and reduction in damage to and pilferage of goods, it took years for the industry to convert ships and ports to efficiently handle containers. The major breakthrough came in 1961, when shippers agreed on standard 20- and 40-foot containers with common fittings permitting their interchange between ships and railroad flatcars.[32]

The city and state were somewhat slow to respond to the trend. The state legislature in 1951 created a special governing body, the Chicago Regional Port District (later changed to Illinois International Port District) to run the Calumet port and issue $24 million in bonds to dredge 70 acres at the south end of Lake Calumet to provide access by larger ships and to build a three-shed intermodal terminal and two new grain elevators there. However, neither the city nor the state was willing to provide regular subsidies similar to what was done at other Great Lakes ports, and the city retained control of Navy Pier. Although it was obvious for a decade that the state's only port needed to jump on the container bandwagon, it wasn't until 1978 that Illinois lent the port district $15 million to acquire the abandoned Youngstown Sheet and Tube steel mill site at the mouth of the Calumet River for conversion into a container-handling facility.[33]

However, Iroquois Landing, as the facility was called, was built too late to capture much traffic and was relegated to a general cargo dock. The *Chicago Tribune* in a series of articles in 1985 accused the Chicago Regional Port District's board of corruption, political cronyism, and conflict of interest, including the fact that John J. Serpico was working both sides of the aisle as chairman of the port district's board while simultaneously serving as president of the Central States Joint Board of the International Union of Allied Novelty and Production Workers, which represented the port's workers. A 1987 study by the then Illinois lieutenant governor George Ryan found that the port suffered from poor management, an ineffective board of directors, poor facilities and maintenance, restrictive union rules, inadequate marketing and promotion, monopoly business practices, and delays in loading and unloading. Although overseas shipping dropped 2 percent at all Great Lakes ports in the preceding fourteen years, it fell by 60 percent in Chicago.[34]

The ineptitude of its port notwithstanding, it is not entirely certain Chicago would have been able to capture much container traffic even if it had been more aggressive. The U.S. railroads were able to provide faster and cheaper service in competition with the Panama Canal and Great Lakes to the point that cargoes traveling between Europe and Asia were transferred from ships to trains at ocean ports and hauled across the North American continent by rail—often through Chicago—to

The widespread adoption of standardized, marine-rail shipping containers in the 1960s helped doom Chicago's port, which was too small and remote to handle containers. The 384-foot *Tropic Quest,* a self-unloader built in 1983, can handle up to five hundred containers and operates far from Chicago in the Caribbean Sea although it is owned by Nicor, a local natural-gas company. (Nicor)

be reloaded on the opposite coast onto container ships as long as 1,000 feet and capable of carrying 6,000 containers.

North American railroads, which handled a combined total of 1,664,929 truck trailers and marine containers in 1965, by 1998 handled 5,419,631 marine shipping containers and 3,353,032 truck trailers.

Container traffic passed that of truck trailers in 1992. The volume of such traffic passing through Chicago was huge: by 1997 more than 700 intermodal trains a week arrived in the city, often passing through on the way to either coast. For the most part they stopped in Chicago only long enough to change crews.[35]

# Epilogue

• People have used water transport ever since they had something uncomfortably heavy or bulky to transport: a couple of Cro-Magnons with a single, large dugout could do the work of ten of their brethren hauling the same amount of goods on their back. An Egyptian reed boat with a crude sail might do the work of twenty men—not faster, but easier and cheaper, and a large Roman *corbita* might do the work of five hundred. Even when slavery provided cheap labor, ships could do the job cheaper.

The exception, of course, is where the waters did not run. The earth's surface may be predominantly water, but there are still thousands of miles of dry land to travel. At some distance from the water, whether it is 25 miles behind a team of oxen or 150 in a tractor-trailer, the economic advantages begin to shift away from water transport and toward the terrestrial beast of burden, whether it brays, swears, or belches smoke. Into the economic equation must also be figured the cost of breaking bulk—transferring the cargo from cart to ship and back again—a labor-intensive task.

At some relative point in the nineteenth century it became cheaper to take the 286-mile land route across the Michigan peninsula to get from Detroit to Chicago than the 633-mile sea route around it. A drummer with a carpetbag and sample case, a person for whom time was money, might have found it more expedient to take a two-day stagecoach trip between the two cities in the 1840s. But what about the immigrant family with four children, household goods, livestock, and farm tools? For them the only alternative to walking along, leading the team hitched to a farm wagon, was a creaking schooner.

That basic economic premise of transportation has not changed much over the years, although the market share of the maritime industry has shrunk as competition from the draft horse, iron horse, horseless carriage, and all their incarnations made their appearance on the scene. The waters are still cheaper when you have easy access to them.

The major change in the economic equation that has occurred over the last two hundred years is the time of transport. Passenger traffic was the most sensitive to time and the first to abandon an old system of travel by water for a new one that delivered faster travel by rail or rubber tire. Next came time-sensitive freight: Chicagoans had never tasted bananas until the Illinois Central Railroad could run its trains fast enough to get an express reefer from the port of New Orleans to the Windy City in two days, a trip that would have taken two weeks by steamboat. The overnight Lake Michigan packets dominated the cross-lake fruit trade until the motor truck came along and took away their business. And today, does a desperately needed computer motherboard travel any other way from Silicon Valley to Chicago than by air?

But try shipping by air from a blending plant on the Calumet River the 10,000 tons of coal needed to fire the power plant that supplies the electricity to the computer factories in Silicon Valley. The trip by water would be 6,000 miles via the Panama Canal, so the coal makes the 2,000-mile trip by train, just as shipping containers traveling between Amsterdam and Yokohama pass through Chicago on the train on their 3,000-mile rail bypass across North America to avoid the long sea route. However, shipping 10,000 tons of limestone the 355 miles from Cleveland to Chicago by rail or truck would be prohibitively expensive, so it travels more than twice as far—752 miles—by water.

The economics of transportation dictate that in the twenty-first century there will continue to be a maritime industry in Chicago just has there was in the past. The runways at O'Hare International Airport were built by concrete hauled to the city by cement boats on the Great Lakes, and the chemicals used in the manufacture of so many products made in Chicago facto-

ries most probably arrived on river barges in 1,500-ton lots. Thus, ships and barges likely will continue to plod on Chicago's rivers and canals, however out-of-sight to the public behind smokestacks and factories. The same geographic and natural advantages that allowed Chicago to dominate the interior of the continent during the age of sail and steam will assure that it remains a vital center for American transportation and commerce, even in the age of the Internet.

# Notes

### Preface

1. Samuel Eliot Morrison, *Admiral of the Ocean Sea* (Boston, 1942), 114–115.

### Chapter 1: The Canoe Routes

1. Chicago had been successively occupied by the Illiniwek, Wea (Miami), and Potawatomi Indians. It was the Potawatomi who finally sold or ceded their lands to the United States. See Stewart Rafert, *The Miami Indians of Indiana* (Indianapolis, IN, 1996), 26–27; R. David Edmunds, *The Potawatomis: Keepers of the Fire,* 15; and William Cronon, *Nature's Metropolis* (New York, 1991), 53–54.

2. John O. Greenwood, *Greenwood's Guide to Great Lakes Shipping* (Cleveland, 1997), table 21-V (distances between points on Lake Michigan), gives the distance between Old Mackinac Point and Gary as 336 miles. See also David M. Solzman, *Chicago River* (Chicago, 1998), 9–23; and John Boatman, *An Anthology of Western Great Lakes Indian History,* ed. Donald L. Fixico (Milwaukee, 1987), 25, citing various accounts in the Wisconsin State Historical collections in Madison based on the manuscripts of Nicholas Perrot describing his visit to the Winnebago in 1667.

3. Milo M. Quaife, *Chicago's Highways Old and New* (Chicago, 1923), 40–41.

4. Timothy J. Kent, *Birchbark Canoes of the Fur Trade* (Ossineke, MI, 1997), 1:116–138; and interview by author, July 8, 1999.

5. Jolliet's oft-quoted observation on the Chicago canal did not survive in his original notes, which were destroyed in a canoeing accident in the Lachine Rapids near Montreal. Father Claude F. Dablon recorded the remarks of both Jolliet and Father Jacques Marquette in his account of the expedition included in *Jesuit Relations,* several versions of which have been published since 1681. See *The Jesuit Relations and Allied Documents: Travels and Explorations of Jesuit Missionaries in New France, 1610–1791,* ed. Reuben G. Thwaites (Cleveland, 1896–1901), 58: 5. A second version of the expedition, a November 11, 1674, letter from Governor Frontenac to Colbert can be found in Pierre Margery, *Découvertes et Établissements des français dans L'Ouest et dans le Sud de l'Amérique Septentrionale, 1614–1754, Mémoires et Documents originaux* (Paris, 1876–1888), 1:257–262. See also Bessie Louise Pierce, *A History of Chicago* (Chicago, 1937), 1:5; David R. Edmunds, *The Potawatomis* (Norman, OK, 1978), 218; and Robert Knight and Lucius H. Zeuch, *The Location of the Chicago Portage Route of the Seventeenth Century* (Chicago, 1928), 1.

6. Brian M. Fagan, *Ancient North America: The Archaeology of a Continent* (London, 1991), 450–453. The Adena culture generally dates between ca. 1400 B.C. and A.D. 200, the Hopewell between ca. 300 B.C. and A.D. 500, and the Mississippian between A.D. 700 and historic times. Antoine de la Mothe Cadillac and Pierre de Leitte, *The Western Country in the 17th Century: The Memoirs of Lamothe Cadillac and Pierre Leitte,* ed. Milo M. Quaife (Chicago, 1947), 78–82, gave an account of the Natchez Mississippian culture in his 1718 memoirs. Dean Snow, *The Archaeology of North America* (New York, 1976), 31–81, indicates strong Olmec influences in the Adena culture and suggests that Pochteca from Teotihuacan may have carried influences from that city as far north as the woodlands of the Mississippi Valley. Fagan, *Ancient North America,* 446–450, on the basis of the themes and motifs decorating pottery and other artifacts, discounts that theory. See also John E. Kelley, "Cahokia and Its Role as a Gateway Center in Interregional Exchange," ed. Thomas E. Emerson and R. Barry Lewis, in *Cahokia and the Hinterlands* (Urbana, IL, 1991), 61–80.

7. Melvin L. Fowler, "The Cahokia Site," in *Explorations into Cahokia Archaeology,* Illinois Archaeological Survey Bulletin, no. 7 (Urbana, IL, 1973), 1–27; Dean Snow, *The Archaeology of North America* (New York, 1976), 59–61; Brian M. Fagan, *Ancient North America* (New York, 1990), 436–41; and David M. Young, "Secret City," *Chicago Tribune Magazine,* June 13, 1976, 18, 55–61. See also Hugh C. Cutler and Leonard W. Blake, "Corn from Cahokia Sites," in *Explorations into Cahokia Archaeology,* 123.

8. Kelley, "Cahokia and Its Role as a Gateway Center," 65–67.

9. The Illiniwek oral tradition did not include any migration legends, and the Kaskaskia chief Jean Baptiste Ducoign told George Rogers Clark in 1780 that his ancestors built the great mound at Cahokia. See Lee Sultzman, ed., "Illinois History," one of a series of tribal histories posted on the Internet at www.dickshovel.com, 3–4; and James Alton James, *The Life of George Rogers Clark* (Chicago, 1928), 497–498.

10. Fowler, "Cahokia Site," 12.

11. Carl J. Ekberg, *French Roots in the Illinois Country* (Urbana, IL, 1998), 33–34; Ray Allen Billington, *Westward Expansion: A History of the American Frontier* (New York, 1949), 122.

12. The distances between Chicago and the oceans are approximate and have changed slightly over the years because of the alternation of shipping channels due to the addition of canals and changes in courses of rivers. Greenwood, *Greenwood's Guide to Great Lakes Shipping,* shipping distance tables 21-I and 21-VIII, lists the distance between Chicago and Montreal as 1,251 miles and between Montreal and Gaspe as 517 miles. U.S. Army Corps of Engineers Water Resources Support Center, *National Waterways Study,* final report (Washington, 1983), D-187, 191, 193, 197, lists the distances of the Mississippi River from the Gulf of Mexico to Baton Rouge, Mississippi, as 233 miles; from Baton Rouge to Cairo, Illinois, as 723 miles; from Cairo to Grafton, Illinois, as 220 miles; the Illinois Waterway from Grafton to Lockport, Illinois, as 291 miles; and the Sanitary and Ship Canal from Lockport to Lake Michigan as 36 miles. Knight and Zeuch, *Location of the Chicago Portage Route,* 35, 93; *Western Country in the 17th Century,* ed. Quaife, 87–88.

13. *Jesuit Relations and Allied Documents,* ed. Thwaites, 58: 5. Also note that since Norman times a league has been about three miles.

14. Francis Parkman, *La Salle and the Discovery of the Great West* (originally published 1869 as one of the seven-volume France and England in North America series, but cited in this instance from a reprint, New York, 1999), 34–36).

15. Ralph Frese, "Canadians and the Canadian Canoe in the Opening of the American Midwest," in *The Canoe in Canadian Cultures,* ed. John Jennings et al. (Ottawa, ON, 1999), 162.

16. Parkman, *La Salle and the Discovery of the Great West,* 8.

17. Frese, "Canadians and the Canadian Canoe," 165; and Joseph L. Peyser, *Jacques LeGardeur De Saint-Pierre* (East Lansing, MI, 1996), 6–7.

18. Parkman, *La Salle and the Discovery of the Great West,* 137, 195–208.

19. Charles J. Balesi, *The Time of the French in the Heart of North America* (Chicago, 1996), 68. Joseph L. Peyser, *Letters from New France: The Upper Country, 1686–1783* (Urbana, IL, 1992), 76–77.

20. Skinner, "Sinews of Empire," 187, among others, asserts there was no post in Chicago during the French period, although there are many references to traders visiting it. Peyser, *Letters from New France,* 114–115, enumerates eighteen soldiers in the garrison of Fort Saint Joseph (now Niles, MI.) in 1723–1725, guarding the Saint Joseph–Kankakee rivers portage. See also Balesi, *Time of the French in the Heart of North America,* 71.

21. Balesi, *Time of the French in the Heart of North America,* 104–105, 128.

22. *Western Country in the Seventeenth Century,* ed. Quaife, 87–90, 166–170.

23. Balesi, *Time of the French in the Heart of North America,* 158. Carl J. Ekberg, *French Roots in the Illinois Country* (Urbana, IL, 1998), 108, indicated Saint Louis and Prairie du Chien were founded as entrepôts for the fur trade.

24. Frese, "Canadians and the Canadian Canoe," 170.

25. Skinner, "Sinews of Empire," 22–24.

26. Kent, *Birchbark Canoes of the Fur Trade,* 1:2–3. Skinner, "Sinews of Empire," 51. Parkman, *La Salle and the Discovery of the Great West,* 137.

27. Kent, *Birchbark Canoes of the Fur Trade,* 1:241.

28. Skinner, "Sinews of Empire," 206. Kent, *Birchbark Canoes of the Fur Trade,* 1:206–210.

29. Skinner, "Sinews of Empire," 194.

30. Ibid., 187.

31. Alan D. Harn, "The LaMoine River Dugout Canoe, Schuyler County, Illinois," *Illinois Archaeology* 11 (1999):187–201.

32. Skinner, "Sinews of Empire," 178–181.

33. Kent, *Birchbark Canoes of the Fur Trade,* 1:87–101.

34. Ibid., 1:89 (table) indicates that the number of licenses increased substantially after 1722 when seventeen were issued. There were thirty licenses each issued in 1723 and 1724, fifty-four in 1725, fifty-three in 1729, sixty-six in 1739, peaking at seventy-eight in 1750.

35. Peyser, *Jacques LeGardeur De Saint-Pierre,* 7. Ekberg, *French Roots in the Illinois Country,* 213–222, notes that beginning in 1713 flotillas of bateaux were used to haul wheat to New Orleans from the Illinois country.

36. Skinner, "Sinews of Empire," viii. The "livre" was both a measure of weight and a currency in New France. The monetary "livre tournois" of the period was worth $10. The weight was equal to 12 ounces.

37. Skinner, "Sinews of Empire," 51–52.

38. Kent, *Birchbark Canoes of the Fur Trade,* 1:241.

39. Quaife, *Chicago and the Old Northwest, 1673–1835,* 296–299. Pierce, *History of Chicago,* 18–19.

40. Quaife, *Chicago and the Old Northwest, 1673–1835,* 226–231. Pierce, *History of Chicago,* 22–23.

41. Pierce, *History of Chicago,* 26.

42. Quaife, *Chicago's Highways Old and New,* 58–59.

43. Ibid., 58–60.

44. Skinner, "Sinews of Empire," 162, 177–179.

## Chapter 2: The Riverboat Era

1. James E. Vance Jr., *Capturing the Horizon* (Baltimore, MD 1990), 110–111.

2. Parkman, *La Salle and the Discovery of the Great West,* 17–19, 78, 132, notes that La Salle in his voyage down the Ohio in the winter of 1669–1670 may have gone as far as its confluence with the Mississippi but more probably only made it to the falls of the Ohio (Louisville). See also Harrison J. MacLean, *The Fate of the Griffon* (Chicago, 1974), 34.

3. Parkman, *La Salle and the Discovery of the Great West,* 229–237.

4. Clarence Walworth Alvord, *The Illinois Country* (Chicago, 1922), 168–189.

5. Ekberg, *French Roots in Illinois Country,* 216–217 n. 20. James E. Davis, *Frontier Illinois* (Bloomington, IN, 1998), 48.

6. Nancy M. M. Surrey, *The Commerce of Louisiana during the French Regime,* 1699–1763 (New York, 1916), 55–58. Ekberg, *French Roots in Illinois Country,* 274–275.

7. Balesi, *Time of the French in the Heart of North America,* 145. Ekberg, *French Roots in Illinois Country,* 280.

8. Snyder, *Selected Writings,* 47–50. John Parkman, *Montcalm and Wolfe* (originally published 1884, but in this instance cited from a reprint, New York, 1983), 873, said the galleys made two round trips a year.

9. Jack K. Bauer, *A Maritime History of the United States* (Columbia, SC, 1988), 156–157. Leland D. Baldwin, *The Keelboat Age on the Western Waters* (Pittsburgh, 1941), 34–35.

10. Bauer, *Maritime History of the United States,* 156.

11. Louis C. Hunter, *Steamboats on the Western Rivers* (originally published 1949; cited here from reprint, New York, 1993), 54–57.

12. Baldwin, *Keelboat Age on the Western Waters,* 46, 53, 179–180.

13. William Havighurst, *Voices on the River: The Story of the Mississippi Waterways* (New York, 1964), 247–248. Baldwin, *Keelboat Age on the Western Waters,* 181, 192–194.

14. William J. Petersen, *Steamboating on the Upper Mississippi* (Iowa City, IA), 68, 223–226.

15. Bauer, *Maritime History of the United States,* 68–70, points out that the name of the vessel was simply *Steam Boat* (later *North River Steam Boat*), not *Clermont,* which was the name of the port it used. Hunter, *Steamboats on the Western Rivers,* 6–10.

16. Hunter, *Steamboats on the Western Rivers,* 11–14.

17. Ibid., 33 (table 1), 17–20.

18. Eloise Engle and Arnold S. Lott, *America's Maritime Heritage* (Annapolis, MD, 1975), 202, notes that the record load of a steamboat was 2,300 tons (9,226 bales of cotton) aboard the *Henry Frank* to New Orleans in 1881.

19. Resolution introduced in Illinois Legislature Concerning the Incorporation of a Canal Company, December 11, 1835, and Amendment to an Act to Incorporate the Beardstown and Sangamon Canal Company, December 12, 1835; Abraham Lincoln, *The Collected Works of Abraham Lincoln* (New Brunswick, NJ, 1953), 1:40.

20. Hunter, *Steamboats on the Western Rivers,* 217, 660 (table 23), 661 (table 24).

21. *Peoria Register,* April 29, 1842.

22. Quaife, *Chicago's Highways Old and New,* 66–71; and Pierce, *History of Chicago,* 1:52–53.

23. Petersen, *Steamboating on the Upper Mississippi,* 245–246. Quaife, *Chicago's Highways Old and New,* 89–91.

24. Robert P. Howard, *Illinois: A History of the Prairie State* (Grand Rapids, MI, 1972), 170; and Petersen, *Steamboating on the Upper Mississippi,* 236.

25. Petersen, *Steamboating on the Upper Mississippi,* 68, 223–226, 373, 377.

26. Hunter, *Steamboats on the Western Rivers,* 521, 654 (table 13), 656–657 (tables 16–17).

27. Jerry O. Potter, *The Sultana Tragedy* (Gretna, LA, 1992), 81–106. Hunter, *Steamboats on the Western Rivers,* 656–657 (table 17).

28. Mark Twain, *Life on the Mississippi* (New York, 1935), 47–48.

29. Ibid., 106.

30. Hunter, *Steamboats on the Western Rivers,* 101, 303, 311, 360–363.

31. Bauer, *Maritime History of the United States,* 167.

32. Robert W. Harrison, *The United States Waterways and Ports: A Chronology,* U.S. Army Corps of Engineers, *National Waterways Study* (Fort Belvoir, VA), 1:8.

33. *Weekly Chicago Democrat,* May 4, June 29, and July 13, 1847. Pierce, *History of Chicago,* 1:395–397, 425–428 (resolutions adopted by the convention), citing J. D. B. DeBow, *Commercial Review of the South and West* 4 (September 1847): 125–127.

34. Lincoln, *Collected Works,* 480–490, speech in the United States House of Representatives on internal improvements, June 20, 1848.

35. Hunter, *Steamboats on the Western Rivers,* 205–212.

36. Ibid., 214–215.

## Chapter 3: The Age of Canals

1. Charles Hadfield, *World Canals Inland Navigation, Past and Present* (New York, 1986), 355, dates the end of America's canal age at 1848 with the completion of the Illinois and Michigan Canal and the Saint Lawrence River locks.

2. Howard, *Illinois,* 155, 193–195. Hadfield, *World Canals,* 314. The *Report of the Board of (I & M) Canal Commissioners* (1833), 4, in attempting to justify construction of the canal made the claim that, even with a 157-mile wagon haul between Peoria and Chicago, the east-west route to New York via the Great Lakes and Erie Canal was cheaper than shipping downriver to New Orleans, then by sea to New York.

3. Vance, *Capturing the Horizon,* 145, said that the primary role of canals after the American railroad network was built was as feeders of raw materials for export. The developmental role shifted to railroads, then highways.

4. Annals, 9th Congress, 2nd session, 95–97, directed the president to prepare "a plan for the application of such means as are within the power of Congress, to the purposes of opening roads and making canals, together with a statement of the undertaking of this nature, which, as objects of public improvement, may require and deserve the aid of Government."

5. Gallatin's four east-west river corridors included connecting (1) the Juniata, a tributary of the Susquehanna, with the Allegheny, the north branch of the Ohio, in Pennsylvania; (2) the Potomac with the Monongahela, the south branch of the Ohio, through Virginia, Maryland, and Pennsylvania; (3) the James to the Kanawha in Virginia; and (4) the Savannah or Santee to some unspecified headwater of the Tennessee in the South. Although the Susquehanna-Ohio was the only one completed as a canal, all four corridors ultimately sustained railroad and highway arteries.

The "northern outlet corridors" also included Gallatin report that ultimately led in the building of the Erie Canal included a connection between the Mohawk River and Lake Ontario and a canal around Niagara Falls to connect Lake Ontario with the Upper Great Lakes.

6. Hadfield, *World Canals,* 275.

7. Shaw, *Canals for a Nation,* 98–107.

8. Thomas C. Cochrane, *Pennsylvania: A Bicentennial History* (New York, 1978), 53, 86, 94. Burgess and Kennedy, *Centennial History,* 11–12. Shaw, *Canals for a Nation,* 75.

9. Ronald E. Shaw, *Erie Water West: A History of the Erie Canal* (Lexington, KY, 1966), 9–10.

10. Ibid., 261.

11. The Erie Canal was closed in 1917 and replaced by the larger New York State Barge Canal.

12. James Rogers Taylor, *The Transportation Revolution, 1815–1860* (New York, 1951), 47–48.

13. Hadfield, *World Canals,* 310, cites the Illinois-Michigan and the 309-mile Ohio and Erie Canal from Portsmouth to Cleveland as being the two most successful western canals.

14. Putnam, *Illinois and Michigan Canal,* 10, infers this was done in the expectation that the new state would be interested in building the canal.

15. The bill also applied to Indiana to build the Wabash and Erie Canal.

16. John Lamb, *I & M Canal: A Corridor in Time* (Romeoville, IL, 1987), 14–15. The entire waterway was 100 miles long because it included a 3-mile section of the Chicago River. Putnam, *Illinois and Michigan Canal,* 18–19. Heise and Edgerton, *Chicago Center for Enterprise,* 1:35. Pierce, *History of Chicago,* 1:44.

17. Andreas, *History of Chicago,* 2:168.

18. *Chicago American,* July 9, 1836.

19. Putnam, *Illinois and Michigan Canal,* 35, 39, 53–58. Howard, *Illinois,* 193–202.

20. Quaife, *Lake Michigan,* 10 (prelude), notes that the surface level of Lake Michigan varies considerably. The lake level between 1860 and 1944 varied by about 5 feet from 578.3 to 583.4 feet above sea level. The mean was 581 feet above sea level.

21. Andreas, *History of Chicago,* 2:168.

22. Putnam, *Illinois and Michigan Canal,* 73–87.

23. Lamb, *Corridor in Time,* 12.

24. Floyd Mansberger and Christopher Stratton, *Canal Boats along the Illinois and Michigan Canal: A Study in Archaeological Variability* (Springfield, IL, 1998), 1, 7–10.

25. Henry Hall, "Ship-building Industry in the United States," in *Tenth Census . . . 1880,* Census Reports (Washington, DC), 8:231–232. John Lamb, "Canal Boats on the Illinois and Michigan Canal," *Journal of the Illinois State Historical Society* 75, no. 3 (August 1978): 211–224.

26. Hall, "Ship-building Industry in the United States," 231–232; Lamb, "Canal Boats on the Illinois and Michigan Canal," 210; Mansberger and Stratton, *Canal Boats along the Illinois and Michigan Canal,* 15, 28, 30.

27. Elisha Sly, "A little History of the Life of Elisha Sly," December 14, 1896, reprinted in the *Newsletter of the Will County Historical Society* (May 1975): 3–4.

28. Putnam, *Illinois and Michigan Canal,* 115–116.

29. U.S. Army Corps of Engineers, Chicago District, report, *History of the Illinois Waterway and Canals* (Chicago, n.d.), 4–5, 8.

30. Lamb, "Canal Boats on the Illinois and Michigan Canal," 220–221.

31. John Lamb, *The "City of Pekin" Story* (Lockport, IL: Illinois Canal Society, 1980). The *City of Pekin,* with a capacity of 95 tons, was one of the best-documented canal boats. It was built in 1875 in Chicago probably without power, later converted to a steam barge, and finally rebuilt before the turn of the century for use on the Illinois River. The boat was abandoned on the canal at Channahon in 1936 and burned in 1941. Lamb, "Canal Boats on the Illinois and Michigan Canal," 220.

32. G. P. Brown, *Drainage Channel and Waterway* (Chicago, 1894), 67. Solzman, *Chicago River,* 225–229.

33. Harry Sinclair Drago, *Canal Days in America* (New York, 1972), 266–267.

34. *Annual Review of Trade and Commerce for St. Louis for 1848,* 7. James Neal Primm, *Lion of the Valley: St. Louis, Missouri* (Boulder, CO, 1981), 166, said the loss of traffic to the I & M Canal was not as great as Saint Louis merchants had feared. Drago, *Canal Days in America,* 266–267.

35. Bauer, *Maritime History of the United States,* 149.

## Chapter 4: Chicago's Rivals

1. Bauer, *Maritime History of the United States,* 151–160.

2. Vance, *Capturing the Horizon,* 104–105, and Ray Allen Billington, *Westward Expansion: A History of the American Frontier* (New York, 1949), 225–244, discuss the political intrigue involved with keeping the Lower Mississippi River open to U.S. shipping before the Louisiana Purchase.

3. Hunter, *Steamboats on the Western Rivers,* 218–219. 500-ton boats could use the Ohio an average of eight months a year in the 1850s.

4. Parkman, *Montcalm and Wolfe* (New York, 1983), 932–954.

5. Joseph S. Wood, "The Idea of a National Road," in *The National Road,* ed. Karl Raitz (Baltimore, MD, 1996), 113–114; Richard Wade, *The Urban Frontier: The Rise of Western Cities* (Cambridge, MA, 1959), 178–179.

6. Wade, *Urban Frontier,* 165–166, 179–180. Cochrane, *Pennsylvania: A Bicentennial History,* 117–142. Hunter, *Steamboats on the Western Rivers,* 106–107.

7. Shaw, *Canals for a Nation,* 229.

8. Carl W. Condit, *The Railroad and the City: A Technological and Urbanistic History of Cincinnati* (Columbus, OH, 1977), 5–99, discusses Cincinnati's ambitious canal- and railroad-building programs. Wade, *Urban Frontier,* 135–136, 185.

9. Shaw, *Canals for a Nation,* 133, 229, concluded that the Cincinnati-Dayton section of the canal was successful in that it encouraged development of southeastern Ohio. See also Billington, *Westward Expansion,* 342–343. Hadfield, *World Canals,* 310, attributes the building of the canal to political considerations.

10. Billington, *Westward Expansion,* 339.

11. Condit, *Railroad and the City,* 6–5.

12. Ibid., 19. By 1861 a chain of railroads built end to end through Indiana led to the start of a 276-mile through operation called the Chicago Short Line or Chicago Air Line between the two cities. Additional three railroad systems linking the two cities were built before the end of the century.

13. Primm, *Lion of the Valley,* 130. Saint Louis may have dominated the Rocky Mountain fur trade as late as the Civil War.

14. Primm, *Lion of the Valley,* 3–4, 113. Logan U. Reavis, *St. Louis, The Future Great City of the World* (Saint Louis, 1870).

15. Primm, *Lion of the Valley,* 139.

16. The steamboat *Zebulon Pike* was smaller than some keelboats in use at the time.

17. Primm, *Lion of the Valley,* 167; Hunter, *Steamboats of the Western Rivers,* 661 (table 24), citing *Western Journal* 2 (1849): 135; 3 (1850): 274; and 7 (1852): 267, and *Proceedings, Board of Supervising Inspectors.*

18. *Chicago Daily Democrat,* January 27, February 23, July 27, and August 23, 1849.

19. Wyatt Winton Belcher, *The Economic Rivalry between St. Louis and Chicago* (New York, 1947), 124, 160, 201.

20. Primm, *Lion of the Valley,* 166. See Hunter, *Steamboats on the Western Rivers,* 49 (table 2), and 661 (table 24), for these and subsequent data on steamboat traffic at Saint Louis.

21. Carlton J. Corliss, *Main Line of Mid America: The Story of the Illinois Central* (New York, 1950), 13–20, discusses Douglas's role in the land grant for the Illinois Central Railroad. Primm, *Lion of the Valley,* 214–215.

22. Belcher, *Economic Rivalry,* 89–91, 167–168. Eastern investment in the Hannibal and Saint Joseph was considerable, and John M. Forbes, the Boston financier who controlled the Burlington, also obtained control of the Hannibal line, making it an extension of the Burlington.

23. Cronon, *Nature's Metropolis,* 295–309.

24. Corliss, *Main Line of Mid America,* 99–104, 126–138.

25. Primm, *Lion of the Valley,* 233; and Belcher, *Economic Rivalry,* 139–157.

## Chapter 5: From Portage to Port

1. George W. Hilton, *Lake Michigan Passenger Steamers* (in press), 11 (manuscript), notes that

only the cities of Green Bay, WI, and Traverse City, MI, have what would be considered adequate natural harbors, because both are at the foot of major bays.

2. Andreas, *History of Chicago,* 1:240.

3. The length of Lake Michigan depends upon the points from which it is measured. Greenwood, *Guide to Great Lakes Shipping,* table 21-V, lists the distance from Old Mackinac Point, MI, to Gary, IN, as 336 miles. Ferdinand C. Lane, *World's Great Lakes* (Garden City, NY, 1945), 165, and Jack L. Hough, *Geology of the Great Lakes* (Urbana, IL, 1958), table 5, both place the length at 307 miles. William Ratigan, *Great Lakes Shipwrecks and Survivors* (Grand Rapids, MI, 1960), 15, notes that the lake's long history of disasters is attributable to its prevailing crosswinds, lack of harbors or refuge, and currents. Hilton, *Lake Michigan Passenger Steamers,* 19.

4. Andreas, *History of Chicago,* 1:240–241.

5. Hough, *Geology of the Great Lakes,* 50–54, citing 1942 and 1945 studies of water temperature by P. E. Church (The annual temperature cycle of Lake Michigan, 1: Cooling from late autumn to the terminal point, 1941–42, University of Chicago Institute of Meteorology, misc. reports, no. 4, 1942; and 2: The annual temperature cycle of Lake Michigan, University of Chicago Institute of Meteorology, misc. reports, no. 18, 1945), indicated the mid-July surface temperature of the lake was 65 to 72 degrees but dropped by 28 degrees at a depth of 70 feet. In spring, the water temperature is 39.2 degrees.

6. Patrick Lapinski, "The *E. M. Ford,*" *Inland Seas* 55 (1999): 91–95, discusses the condition of the cement boat *E. M. Ford,* which was launched in 1898 and still in commission in 1999. Richard Gebhart, "Still Working—a Grand Old Lady of the Lakes," *Inland Seas* 47 (1991): 257–264, noted that the *J. B. Ford,* which was built in 1904 as the *Edwin F. Holmes,* was still afloat and used as a floating cement silo in 1991. Bradley A. Rodgers, *Guardian of the Great Lakes* (Ann Arbor, MI, 1996), 4, 131, 136, discusses how an iron paddle-wheel frigate, the USS *Michigan,* was launched on Lake Erie in late 1843, made its final voyage in 1923 (after being renamed *Wolverine*), and was scrapped in 1949.

7. Hough, *Geology of the Great Lakes,* 35, gives the tide on Lake Michigan at 0.14 feet.

8. Ibid., 45.

9. Lane, *World's Great Lakes,* 159; and Hough, *Geology of the Great Lakes,* 49.

10. Hilton, *Lake Michigan Passenger Steamers,* 20 and 24–25, citing the *Holland City News* of February 15 and March 8, 1873.

11. Heise and Edgerton, *Chicago Center for Enterprise,* 1: 63–64, citing the *Chicago Daily Journal* of March 13, 1849.

12. Quaife, *Lake Michigan,* 114.

13. Quaife, *Lake Michigan,* 116, 119. The *Adams* earned the government $421.93 in charges for private freight, compared to $1,481.67 for hauling public property in 1807.

14. Cronon, *Nature's Metropolis,* xiii–xvii. Quaife, *Lake Michigan,* 149–150.

15. *Chicago Democrat,* July 20 and August 17, 1836.

16. *Chicago Democrat,* July 16, 1834. Mary Jane Judson Rice, *Chicago: Port to the World* (Chicago, 1969), 25; Harlan Hatcher, *The Great Lakes* (London, 1944), 208–211.

17. Andreas, *History of Chicago,* 2:240. The lighthouse collapsed before going into service and was rebuilt in 1832.

18. *Chicago Daily American,* September 10, 1841.

19. Lincoln, *Collected Works,* 1:480–490, contains his comments on the issue in his speech before the House of Representatives, June 20, 1848.

20. Andreas, *History of Chicago,* 2:73–74.

21. Theodore J. Karamanski, "The Marseilles of Lake Michigan," *Chicago History* 28, no. 3 (spring 2000): 47–50.

22. Putnam, *Illinois and Michigan Canal,* 161.

23. Solzman, *Chicago River,* 164. Edward Greer, *Big Steel: Black Politics and Corporate Power in Gary, Indiana* (New York, 1979), 54, notes that the high cost of downtown land—up to $3.5 million an acre in 1890—was a major factor in the decision by various heavy industries, like steel, to locate in the south Chicago area.

24. Pierce, *History of Chicago,* 2:114–116. Andreas, *History of Chicago,* 3:471–474.

25. *Chicago Tribune,* February 20, 1868, and January 3, 1869; Harold M. Mayer, *The Port of Chicago and the St. Lawrence Seaway* (Chicago, 1957), 13.

## Chapter 6: Schooners and the Reign of Sail

1. James L. Elliott, *Red Stacks over the Horizon* (Grand Rapids, MI, 1967), 27, 31–32. *Historical Collections of the Great Lakes,* master registry sheet of steamship *Comet* (Bowling Green, OH, 2000).

2. Morison, *Admiral of the Ocean Sea: A Life of Christopher Columbus* (Boston, 1942), 115–123. The *Pinta* and *Santa Maria* were rigged in *vela rondonda* (square sails) when Columbus acquired their services, but the *Nina* was rerigged from a *caravela latina* (lateen) configuration (large triangular sails on yards attached at their midpoint to the mast) to a square configuration in the Canary Islands after the 1492 voyage had begun.

3. MacLean, *Fate of The Griffon,* 39–45, concluded from a January 23, 1679, letter by La Salle referring to two masts on the ship (main and "mizaine," or "mizzen" in contemporary use) and examination of the vessel's supposed wreckage in 1955 at Russell Island in Lake Huron that it was a brigantine. Kenneth S. Atkins, "Le *Griffon:* A New View," *Inland Seas* 46, no. 3 (fall 1990): 162–169, upon reexamination of the evidence that the ship was a barque with foremast and mainmast.

4. David R. MacGregor, *The Schooner: Its Design and Development from 1600 to the Present* (London, 1997), 13–15.

5. Ibid., 19.

6. Baldwin, *Keelboat Age on Western Waters,* 159–163.

7. Ibid., 164–174.

8. Quaife, *Lake Michigan,* 100–105, 114, describes the *Adams* as a "snow," a contemporary term referring to a brig with a somewhat unusual sail configuration, but Andreas, *History of Chicago,* 2:240, said it was a schooner. The confusion may originate from the fact that the *Adams* was captured by the British in 1812 and may have been reconfigured.

9. Mansfield, *History of the Great Lakes,* 62–63, 185. Quaife, *Lake Michigan,* 115.

10. Franz Anton Ritter von Gerstner, *Early American Railroads* (Berkeley, CA, 1997), 415; originally published in Germany in 1842.

11. Mansfield, *History of the Great Lakes,* 428.

12. Andreas, *History of Chicago,* 2:242.

13. Mansfield, *History of the Great Lakes,* 439.

14. Robert Shipley and Fred Addis, *Schooners* (Saint Catherines, ON, Canada, 1991), 11.

15. Andreas, *History of Chicago,* 2:241. The Newberry steamer *Michigan* made it over the bar and into the river earlier in 1834, and the owners of the yacht *Westward Ho* had it dragged over the bar in 1833 by eight yoke of oxen.

16. The reuse of names on Great Lakes vessels was common. Three vessels bore the name *Dean Richmond,* including a two-masted schooner built in Cleveland in 1855 and destroyed later the same year in a storm 5 miles north of Racine, Wisconsin; a schooner built the next year that made the first trans-Atlantic trip from Chicago and was sold to British interests upon its arrival in Liverpool in 1856; and the wooden propeller built in 1864 and sunk in 1893 in a storm on Lake Erie near Dunkirk, New York, with a loss of twenty or twenty-one persons.

17. Mansfield, *History of the Great Lakes,* 191–192; Jacques LesStrang, *Cargo Carriers of the Great Lakes* (Boyne City, MI, 1985), 47–51.

18. Henry N. Barkhausen, *Great Lakes Sailing Ships* (Milwaukee, WI, 1947), 2; Hatcher, *Great Lakes,* 229.

19. *Denver Times,* November 27, 1911; *Manitowoc Herald,* December 1, 1911; *American Shipbuilder,* May 19, 1904.

20. Ship Information and Data Record, Herman G. Runge Collection at Milwaukee Public Library, Off. no. 4349.

21. *American Shipbuilder,* May 19, 1904.

22. Mansfield, *History of the Great Lakes,* 439. Gerstner, *Early American Railroads,* 415, 419.

23. Shipley and Addis, *Schooners,* 39, indicate that crews of five or six were common and that the cook, often a woman, was expected to assist in seafaring duties. Eloise Engle and Arnold S. Lott, *America's Maritime Heritage* (Annapolis, MD, 1975), 266. Large oceanic schooners by 1900 were operating with a crew of ten men, in contrast to one hundred required on a large square-rigged clipper ship. Gerstner, *Early American Railroads,* 415–424.

24. Mansfield, *History of the Great Lakes,* 440, citing data from the commissioner of the U.S. Bureau of Navigation.

25. Barkhausen, *Great Lakes Sailing Ships,* 2. Richard Palmer, "Men Who Sought Stone for Their Daily Bread," *Inland Seas* 47, no. 4 (winter 1991): 251–252. The crews of old schooners, using long poles, fished stones off the shallow bottom of Lake Ontario near the shore. The limestone was sold in Toronto for building foundations.

26. William Ratigan, *Great Lakes Shipwrecks and Survivors* (Grand Rapids, MI, 1960), 38–39, and Jay Gourley, *The Great Lakes Triangle* (Greenwich, CT, 1977), 58–60, provide accounts of the legend ranging from popular history (Ratigan) to the ludicrous (Gourley).

27. Fred Neuschel, *August and Herman Schuenemann: Tree Captains of Lake Michigan,* privately published (Algoma, WI, 1993), 8–15.

28. Ibid., 18–19.

29. Ibid., 21–23.

30. *Chicago Tribune,* November 11, 1897; and Ship Information and Data Record, Herman G. Runge Collection, Milwaukee Public Library, Off. no. 115781.

31. Neuschel, *August and Herman Schuenemann,* 26–27.

32. Herman G. Runge Collection, Milwaukee Public Library, Off. nos. 110024 and 110087. Estate of Herman Schuenemann, Cook County Probate Court, gen. no. 10115, docket 133, 20.

33. *Chicago Tribune,* November 23, 1913; November 28, 1914; December 6, 1921; November 30, 1923; December 13, 1934. Neuschel, *August and Herman Schuenemann,* 28–32.

34. Shipley and Addis, *Schooners,* 39–44.

35. LesStrang, *Cargo Carriers of the Great Lakes*, 14. Richard Palmer, *Inland Seas* 46, no. 2 (spring 1990): 6–9, indicates that the schooner *Lyman M. Davis* served during the 1931 season carrying cargo between Oswego and Kingston, Ontario, on Lake Ontario.

## Chapter 7: Traveling by Water

1. *Chicago Daily American,* November 6, 1841; *Chicago Democrat,* June 29, 1842.

2. *Daily Democrat,* November 10, 1847.

3. Henry Rowe Schoolcraft, *Travels Through the Northwestern Regions of the United States* (New York, 1925; cited here from reprint, Ann Arbor, MI, 1966), 378–394.

4. Charles Dickens, *American Notes for General Circulation* (London, 1842; cited here from New York, 1985, edition), 111, 113, 186–188, 190–193, 198, 200–201, 203, 216, 234, 239–242.

5. See Arthur Cunynghame, *A Glimpse at the Western Republic* (London, 1851), 76–77; and Carl Culmann, "Notes on a Journey to Belgium, France, England, Ireland and U.S.A. in 1848–50," Library of the Swiss Federal Institute of Technology, Zurich, in translation by Max A. Steinhaus in the Chicago Historical Society collection.

6. The captain may have been James J. Perry, who was an investor in and master of a 236-ton, Pittsburgh-built steamboat of that name. The vessel, which was used in the Pittsburgh-Cincinnati trade, was 172 feet long, 25 feet wide, and drew 5.7 feet of water. Dickens's fears of a boiler explosion proved unfounded. The *Messenger* was succeeded in 1849 by *Messenger 2,* which gained some degree of fame in 1851 when the showman P. T. Barnum and Jenny Lind attracted a crowd along the banks of the Ohio River during their trip on the vessel from Cincinnati to Pittsburgh. Frederick Way Jr., *Way's Packet Directory, 1848–1994* (Athens, OH, 1983), 319–320.

7. Lincoln, *Collected Works,* 1:6, 13, and 4:63.

8. Wayne C. Temple, *Lincoln's Connections with the Illinois and Michigan Canal, His Return from Congress in 1848, and His Invention* (Springfield, IL, 1986.)

9. Harry E. Pratt, ed., *Illinois as Lincoln Knew It: A Boston Reporter's Record of a Trip in 1847* (Springfield, IL, 1938) contains letters written by the Boston newspaper reporter J. H. Buckingham, who had covered the River and Harbor Convention, left for Saint Louis after the meeting closed, and accompanied Lincoln between Peoria and Springfield.

10. Temple, *Lincoln's Connections,* 26–27.

11. Lincoln, *Collected Works,* 4:143.

12. Temple, *Lincoln's Connections,* 41. The *Globe*'s return trip to Buffalo took six days.

13. Ibid., 41. Although there is no extant record of the canal trip, a reference in the October 7, 1848, *Chicago Daily Democrat* that "Hon. Abraham Lincoln, M.C., and his family *passed down* [emphasis mine] to Springfield this morning, on his way home from Congress" indicates to Temple the

trip was by canal. The term "passed" was common newspaper usage referring to travel by water. The remainder of the details of the trip was reconstructed by Temple from records of the activities on the canal and river in those days. It is known that Lincoln made a political speech in Peoria on October 9, 1848.

14. Rudyard Kipling, *American Notes: Rudyard Kipling's West* (Norman, OK, 1981), 48, 77, 129; originally published in a pirated edition in 1891.

15. Robert B. Shaw, *A History of Railway Accidents, Safety Precautions, and Operating Practices,* 2d ed. (Potsdam, NY, 1978), 61–64; and Helen Louise Plaster Stoutmeyer, *The Train That Never Arrived* (Fairbury, IL, 1970), 6–49. Stoutmeyer said the death toll may be understated because a number of victims were returned to their homes and died later of injuries.

16. Fred Whitlark, "The *Seeandbee* Remembered," *Inland Seas* 47, no. 1 (spring 1991): 2–15.

17. Greenwood, *Greenwood's Guide to Great Lakes Shipping,* 3-2, 3-3, 3-4.

18. Charles F. Conrad, owner of the Lake Michigan Carferry Service, interview by author, August 4, 1992; and cross-lake trip by the author aboard the *Badger,* August 5, 1992.

## Chapter 8: Disasters

1. Herman Melville, *Moby Dick or the White Whale* (New York, 1979), 223–224; originally published in 1851.

2. Hilton, *Eastland,* 134–136.

3. Hunter, *Steamboats on the Western Rivers,* 272, 287 (table), citing *Cist's Weekly Advertiser* (Cincinnati, OH), July 16, 1852; and S. Doc. 18, 30th Cong., 2d sess., 36–48.

4. *Baltimore Gazette,* November 10 and 14, 1837. *National Intelligencer,* November 10 and 15, 1837.

5. *Memphis Eagle,* January 30, 1851. *Louisville Courier,* January 31 and February 3, 1851. Hunter, *Steamboats on the Western Rivers,* 192–199, 273–274.

6. H. W. Humphrey and George W. Barrette, *The Columbia Disaster* (Peoria, IL, 1918), 3–16; privately published, collection of the Peoria Public Library.

7. Hunter, *Steamboats on the Western Rivers,* 278–279.

8. In contrast to the *Monmouth* disaster, which received very little attention in the press because few white persons were involved, the *Ben Sherrod* fire got nationwide coverage because of the reckless conduct of the *Ben Sherrod* and *Alton* captains and crews and entailed a subsequent public investigation in Memphis. Stories were carried in the *New Orleans True American* on May 11, 1837; the *Natchez Mississippi Free Trader* on May 18, the *Baltimore Gazette* on May 19, and the *Boston Daily Advertiser* on May 30. The *Baltimore Gazette* also carried stories on the *Monmouth* disaster on November 11 and 14, 1837. Hunter, *Steamboats on the Western Rivers,* 276–282.

9. Twain, *Life on the Mississippi,* 97–101.

10. Hunter, *Steamboats on the Western Rivers,* 521, 537, citing 1880 census data, which he opined are little more than an estimate based on newspaper accounts.

11. The *Sultana* explosion illustrates the difficulty of ascertaining the death toll by means of a body count in early maritime disasters, because many bodies were certainly washed downstream and never found or victims somehow managed to reach shore only to die undiscovered of their injuries. U.S. War Department, *War of Rebellion: A Compilation of the Official Records of Union and Confederate Armies* (Washington, DC, 1880–1901), ser. 1, vol. 48, part 1, p. 27. Brigadier General William Hoffman, the U.S. Army commissary general of prisoners, in his May 19, 1865, report estimated the number of dead at 1,238. Charles Hocking, *Dictionary of Disasters at Sea during the Age of Steam* (London: Lloyd's Registry, 1969), 266–267, puts the death toll at 1,653. Hunter, *Steamboats on the Western Rivers,* 543, places it at "more than 1,500." Frederick Way Jr., *Way's Packet Directory,* said the official custom record was 1,600 but the number was probably rounded. He used 1,547, with 1,100 of them soldiers. Jerry O. Potter, *Sultana Tragedy,* 131, said the death toll may have been as high as 1,800.

12. Potter, *Sultana Tragedy,* 51, 131, 141, citing, on p. 141, the *Memphis Daily Bulletin* of May 21, 1865.

13. Hunter, *Steamboats on the Western Rivers,* 529–533.

14. Ibid., 537–546.

15. Pierce, *History of Chicago,* 1:47; Dennis L. Noble, *A Brief History of U.S. Coast Guard Operations, Great Lakes* (Washington, 1989), 2.

16. Rodgers, *Guardian of the Great Lakes,* 48.

17. Noble, *Brief History,* 5–8. William Ratigan, *Great Lakes Shipwrecks and Survivors* (Grand Rapids, MI, 1969), 15, 68–69.

18. Ratigan, *Great Lakes Shipwrecks,* 43–49; Noble, *Brief History,* 9; Brendon Baillod, "The Wreck of the Steamer *Lady Elgin,*" *Great Lakes Shipwreck Research* (www.execpc.com/~bbaillod), *Lady Elgin,* 3–4.

19. Noble, *Brief History,* 9.

20. *Milwaukee Sentinel,* September 10, 1860; *Chicago Tribune,* September 10–14, 1860.

21. Baillod, "The Wreck of the Steamer *Lady Elgin,*" 2–3, 43–49.

22. Hilton, *Eastland,* 1–13. The Board of Trade's 1894 revisions to the Merchant Shipping Act required British-flag passenger vessels in excess of 10,000 tons to carry lifeboats with a capacity of 550 regular passengers and crew and an additional 400 if immigrants (steerage) were carried. The *Titanic's* licensed passenger capacity was 2,603, and she carried only 1,320 on her fateful maiden voyage.

23. Hilton, *Eastland,* 80–81.

24. *Chicago Tribune,* July 25–30 and August 1, 1915; *Chicago Evening Post,* July 26–29, 1915; *Chicago Examiner,* July 25, 1915; Hilton, *Eastland,* 46–53, 80–85.

25. Andreas, *History of Chicago,* 1:243.

26. *Chicago Tribune,* November 9, 1860. Temple, *Lincoln's Connections,* 87–88.

27. Richard F. Palmer, "Captain Joseph Gilson—Unsung Hero of the Chicago Fire," *Inland Seas* 55, no. 2 (summer 1999): 132–133. Mansfield, *History of the Great Lakes,* 659–660.

28. *Chicago Tribune,* April 11, 1868.

29. Ratigan, *Great Lakes Shipwrecks,* 51–53.

30. Ibid., 53–57, 195–200.

31. Andreas, *History of Chicago,* 1:243. Mansfield, *History of the Great Lakes,* 610–671. Robert J. Hemming, *Ships Gone Missing: The Great Lakes Storm of 1913* (Chicago, 1992), 5, 59–60.

32. Gourley, *Great Lakes Triangle,* 58–60. Neuschel, *August and Herman Schuenemann,* 31–34. Probate file of Herman Schuenemann, Circuit Court of Cook County, gen. no. 10115, docket 133, 20.

33. Dwight Boyer, *Ghost Ships of the Great Lakes* (New York, 1968), 176–188, 246–264.

34. CQD was the original wireless distress signal, dating from 1904 and standing for "all stations" (CQ) "distress" (D) but popularly interpreted to mean "Come Quickly Danger." In 1908 it was officially superceded as the international distress signal by SOS, sent in Morse Code as three dots, three dashes, and three dots, which was easier to transmit and interpret. The CQD and SOS signals were used interchangeably for years, and the *Titanic* in 1912 sent both just before she foundered. SOS has been superceded by "Mayday," from the French *M'aidez* (Help me), because it is more distinguishable over the voice radios that replaced the Morse wireless signals (Peter Kemp, *The Oxford Companion to Ships and the Sea* [Oxford, England, 1988]).

35. George W. Hilton, *The Great Lakes Car Ferries* (Berkeley, CA, 1962), 130–131, 262.

36. Boyer, *Ghost Ships of the Great Lakes,* 81–98; Hilton, *Great Lakes Car Ferries,* 178–179, 265; Ratigan, *Great Lakes Shipwrecks,* 41–42. The text of the message by the purser A. R. Sadon, verified as being in his handwriting, reads: "The ship is taking water fast. We have turned around and headed for Milwaukee. Pumps are working but sea gate is bent in and can't keep the water out. Flicker is flooded. Seas are tremendous. Things look bad."

37. Ratigan, *Great Lakes Shipwrecks,* 16–36.

38. Alida Malkus, *Blue-Water Boundary* (New York, 1960), 259–260.

## Chapter 9: Pirates

1. Mark Twain, *Adventures of Tom Sawyer* (New York, 1935), 324.

2. Ibid., 397.

3. Baldwin, *Keelboat Age on the Western Waters,* 14, 16, 116–117.

4. Otto A. Rothert, *The Outlaws of Cave-in-Rock* (Carbondale, IL, 1996), 317–318; originally published, Cleveland, OH, 1924.

5. Ibid., 43–44.

6. Ibid., 47, 176, 203–252. Baldwin, *Keelboat Age on the Western Waters,* 119–125.

7. *Springhouse* 6, no. 4 (August 1989), 27–34. Rothert, *Outlaws of Cave-in-Rock,* 49–51, 56, 60–94, 122, 246–257.

8. Baldwin, *Keelboat Age on the Western Waters,* 132–133, 172.

9. Cronon, *Nature's Metropolis,* 169–206. Putnam, *Illinois and Michigan Canal,* 102 n.

10. *Detroit Daily Free Press,* August 3, 1853. Rodgers, *Guardian of the Great Lakes,* 46–47.

11. Ibid., 48–54.

12. Lucille Kane, "Federal Protection of the Timber Trade in the Upper Great Lakes States," *Agricultural History* 23, no. 2 (April 1949): 136–139.

13. Milo Quaife, *The Kingdom of St. James* (New Haven, 1930), discusses Strang and his sect in some detail.

14. Richard Palmer, "Mormon Pirates of Beaver Island," *Inland Seas* 54, no. 3 (fall 1998): 195–198; Ratigan, *Great Lakes Shipwrecks,* 39, 40; John Gallagher, a retired Coast Guard lighthouse keeper at Saint James, Michigan, and witness to the *J. Oswald Boyd* explosion, interview by author, July 1999.

15. Paul G. Connors, "America's Emerald Isle: The Cultural Invention of the Irish Fishing Colony on Beaver Island, Michigan" (Ph.D. diss., Loyola University Chicago, 1999), 410–421.

16. Ibid., 85–103

17. Ibid., 98–102. Rodgers, *Guardian of the Great Lakes,* 71.

18. Quaife, *Lake Michigan,* 246–247; Rodgers, *Guardian of the Great Lakes,* 72–75.

19. Connors, "America's Emerald Isle," 108–12.

20. Rodgers, *Guardian of the Great Lakes,* 80–84. Theodore J. Karamanski, *Rally 'round the Flag* (Chicago, 1993), 214–223.

21. Rodgers, *Guardian of the Great Lakes,* 86–87.

22. Ibid., 87–90.

23. Ibid., 91.

24. Andreas, *History of Chicago,* 3:295; Connors, "America's Emerald Isle," 302–303.

25. Ibid., 311–312.

26. Ibid., 322–324.

27. Ibid., 324–327.

28. Ibid., 337–347.

29. Victoria Brehm, *Sweetwater, Storms, and Spirits* (Ann Arbor, MI, 1990), 146–147; Connors, "America's Emerald Isle," 373–377.

30. Richard F. Palmer, "The Rum Runners," *Inland Seas* 45, no. 4 (winter 1989): 247–248.

31. Kathleen Warnes, "Rumrunning on the Detroit River," *Inland Seas* 53, no. 3 (fall 1997): 170–177.

32. Stevenson Swanson, ed., *Chicago Days: 150 Defining Moments in the Life of a Great City* (Chicago, 1997), 50–51, is a short and amusing account.

## Chapter 10: Steam and Steel

1. John H. White Jr., *American Railroad Freight Car* (Baltimore, 1993), 70, 117–120.

2. Henry Hodges, *Technology in the Ancient World* (New York, 1970), 216; Bauer, *Maritime History of the United States,* 68–71; Hunter, *Steamboats on the Western Rivers,* 122–126.

3. Vance, *Capturing the Horizon,* 435–439.

4. Bauer, *Maritime History of the United States,* 68–71; Hunter, *Steamboats on the Western Rivers,* 122–126.

5. Hunter, *Steamboats on the Western Rivers,* 65–94.

6. Ibid., 167–170.

7. American Waterways Operators, *Big Load Afloat* (Washington, DC, 1965), 17; William J. Petersen, *Towboating on the Mississippi* (Cranbury, NJ, 1979), 77. Federal Barge Line's steam towboat *Illinois* was converted from stern-wheel to twin screws sometime before 1937.

8. Putnam, *Illinois and Michigan Canal,* 20–21.

9. Andreas, *History of Chicago,* 1:171; Heise and Edgerton, *Chicago: Center for Enterprise,* 56 n; John Lamb, "Canal Boats on the Illinois and Michigan Canal," 71, no. 3 (August 1978): 220.

10. Lamb, "Canal Boats on the Illinois and Michigan Canal," 220–223; Lamb, *The "City of Pekin" Story,* 1–5. The *City of Pekin* conformed to the standard I & M Canal boat size, 99 feet long and 17 feet wide.

11. Hilton, *Eastland,* 32–33.

12. Shipley, *Schooners,* 54–55; Barkhausen, *Great Lakes Sailing Ships,* 11.

13. Mansfield, *History of the Great Lakes,* 394, 439; Bauer, *Maritime History of the United States,* 186.

14. LesStrang, *Cargo Carriers of the Great Lakes,* 35.

15. Mansfield, *History of the Great Lakes,* 428; Elliott, *Red Stacks over the Horizon,* 27–31.

16. Whitlark, "The Seeandbee Remembered," 2–15; *Chicago Tribune,* October 24, 1943.

17. Bauer, *Maritime History of the United States,* 97, 99; Mansfield, *History of the Great Lakes,* 403.

18. LesStrang, *Cargo Carriers of the Great Lakes,* 38; Mansfield, *History of the Great Lakes,* 439 sqq (tables).

19. Barkhausen, *Great Lakes Sailing Ships,* 2; Mansfield, *History of the Great Lakes,* 404.

20. Quaife, *Lake Michigan,* 161–162.

21. Elliott, *Red Stacks over the Horizon,* 39–41.

22. Rodgers, *Guardian of the Great Lakes,* 20, 131–132.

23. Bauer, *Maritime History of the United States,* 95–96.

24. Mansfield, *History of the Great Lakes,* 412–413; Bauer, *Maritime History of the United States,* 95–96; LesStrang, *Cargo Carriers of the Great Lakes,* 25.

25. Bauer, *Maritime History of the United States,* 96; Rodgers, *Guardian of the Great Lakes,* 35.

26. Rodgers, *Guardian of the Great Lakes,* 17; Bauer, *Maritime History of the United States,* 96; LesStrang, *Cargo Carriers of the Great Lakes,* 25; Elliott, *Red Stacks over the Horizon,* 37.

27. LesStrang, *Cargo Carriers of the Great Lakes,* 25; Mansfield, *History of the Great Lakes,* 439 sqq (tables), citing U.S. Bureau of Navigation data.

28. Andreas, *History of Chicago,* 3:387, 471; Mansfield, *History of the Great Lakes,* 342.

29. Bauer, *Maritime History of the United States,* 198; LesStrang, *Cargo Carriers of the Great Lakes,* 38–45; Mansfield, *History of the Great Lakes,* 416.

30. Elliott, *Red Stacks over the Horizon,* 128–130.

31. LesStrang, *Cargo Carriers of the Great Lakes,* 53, 72.

32. Eric Hirisamaki, "The Hulett Story," *Inland Seas* 47, no. 2 (summer 1991): 82–95.

33. Cronon, *Nature's Metropolis,* 107–109.

34. Ibid., 112–113.

## Chapter 11: Sails or Rails?

1. John F. Stover, *American Railroads* (Chicago, 1961), 158.

2. Harold M. Mayer, "The Railway Pattern of Metropolitan Chicago" (Ph.D. diss., University of Chicago, 1943), 14.

3. Albro Martin, *Railroads Triumphant* (London, 1992), 240; Cronon, *Nature's Metropolis,* 60–61.

4. Putnam, *Illinois and Michigan Canal,* 23.

5. Andreas, *History of Chicago,* 2:246. The railroads were proposed between Vincennes and Saint Louis; Cairo, LaSalle, and Galena (the eventual Illinois Central); the Southern Cross from Alton to Mount Carmel and Shawneetown; the Northern Cross from Quincy to Springfield and Lafayette, Indiana; an Illinois Central branch to Terre Haute, Indiana; a Southern Cross branch to Belleville; Peoria to Warsaw on the Mississippi River; and Bloomington to Mackinaw, with a branch to Pekin. Howard, *Illinois,* 196–202; George M. McConnel, "Recollections of the Northern Cross Railroad," *Transactions of the Illinois State Historical Society* 13 (Springfield, IL, 1908): 145–152.

6. Andreas, *History of Chicago,* 1:247; H. Roger Grant, *The North Western: A History of the Chicago and North Western Railway System* (DeKalb, IL, 1996), 12–13.

7. W. H. Stennett, *Yesterday and To-day* (Chicago, 1905), 10, said that an estimate by Richard P. Morgan, the engineer hired by the Galena in 1847, put the cost of building to New Buffalo, Michigan, at $329,000. William B. Ogden, *Galena and Chicago Union Railroad Co. Annual Report of 1848,* 7, estimated the cost of the 41-mile line from Chicago to Elgin at $342,000. F. Howe, the Galena secretary and treasurer, noted on page 20 of the same annual report that the railroad had by April 1, 1848, obtained stock subscriptions (pledges) of $351,800, but only $20,817 in cash.

8. Alvin F. Harlow, *The Road of the Century: The Story of the New York Central* (New York, 1947), 220.

9. Ibid., 254. The Michigan Southern, founded in 1831 and only later to be known as the Lake Shore Railroad, gained access to the Illinois State Line by acquiring the dormant charter of the Northern Indiana Railroad that Ogden had sought in 1847 to extend his Galena and Chicago Union eastward. The Northern Indiana had originally been chartered in 1835 as the Buffalo and Mississippi Railroad with the intention of building a line from Maumee Bay (Toledo) to the Illinois River at La Salle, bypassing Chicago in the process.

10. Cronon, *Nature's Metropolis,* 82–83.

11. Harold Mayer and Richard C. Wade, *Chicago: Growth of a Metropolis* (Chicago, 1969) 28–30; *Railway Age,* July 12, 1889, 455; Slason Thompson, *A Short History of American Railroads* (Chicago, 1925), 217–218.

12. Charles Warren, *The Supreme Court in United States History* (Boston, 1922), 578–579; *Munn v Illinois,* 4 U.S. 113.

13. Condit, *Railroad and the City,* 19; Cronon, *Nature's Metropolis,* 112.

14. International Harvester Company, *Roots in Chicago,* centennial corporate history (Chicago, 1947), 12.

15. White, *American Railroad Freight Car,* 117; Hunter, *Steamboats on the Western Rivers,* 25.

16. Pierce, *History of Chicago,* 1:77 n. 7, citing *Hunt's Merchants' Magazine* 6 (February 1842), 189, and the *Chicago Democrat,* May 14, 1845; Temple, *Lincoln's Connections,* 39.

17. Hunter, *Steamboats on the Western Rivers,* 335–337; *Report of the Postmaster General,* 35th Cong., 1st sess., December 1, 1857, S. Doc. 2, 982–984.

18. Pierce, *History of Chicago,* 492 (table), citing the *Daily Democratic Press, Annual Review* (1852), 10–11. Chicago Board of Trade, *Second Annual Statement* (Chicago, 1859), 83–104.

19. Chicago Board of Trade, *Second Annual Statement,* 83–104.

20. U.S. Department of Transportation, *America's Highways 1776–1976: A History of the Federal Aid Program* (Washington, DC, 1976), 12; Stover, *American Railroads,* 34.

21. Thompson, *Short History of American Railways,* 45–47; Vance, *Capturing the Horizon,* 125–128; Harry Sinclair Drago, *Canal Days in America* (New York, 1972), 249.

22. Andreas, *History of Chicago,* 1:148–149.

23. Putnam, *Illinois and Michigan Canal,* 104–113, 110–112, 115–116. The canal's trade in 1850 included 417,000 bushels of wheat, 318,000 bushels of corn, and 5.7 million pounds of sugar, all primarily eastbound, and 10.4 million pounds of merchandise and 38.7 million board feet of lumber predominantly westbound.

24. Putnam, *Illinois and Michigan Canal,* 112; Lamb, "Canal Boats on the Illinois and Michigan Canal," 220–221.

25. White, *American Railroad Freight Car,* 172.

26. Putnam, *Illinois and Michigan Canal,* 115–116.

27. Corliss, *Main Line of Mid America,* 58, 173–175.

28. Petersen, *Towboating on the Mississippi,* 9; Hunter, *Steamboats on the Western Rivers,* 547–561, 564, 662 (table 25).

29. Hunter, *Steamboats on the Western Rivers,* 561–567, 570–571, 661 (table 24).

30. White, *American Railroad Freight Car,* 173; Hunter, *Steamboats on the Western Rivers,* 580.

31. White, *American Railroad Freight Car,* 29.

32. Everett Chamberlin, *Chicago and Its Suburbs* (Chicago, 1874), 279–292 (tables); Cronon, *Nature's Metropolis,* 97–206, discusses the Chicago lumber and grain trade in detail. Martin, *Railroads Triumphant,* 168; Andreas, *History of Chicago,* 1:73–74 (table).

33. Mansfield, *History of the Great Lakes,* 530. Chamberlin, *Chicago and Its Suburbs,* 279–292 (tables).

34. Chicago Board of Trade, *Fourteenth Annual Report,* 87–109.

35. Andreas, *History of Chicago,* 3:387, 471–475.

36. L. Klein, "Notes on Steam Navigation upon the Northern Great Lakes," *Inland Seas* 48, no. 1 (spring 1992): 55–58 (reprinted from *American Railway Journal,* May 15 and June 1, 1841); Mansfield, *History of the Great Lakes,* 397.

37. Mansfield, *History of the Great Lakes,* 408.

38. Mansfield, *History of the Great Lakes,* 408.

39. Michael Krieger, *Where Rails Meet the Sea* (New York, 1998), 57–61.

40. Krieger, *Where Rails Meet the Sea,* 64–67.

41. George W. Hilton, *The Great Lakes Car Ferries* (Berkeley, CA, 1962), 1–3, 55–71.

42. Karl Zimmermann, *Lake Michigan's Railroad Car Ferries* (Andover, NJ, 1993), 19–28, indicates that by the time the Chesapeake and Ohio, on March 18, 1975, petitioned the Interstate Commerce Commission to abandon service, its car ferry fleet had been reduced from eight ships to three and was losing $4 million a year. Krieger, *Where Rails Meet the Sea,* 76–83.

## Chapter 12: The San, Cal-Sag, and Hennepin

1. Vance, *Capturing the Horizon,* 41, 46–49.

2. U.S. Army Corps of Engineers, *Waterborne Commerce of the United States,* part 3, *Waterways and Harbors, Great Lakes, Port of Chicago,* 12.

3. Ronald Tweet, "The Continuing Journey of the Hennepin Canal," in *The Illinois and Mississippi Canal: History of the Rock Island District Corps of Engineers, 1866–1975,* internal report of the U.S. Army Corps of Engineers, Rock Island, IL (undated reprint by the Illinois Department of Natural Resources), 2.

4. "Distances on the Hennepin Canal," mileage chart in the files of the Hennepin Canal Parkway State Park, Sheffield, IL.

5. Tweet, "Continuing Journey of the Hennepin Canal," 4–5.

6. Judi Jacksohn, "What the Census Revealed in Bureau County," undated monograph in the files of the Hennepin Canal Parkway State Park, Sheffield, IL, 1, 19; Putnam, *Illinois and Michigan Canal,* 161–162.

7. Hunter, *Steamboats on the Western Rivers,* 82–83, 573; Joy Morton, president of Morton Salt Company, letter to Lieutenant Colonel W. V. Johnson, U.S. Army Corps of Engineers, November 15, 1915.

8. G. P. Brown, *Drainage Channel and Waterway* (Chicago, 1894), 276–277.

9. Lamb, "Canal Boats on the Illinois and Michigan Canal," 220–221; Brown, *Chicago Drainage Channel and Waterway,* 67, 232–241.

10. Pierce, *History of Chicago,* 2:329–332.

11. Donald L. Miller, *City of the Century* (New York, 1996), 427–430; Brown, *Chicago Drainage Channel and Waterway,* 20–21.

12. Ray Ginger, *Altgeld's America* (New York, 1958), 76; Miller, *City of the Century,* 428.

13. Swanson, *Chicago Days,* 76–77; Miller, *City of the Century,* 427–430.

14. Solzman, *Chicago River,* 33–34, 53.

15. Emily J. Harris, "Meeting of the Waters," *Chicago History* 27, no. 3 (winter 1998–1999), 37; City of Chicago, *Straightening of the Chicago River* (Chicago, 1926), 9–10. The straightening, which had been suggested by Daniel Burnham in his master plan for the city, involved digging a new channel 850 feet west of the bend, diverting the river into it, and filling in the old channel.

16. Solzman, *Chicago River,* 48–52; *Chicago Tribune,* September 22, 1926.

17. Tweet, "Continuing Journey," 2–3; Brown, *Chicago Drainage Channel and Waterway,* 276–277, 288.

18. U.S. Army Corps of Engineers, *Illinois Waterway* (Washington, DC, 1979), brochure.

19. Michael C. Robinson, "History of Navigation in the Ohio River Basin," in U.S. Army Corps of Engineers, *National Waterways Study* (Washington, DC, 1983), 28.

20. See U.S. Army Corps of Engineers Water Resources Support Center, *National Waterways Study: A Framework for Decision Making,* final report (Washington, DC, 1993), D-197, for dimensions of the Illinois Waterway; and Illinois Department of Transportation, Division of Water Resources, *The Barge Transportation System Serving Illinois* (Chicago, 1990), 1, for data on barges.

21. *Waterways Journal* 46, no. 9 (May 27, 1933).

22. Illinois Department of Transportation, *Illinois Waterborne Shipping Database 1991,* 35, 44, 54; and *Illinois Waterborne Commerce Statistics 1995,* 31.

23. U.S. Army Corps of Engineers, *Waterborne Commerce of the United States,* part 3, *Waterways and Harbors, Great Lakes, Port of Chicago, Sanitary and Ship Canal,* 1933, 1946, 1955, 1970.

24. Mayer, *Port of Chicago,* 21–22.

25. Ibid., 169.

26. Data calculated from U.S. Army Corps of Engineers, *Waterborne Commerce of the United States,* part 3, *Waterways and Harbors, Great Lakes, Port of Chicago, Sanitary and Ship Canal, and Calumet Sag Channel,* 1964, 1970, 1994, 1996. The data were recalculated to eliminate double counting of shipping using both canals.

## Chapter 13: The River Renaissance

1. Paul W. MacAvoy and John W. Snow, eds., *Railroad Revitalization and Regulatory Reform,* American Enterprise Institute for Public Policy Research report (Washington, DC, 1977), 20, 115–148, includes an admission by the U.S. Transportation Department that federal transportation policies after World War II were "unbalanced" in favor of waterways and motor trucks and against railroads. Jesse J. Friedman and Associates, *Federal Aid to Railroads,* 3 vols., (Washington, DC, 1978–1980); Friedman was commissioned by the Water Transport Association and American Waterways Operators during the time Congress was considering railroad deregulation to show how the railroads had already benefited from government subsidies. Glover Wilkins, "It Took a Lot of Politicking to Keep the Tenn-Tom Afloat," *Waterways Journal* 102, no. 13 (June 29, 1987): 21, 36, 46, is an account of the lobbying for and against the waterway.

2. Donald C. Sweeney, affidavit of February 2, 2000, filed with Office of Special Counsel, U.S. Department of Defense, Washington, DC; *Saint Louis Post Dispatch,* "One economist traded security for uncertainty when he blew the whistle on an Army Corps of Engineers Study," March 19, 2000; *Chicago Tribune,* "Army Engineers defend lengthening river locks," October 31, 2000; *Washington Post,* "Review set with industry in mind," February 24, 2000; Izaak Walton League, National Audubon Society, National Wildlife Federation, Sierra Club, and Taxpayers for Common Sense, joint press release, Washington, DC, February 14, 2000. Office of Special Counsel, U.S. Department of Defense, Washington, DC, press release, December 6, 2000.

3. Donald F. Wood and James C. Johnson, *Contemporary Transportation,* 5th ed. (Upper Saddle River, NJ, 1996), 39–42, gives a concise summary of government subsidy policy of the various transportation modes.

4. Eno Transportation Foundation, *Transportation in America 1997* (Lansdowne, VA, 1997), 11 (domestic intercity ton-miles by mode). In 1996 rails handled 40 percent; trucks, 27.7 percent; oil pipelines, 17.7 percent; Great Lakes and rivers 14.2 percent; and air 0.4 percent.

5. *Pennsylvania v Wheeling and Belmont Bridge Co.,* 13 How. 518; Warren, *Supreme Court in United States History,* 2:234–236.

6. Martin, *Railroads Triumphant,* 327, summarizes the railroad's account of the incident. Primm, *Lion of the Valley,* 294, discusses the steamboat industry's version. Albert Beveridge, *Abraham Lincoln: 1809–1858* (Boston, 1928), 1:598–605; and John J. Duff, *A. Lincoln: Prairie Lawyer* (New York, 1960), 332–345, give accounts of the trial based on Chicago and Saint Louis newspaper clippings. The official record was destroyed in the 1871 Chicago fire. Duff identified the boy who assisted Lincoln as Benjamin Brayton Jr., the son of the railroad's bridge engineer, but also suggested Lincoln hired a local steamboat to test the currents by passing back and forth beneath the bridge.

7. Beveridge, *Abraham Lincoln,* 603.

8. Howard, *Illinois,* 362–364, 370–371; John F. Stover, *American Railroads* (Chicago, 1961), 127–131. Wood and Johnson, *Contemporary Transportation,* 45–59, give a summary of government regulatory policy in the nineteenth and twentieth centuries.

9. Chicago Board of Trade, *Second Annual Statement* (Chicago, 1859), 83–104, and *Fourteenth Annual Report* (Chicago, 1871), 86–109; John H. White Jr., *American Railroad Freight Car,* 24, 68, 137.

10. Floyd M. Clay, *History of Navigation on the Lower Mississippi,* U.S. Army Corps of Engineers, *National Waterway Study* (Washington, DC, 1983), 26–27; L. P. Struple, "From Sternwheelers to Props, Steam to Diesel," *Waterways Journal* 101, no. 13 (June 29, 1987): 82 (excerpt from a 1967 presentation to the U.S. Senate Surface Transportation Subcommittee); Hunter, *Steamboats on the Western Rivers,* 567–574.

11. Frederick Way Jr., "Remembering the Ups and Downs of the 1900s," *Waterways Journal* 102, no. 13 (June 29, 1987): 15.

12. Michael C. Robinson, *History of Navigation in the Ohio River Basin,* U.S. Army Corps of Engineers, *National Waterway Study,* Washington, DC, 1983, 28–29; Putnam, *Illinois and Michigan Canal,* 142, 162–163. Tons transported on the I & M were 1901—81,456; 1902—35,824; 1903—62,894;

1904—47,616; 1905—38,820; 1906—35,480; 1907—80,616; 1908—312,500; 1909—352,600; 1910—374,500.

13. Susan Howarth Eastman, "An Overview to Inland Waterways Transportation," *Waterways Journal* 102, no. 13 (June 29, 1987): 10; Robinson, *History of Navigation*, 26–29; Charles F. Lehman, "Many Believe Rail/Barge Merger for the Best," *Waterways Journal* 102, no. 13 (June 29, 1987): 22.

14. White, *American Railroad Freight Car*, 104, 113; Martin, *Railroads Triumphant*, 354–358.

15. *Chicago Tribune*, "That Throttling Town," October 26, 1997, transportation sec., and "Rare Birds," November 29, 1998, transportation sec.

16. Stover, *American Railroads*, 183–190.

17. William Havighurst, *Voices on the River: The Story of the Mississippi Waterways* (New York, 1914), 259. Peter Fanchi Jr., "FBL: A Barge Line Whose Time Had Arrived," *Waterways Journal* 102, no. 13 (June 29, 1987): 44, 47. Eastman, "An Overview to Inland Waterways Transportation" 28.

18. Fanchi, "FBL: A Barge Line Whose Time Had Arrived," 44.

19. Way Jr., "Remembering the Ups and Downs of the 1900s," 15. Eastman, "An Overview to Inland Waterways Transportation" 31, 35.

20. Fanchi, "FBL: A Barge Line Whose Time Had Arrived," 44.

21. Struple, "From Sternwheelers to Props," 82.

22. *Waterways Journal* 102, no. 13 (April 16, 1898; reprint, June 29, 1987): 126; Haskell Green, captain of the *Crescent City*, interview by author aboard the towboat on the Illinois River at Utica, IL, October 28, 1980; Struple, "From Sternwheelers to Props," 82.

23. Robinson, "History of Navigation," 38 (profile of Ohio River navigation pools). The Ohio River required twenty dams to create a navigation channel between Pittsburgh and Cairo. U.S. Army Corps of Engineers, "A Framework for Decision Making," *National Waterways Study*, final report (Washington, DC, 1993), app. D, 203–208. The entire Ohio River system, which includes the tributary Allegheny (eight), Monongahela (nine), Kanawha (three), Kentucky (fourteen), Green (three), and Cumberland (four) Rivers, but not the Tennessee River (ten), collectively has a total of sixty-three dams.

24. U.S. Army Corps of Engineers, *National Waterways Study*, final report, app. D, 183–188, 196–198.

25. *Chicago Tribune*, October 14, 1978, and October 24, 1979; John W. Lambert, "Locks and Dam 26 Was Focal Point of Conflict," *Waterways Journal* 102, no. 13 (June 29, 1987): 77, 81.

26. Illinois Department of Transportation, *Illinois Waterborne Commerce Statistics, 1970–1995* (Chicago, 1997), 29, 31.

27. *Chicago Tribune*, July 25, 1953; Fanchi, "FBL: A Barge Line Whose Time Had Arrived," 44; Eastman, "An Overview of Inland Waterways Transportation," 58, 62.

28. Petersen, *Towboating on the Mississippi*, 97, 174–181.

29. *Chicago Tribune*, April 10, 1949.

30. Marvin J. Barloon, *Water Transportation: Productivity and Policy* (Washington, DC: National Environmental Development Association, 1978), 8–9, 12–13. There is considerable disagreement by the barge and railroad industries over the relative cost efficiencies of their modes, although there is general agreement that barges are cheaper. Barloon states that, based on calculations he made in 1976, the rule of thumb is that barges can haul the same freight for a quarter of the cost of railroads and a twentieth of the cost of motor trucks (8–9). On the other hand, the railroad industry claims that the cost advantage of barges would be considerably less if the industry had to absorb the capital costs of the navigation system, including the locks and dams, which is heavily subsidized by the federal government.

## Chapter 14: Decline of the Great Lakes

1. Gary S. Dewar, "The Pittsburgh Supers," *Inland Seas* 48, no. 1 (spring 1992): 2–19; LesStrang, *Cargo Carriers of the Great Lakes*, 67–71; *Greenwood's Guide to Great Lakes Shipping* (1995), 1-4 to 1-24.

2. Anthony J. Watts, *Japanese Warships of World War II* (New York, 1967), 31; Greenwood, *Greenwood's Guide to Great Lakes Shipping*, 5–6; and C. E. Tripp and G. H. Plude, "One-Thousand-Foot Great Lakes Self-Unloader: Erie Marine Hull 101" (paper presented to Great Lakes and Rivers Section of the Society of Naval Architects and Marine Engineers, January 21, 1971, 4), who give the following dimensions for the 1971 thousand-footer *Stewart J. Cort* and the battleship *Yamato*:

| Ship | Overall Length | Beam | Draft | Displacement* (loaded) |
|------|------|------|-------|----------------|
| *Stewart J. Cort* | 1,000' | 104'7 1/4" | 27'10" | 68,330 tons |
| *Yamato* | 863' | 127 3/4' | 35 1/2' | 71,659 tons |

*Displacement is the weight of the water displaced by the ship's hull when fully loaded.

3. Hatcher, *Great Lakes,* 328–329; LesStrang, *Cargo Carriers of the Great Lakes,* 16; *Rouse Simmons,* Ship Information and Data Record, Herman G. Runge Collection, Milwaukee Public Library, Off. nos. 110024, 110087.

4. LesStrang, *Cargo Carriers of the Great Lakes,* 16, 27, 38–44. Peter Van Der Linden, *Great Lakes Ships We Remember* (Cleveland, 1984), 2:104–105, gives the dimensions of the whaleback steamer John Erickson, built in 1856, as length 390 feet, beam 48.2 feet, draft 22 feet, with a gross registered tonnage of 3,200 tons. Greenwood, *Greenwood's Guide to Great Lakes Shipping* (1995), 2–9, identified the *E. M. Ford,* a cement boat, as the oldest registered ship on the Great Lakes and gave its dimensions (overall length, beam, and draft in feet) as 428 by 50 by 21.

5. LesStrang, *Cargo Carriers of the Great Lakes,* 50; *Canals of the United States and Canada,* part 4, chap. 1.

6. Lake Carriers Association, *Annual Report* (Cleveland, OH, 1910), 4–7.

7. LesStrang, *Cargo Carriers of the Great Lakes,* 57–58.

8. Ibid., 131–133.

9. Greenwood, *Greenwood's Guide to Great Lakes Shipping* (1995), 8-4-5 (vessel longevity table).

10. Ibid., 137, 151.

11. Robert A. Bludworth, president of Marine Specialities Company, Friendswood, Texas, interview by author, July 7, 1997; Robert Hill, marine architect of Ocean Tug and Barge Engineering, interview by author, July 8, 1997; Jeffrey N. Covinsky, president of Hannah Marine Corporation, interview by author, July 7, 1997; *American Tugboat Review* (1997): 15–20.

12. Rick Tammaro, port engineer for Amoco Corporation's Coastwide Trading Company, Texas City, Texas, interview by author, August 8, 1997.

13. Covinsky, interview.

14. *Chicago Tribune,* August 14, 1997; Greenwood, *Greenwood's Guide to Great Lakes Shipping,* 4-3 (table); George W. Hilton, *Great Lakes Car Ferries,* 264; Michael C. Caliendo, director of operations of Andrie, Muskegon, Michigan, interview by author aboard the *Integrity-Jacklyn M.* on Lake Michigan between Milwaukee and Chicago, August 5, 1997.

15. George W. Hilton, *Lake Michigan Passenger Steamers* (in press) is a detailed account of the Lake Michigan packet industry.

16. Hilton, *Eastland,* 63–80; Hilton, *Lake Michigan Passenger Steamers,* 59–60, 80–81.

17. Elliott, *Red Stacks over the Horizon,* 17–18.

18. Hilton, *Lake Michigan Passenger Steamers,* 157; Elliott, *Red Stacks over the Horizon,* 39–45, 112, 166–167.

19. Elliott, *Red Stacks over the Horizon,* 166–167, makes the claim that the Goodrich line by 1900 did a larger volume of passenger business than any shipping company on the Great Lakes.

20. Ibid., 213–214, quoting Albert W. Goodrich, dates the beginning of the decline of lake passenger service to the passage of La Follette's act. Hilton, *Lake Michigan Passenger Steamers,* 207–242, blames much of the decline on the development of the motor truck and automobile.

21. Ibid., 276–280. The Goodrich Transit Company's ships were sold for a fraction of the remaining balances on their mortgages.

22. Fred Whitlark, "Seeandbee Remembered," 2–15.

23. Richard H. Braun, "The Georgian Bay Line," *Inland Seas* 54, no. 3 (fall 1998): 175–183.

24. Chicago, Duluth and Georgian Bay Transit Company's consolidated financial statement for the year ended December 31, 1940; *Jane's Fighting Ships* (London, 1944–45), 507.

25. Nancy A. Schneider, "The Magnificent Noronic," *Inland Seas* 52, no. 4 (winter 1996): 241–249; E. J. Goebel, president of the Chicago, Duluth and Georgian Bay Transit Company, letters to stockholders, September 29 and November 1, 1967, and January 18 and February 9, 1968.

26. American Classic Voyages Company, form 10K filed with the U.S. Securities and Exchange Commission for the year ending December 31, 1998, 3.

27. Delta Queen Steamboat Company, stock prospectus filed with the U.S. Securities and Exchange Commission (SEC), March 12, 1992, 40, 47; American Classic Voyages Company, stock prospectus filed with the SEC, April 22, 1999, 32; American Classic Voyages Company, form 10K filed with the SEC for the year ending December 31, 1999, 7.

28. American Classic Voyages Company, form 10K filed with the SEC for the year ending December 31, 1998, 6–7, and December 31, 1999, 7, 21. The company reported the following financial data to the SEC in 1999 (in thousands of dollars):

|                     | 1999      | 1998    | 1997    | 1996     | 1995    |
|---------------------|-----------|---------|---------|----------|---------|
| Revenues            | 208,717   | 192,225 | 177,884 | 190,408  | 188,373 |
| **Net income (loss)** | **(1.750)** | **157** | **2,429** | **(17,636)** | **(9,671)** |

29. Kristen Malley, investor relations representative, Nicor, letter to author, May 8, 2000; "History of Tropical Shipping" (May 15, 2000), www.tropical.com/about/history.htm; Nicor, form 10K filed with the SEC for the year ending December 31, 1999, 4, 13–19.

30. Ralph C. Epstein, *GATX: A History of the General American Transportation Corp., 1898–1948* (New York, 1948), 1–5, 92, 174–175. GATX is the abbreviated version of General American Tank Car Corporation formed in 1916 when the firm began selling stock to the public. The X in the name is the symbol used by railroads to identify cars they do not own.

31. American Steamship Company, report published by the company (Buffalo, NY, ca. 1998), 3–4; GATX Corporation, annual report to shareholders (1994), 20–23.

32. Deadweight tonnage is the cargo capacity of a vessel measured in tons of 2,240 pounds when loaded to its freeboard capacity.

33. *American Steamship Company Vessel Service Data* (Buffalo, NY, 1994); GATX Corporation, form 10K filed with SEC for the year ending December 31, 1997, 3; *A History of American Steamship Co.* (Buffalo, NY, undated), 4–5.

34. "Hannah Marine Corporation: Forty-five Years of Service," *Seaway Review* 22, no. 2 (1993): 15–17.

## Chapter 15: Chicago's Lost Opportunities

1. Illinois Department of Transportation, *Illinois Waterborne Commerce Statistics 1970–1995* (Chicago, 1997), 64–72, gives tonnages of goods shipped from Chicago and Saint Louis (in parens.) as follows:

1970—50,806,000 (21,784,000); 1975—45,184,000 (26,073,000); 1980—35,501,000 (28,189,000); 1984—25,895,000 (30,910,000); 1985—24,204,000 (30,445,000); 1990—25,392,000 (34,745,000); 1995—28,344,000 (38,611,000).

2. U.S. Army Corps of Engineers, *Waterborne Commerce of the United States,* part 3, *Waterways and Harbors, Great Lakes* (Washington, DC, 1990), 26–29.

3. Army Corps of Engineers, *Waterborne Commerce of the United States,* part 3, *Waterways and Harbors, Great Lakes* (Washington, DC, 1997), Port of Chicago, Table of Freight Traffic, 11–12.

4. Malkus, *Blue-Water Boundary* (New York, 1960), 257; Greenwood, *Greenwood's Guide to Great Lakes Shipping* (1997), 1–24.

5. *Chicago Tribune,* April 10, 1949, business sec.

6. Hatcher, *Great Lakes,* 358; *Chicago Tribune,* "One-hundred-first Street Shipyard set to close after ninety years," November 4, 1981, business sec.

7. Mayer, *Port of Chicago,* 14; Chicago Harbor Commission, *Report to the Mayor and Aldermen of the City of Chicago* (Chicago, 1909).

8. Mayer, *Port of Chicago,* 17.

9. Ibid., 221–226.

10. Elliott, *Red Stacks over the Horizon,* 213–214; *Chicago Tribune,* November 29, 1998, transportation sec.; Albert Mroz, *The Illustrated Encyclopedia of American Trucks and Commercial Vehicles*

(Iola, WI, 1996), 219–220; Hilton, *Lake Michigan Passenger Steamers,* 207–208.

11. *Chicago Tribune,* "Cruise ship operator may revive Great Lakes voyages," September 15, 1998, business sec.

12. *Chicago Tribune,* "Tug plus barge is more than a ship," August 14, 1997, business sec.; Greenwood, *Greenwood's Guide to Great Lakes Shipping* (1997), 6–2; Quebec and Ontario Transportation Company press releases, December 21, 1983, and January 24, 1984.

13. Daniel Injerd, Illinois Department of Natural Resources, letter to Al Ames, Great Lakes regional director of U.S. Maritime Administration, December 30, 1997, attachment 6.

14. Solzman, *Chicago River,* 164–165.

15. Arend Van Vlissengen, *Report on a Plan for the Construction of a Harbor at Lake Calumet, Chicago, and the Public Need of Such a Harbor* (Chicago, 1920).

16. Mayer, *Port of Chicago,* 179–188.

17. Ibid., 179–188.

18. Bauer, *Maritime History of the United States,* 202–203.

19. Andreas, *History of Chicago,* 2:243; LesStrang, *Cargo Carriers of the Great Lakes,* 27; Rodgers, *Guardian of the Great Lakes,* 83.

20. Mayer, *Port of Chicago,* 58–59; LesStrang, *Cargo Carriers of the Great Lakes,* 47–51.

21. U.S. Army Corps of Engineers, *Waterborne Commerce of the United States,* part 3, *Waterways and Harbors, Great Lakes* (Washington, DC, 1955, 1959), Port of Chicago, Table of Freight Traffic, 69–74; Mayer, *Port of Chicago,* 60–67.

22. Rene de Kerchove, *International Maritime Dictionary* (New York, 1948), 107. The standard class of vessels known as *C-2* was designed by the U.S. Maritime Commission at 459 feet long, a beam of 63 feet, and a loaded draft of 25 feet.

23. Malkus, *Blue-Water Boundary,* 258–291.

24. U.S. Army Corps of Engineers, *Waterborne Commerce of the United States,* part 3, *Waterways and Harbors, Great Lakes,* Port of Chicago, Table of Freight Traffic (1965), 26–56; (1990), 2–13.

25. Illinois Department of Transportation, Division of Natural Resources, *Illinois Waterborne Commerce Statistics, 1970–1995,* 64.

26. *Chicago Tribune,* "Trickling down: Great Lakes shipping loses steam," October 25, 1992, business sec.; Bauer, *Maritime History of the United States,* 202–204; U.S. Department of Transportation, Saint Lawrence Seaway Development Corporation (Washington, DC), traffic tonnage tables from annual reports for the years 1978–1998. Data for 1999 were estimated.

27. Illinois Department of Transportation, *Illinois Waterborne Shipping Database 1991* (Chicago, 1991), 17 (table 7), 26 (table 16).

28. *Chicago Tribune,* "Trickling down: Great Lakes shipping loses steam," October 25, 1992, business sec.

29. Illinois Department of Transportation, *Illinois Waterborne Commerce Statistics, 1970–1995,* 62–63; Saint Lawrence Seaway Authority, *The St. Lawrence Seaway Traffic Report, 1991 Navigation Season* (Washington, DC, 1991), 14 (table of traffic by origin and destination).

30. Illinois Department of Transportation, *Illinois Waterborne Shipping Database 1991,* 36 (table 26), 37 (table 27), 41 (table 32).

31. *Chicago Tribune,* "Trickling down: Great Lakes shipping loses steam"; John R. Dobrzynski, manager of transportation of the Board of Trade, Chicago, interview by author, August 18, 1992; James A. Johnson, chief of ports management section of Illinois Department of Transportation, Chicago, interview by author, August 17, 1992; Robert L. Gardner, vice president and general manager of Conticarriers and Terminals, Chicago, interview by author, August 21, 1992.

32. William D. Middleton, *North Shore: America's Fastest Interurban* (San Marino, CA, 1964), 93–95; Bauer, *Maritime History of the United States,* 316–318; Twain Braden, "Maritime Milestones," *American Ship Review* (Portland, ME), no. 38 (1998): 80.

33. *Chicago Tribune,* May 14 and 15, 1978.

34. *Chicago Tribune,* August 11, 16, 17, 1885; June 4, 1987.

35. Association of American Railroads, *Railroad Facts* (Washington, 1999), 29; Belt Railroad Company of Chicago, *Chicago Terminal Assessment Study,* 2d ed. (Chicago, 1997–1998), train/engine operations summary table (n.p.).

# Bibliography

The following is a list of hardbound publications in general circulation, government reports widely circulated, and significant research by scholars on various transportation topics. Statistical summaries, periodicals, and unpublished studies are generally cited in the notes.

Alvord, Clarence Walworth. *The American West: The Illinois Country, 1673–1818*. Chicago, 1965.

American Waterways Operators. *Big Load Afloat*. Washington, DC, 1965.

Andreas, A. T. *History of Chicago from the Earliest Period to the Present Time*. 3 vols. Chicago, 1884.

———. *A History of Cook County, Illinois, from the Earliest Period to the Present Time*. Chicago, 1884.

Andrews, Wayne. *Battle for Chicago*. New York, 1946.

Baldwin, Leland D. *The Keelboat Age on the Western Waters*. Pittsburgh, 1941.

Balesi, Charles J. *The Time of the French in the Heart of North America*. Chicago, 1996.

Barkhausen, Henry N. *Great Lakes Sailing Ships*. Milwaukee, 1947.

Bauer, K. Jack. *A Maritime History of the United States*. Columbia, SC, 1988.

Beasley, Norman. *Freighters of Fortune: The Story of the Great Lakes*. New York, 1930.

Beeson, Harvey C. *Beeson's Marine Directory of the Northwestern States*. Chicago, 1888–1921.

Belcher, Wyatt Winton. *The Economic Rivalry between Chicago and St. Louis, 1850–1880*. New York, 1947.

Beveridge, Albert J. *Abraham Lincoln, 1809–1858*. Boston, 1928.

Billington, Ray Allen. *Westward Expansion: A History of the American Frontier*. New York, 1949.

Boorstin, Daniel J. *The Americans: The National Experience*. New York, 1965.

Brown, G. P. *Chicago Drainage Channel and Waterway*. Chicago, 1894.

Buckingham, J. H. *Illinois as Lincoln Knew It*. Ed. Harry E. Pratt. Springfield, IL, 1938.

Burgess, George H., and Kennedy, Miles C. *Centennial History of the Pennsylvania Railroad Co*. Philadelphia, 1949.

Burman, Ben Lucien. *Looking Down That Winding River*. New York, 1973.

Carver, Jonathan. *Jonathan Carver's Travels Through North America, 1766–1768*. London, 1778. Reprint, New York, 1993.

Chamberlin, Everett. *Chicago and Its Suburbs*. Chicago, 1874. Reprint, New York, 1974.

Chandler, Alfred D., Jr. *The Visible Hand: The Managerial Revolution in American Business*. Cambridge, MA, 1977.

Clarke, Thomas Curtis, et al. *The American Railway*. 1888. Reprint, New York, 1972.

Clay, Floyd M. *History of Navigation on the Lower Mississippi*. U.S. Army Corps of Engineers. *National Waterways Study*. Washington, DC, 1983.

Clutton-Brock, Juliet. *Horse Power: A History of the Horse and the Donkey in Modern Society*. Cambridge, MA, 1992.

Cochrane, Thomas C. *Pennsylvania: A Bicentennial History*. New York, 1978.

Condit, Carl W. *The Railroad and the City: A Technological and Urbanistic History of Cincinnati*. Columbus, OH, 1977.

Connors, Paul G. "America's Emerald Isle: The Cultural Invention of the Irish Fishing Colony on Beaver Island, Mich." Ph.D. diss., Loyola University, 1999.

Corliss, Carlton J. *Main Line of Mid-America: The Story of the Illinois Central*. New York, 1950.

Cronon, William. *Nature's Metropolis*. New York, 1991.

Currey, J. Seymour. *Chicago: Its History and Builders*. 2 vols. Chicago, 1912.

Damase, Jacques. *Carriages*. Trans. William Mitchell. New York, 1968.

Davis, James E. *Frontier Illinois*. Bloomington, IN, 1998.

Dayton, Fred Irving. *Steamboat Days*. New York, 1925.

Drago, Harry Sinclair. *Canals Days in America*. New York, 1972.

Duff, John J. *A. Lincoln: Prairie Lawyer*. New York, 1960.

Eastman, Susan Howarth. "An Overview of Inland Waterways Transportation." *Waterways Journal* 102, 13 (June 29, 1987).

Edmunds, R. David. *The Potawatomis: Keepers of the Fire*. Norman, OK, 1978.

Ekberg, Carl J. *French Roots in the Illinois Country*. Urbana, IL, 1998.

Elliott, James. *Red Stacks over the Horizon*. Grand Rapids, MI, 1967.

Emerson, Thomas E., and R. Barry Lewis. *Cahokia and the Hinterlands*. Urbana, IL, 1991.

Epstein, Ralph C. *GATX: A History of the General American Transportation Corporation*. New York, 1948.

Fagan, Brian M. *Ancient North America: The Archaeology of a Continent*. London, 1991.

Feltner, Charles E., and Jeri Baron Feltner. *Great Lakes Maritime History: Bibliography and Sources of Information*. Dearborn, MI, 1982.

Fowler, Melvin L. *Cahokia, Ancient Capital of the Midwest*. Menlo Park, CA, 1974.

Fowler, Melvin L., with Bilione Whiting Young. *Cahokia, the Great American Metropolis*. Urbana, IL, 2000.

Gerstner, Franz Anton Ritter von. *Early American Railroads*. Berkeley, CA, 1997. Originally published as *Die innern Communicationen der Vereinigten Staaten von Nordamerica*. 2 vols. Vienna, 1842–1843.

Grant, H. Roger. *The North Western: A History of the Chicago and North Western Railway System*. DeKalb, IL, 1996.

Greenwood, John O. *Greenwood's Guide to Great Lakes Shipping*. Cleveland, 1997.

Hadfield, Charles. *The Canal Age*. New York, 1968.

———. *World Canals Inland Navigation, Past and Present*. New York, 1986.

Harlow, Alvin F. *The Road of the Century: The Story of the New York Central*. New York, 1947.

Harn, Alan D. *The Prehistory of the Dickson Mounds*. Springfield, IL: Illinois State Museum, 1971.

Hatcher, Harlan. *The Great Lakes*. London, 1944.

Havighurst, Walter. *The Long Ships Passing: History of the Great Lakes*. New York, 1942.

———. *Voices on the River: The Story of the Upper Mississippi Waterways*. New York, 1964.

Hawgood, John A. *America's Western Frontiers: The Exploration and Settlement of the Trans-Mississippi West*. New York, 1967.

Heise, Kenan, and Michael Edgerton. *Chicago: Center for Enterprise*. 2 vols. Woodland Hills, CA, 1982.

Hemming, Robert J. *Gales of November: The Sinking of the Edmund Fitzgerald*. Chicago, 1981.

———. *Ships Gone Missing: The Great Lakes Storm of 1913*. Chicago, 1992.

Hilton, George W. *The Great Lakes Car Ferries*. Berkeley, CA, 1962.

———. *Eastland: Legacy of the Titanic*. Stanford, CA, 1995.

———. *Lake Michigan Passenger Steamers*. In press.

Hough, Jack L. *Geology of the Great Lakes*. Urbana, IL, 1958.

Hunter, Louis C. *Steamboats on the Western Rivers: An Economic and Technological History*. Cambridge, MA, 1949.

John Jennings et al., eds. *The Canoe in Canadian Culture*. Peterborough, ON, Canada, 1999.

Johnson, Bob, ed. *Short Lines: A Collection of Classic American Railroad Stories*. New York, 1996.

Karamanski, Theodore J. *Rally 'round the Flag: Chicago and the Civil War*. Chicago, 1993.

Kent, Timothy J. *Birchbark Canoes of the Fur Trade*. 2 vols. Ossineke, MI, 1997.

Kemp, Peter, ed. *The Oxford Companion to Ships and the Sea*. Oxford, England, 1988.

Kipling, Rudyard. *American Notes*. Norman, OK, 1981. Original, unauthorized publication, New York, 1891.

Knight, Robert, and Lucius H. Zeuch. *The Location of the Chicago Portage Route of the Seventeenth Century*. Chicago: Chicago Historical Society, 1928.

Krieger, Michael. *Where Rails Meet the Sea*. New York, 1998.

Lande, Lawrence M. *The Development of the Voyageur Contract, 1686–1821*. Montreal, 1989.

Lane, Ferdinand C. *The World's Great Lakes*. Garden City, NY, 1948.

LesStrang, Jacques. *Cargo Carriers of the Great Lakes*. Boyne City, MI, 1985.

MacGregor, David R. *The Schooner: Its Design and Development from 1600 to the Present*. London, 1997.

MacLean, Harrison John. *The Fate of The Griffon*. Chicago, 1974.

Malkus, Alida. *Blue-Water Boundary*. New York, 1960.

Mansfield, J. B. *History of the Great Lakes*. 2 vols. Chicago, 1899. Reprint, Cleveland, 1972.

Martin, Albro. *Enterprise Denied: Origins of the Decline of American Railroads, 1897–1910*. New York, 1971.

———. *Railroads Triumphant*. Oxford, England, 1992.

Mayer, Harold M. *The Railway Pattern of Metropolitan Chicago*. Ph.D. diss., University of Chicago, 1943.

———. *The Port of Chicago and the St. Lawrence Seaway*. Chicago, 1957.

Mayer, Harold M., and Richard C. Wade. *Chicago: Growth of a Metropolis*. Chicago, 1969.

Miller, Donald L. *City of the Century*. New York, 1996.

Miller, Ross. *American Apocalypse*. Chicago, 1990.

Moses, John, and Joseph Kirkland. *History of Chicago*. 2 vols. New York, 1895.

Neuschel, Fred. *August and Herman Schuenemann: Tree Captains of Lake Michigan*. Privately published, Algoma, WI, 1993.

Overton, Richard C. *Burlington Route*. New York, 1965.

Parkman, Francis. *France and England in North America*. 2 vols. Ed. David Levin. New York, 1983. Originally published in 7 vols., New York, 1865–1892.

Petersen, William J. *Steamboating on the Upper Mississippi*. Iowa City, IA: State Historical Society of Iowa, 1968.

———. *Towboating on the Mississippi*. Cranbury, NJ, 1979.

Peyser, Joseph L. *Letters from New France: The Upper Country, 1686–1783*. Urbana, IL, 1992.

———. *Jacques Legardeur de Saint-Pierre*. East Lansing, MI, 1996.

Pfeiffer, John E. *Indian City on the Mississippi*. New York, 1974.

Pierce, Bessie Louise. *A History of Chicago*. 2 vols. Chicago, 1937.

Potter, Jerry O. *The Sultana Tragedy: America's Greatest Maritime Disaster*. Gretna, LA, 1997.

Primm, James Neal. *Lion of the Valley: St. Louis, Missouri*. Boulder, CO, 1981.

Putnam, James William. *The Illinois and Michigan Canal*. Chicago, 1918.

Quaife, Milo M. *Chicago and the Old Northwest: 1673–1835*. Chicago, 1913.

———. *Chicago's Highways Old and New: From Indian Trail to Motor Road*. Chicago, 1923.

———. *Lake Michigan*. Indianapolis, 1944.

———, ed. *The Western Country in the 17th Century: The Memoirs of Lamothe Cadillac and Pierre Leitte*. Chicago, 1947.

Rafert, Stewart. *The Miami Indians of Indiana*. Indianapolis: Indiana Historical Society, 1996.

Raitz, Karl, ed. *The National Road*. Baltimore, MD, 1996.

Ratigan, William. *Great Lakes Shipwrecks and Survivors*. Grand Rapids, MI, 1960.

Rice, Mary Jane Judson. *Chicago: Port to the World*. Chicago, 1969.

Robinson, Michael C. *History of Navigation in the Ohio River Basin*. U.S. Army Corps of Engineers. *National Waterways Study*. Washington, DC, 1983.

Rodgers, Bradley A. *Guardian of the Great Lakes: The U.S. Paddle Frigate Michigan*. Ann Arbor, MI, 1996.

Rothert, Otto A. *The Outlaws of Cave-in-Rock*. Cleveland, OH, 1924. Reprint, Carbondale, IL, 1996.

Scanlan, Charles M. *The "Lady Elgin" Disaster, September 8, 1860*. Privately published, Milwaukee, WI, 1928.

Schoolcraft, Henry Rowe. *Travels through the Northwest Regions of the United States*. 1821. Reprint, Ann Arbor, MI, 1966.

Schuberth, Christopher J. *A View of the Past: An Introduction to Illinois Geology*. Springfield, IL: Illinois State Museum, 1986.

Shaw, Ronald E. *Erie Water West: A History of the Erie Canal, 1792–1854*. Lexington, KY, 1966.

———. *Canals for a Nation: The Canal Era in the United States, 1790–1860*. Lexington, KY, 1990.

Shipley, Robert, and Fred Addis. *Schooners*. Saint Catherines, ON, Canada, 1991.

Skinner, Claiborne Adams. "The Sinews of Empire: The Voyageurs and the Carrying Trade of the *Pays d'en Haut*, 1681–1754." Ph.D. diss., University of Illinois, Chicago, 1990

Snow, Dean. *The Archaeology of North America*. New York, 1976.

Snyder, John Francis. *Selected Writings of John Francis Snyder*. Ed. Clyde C. Walton. Springfield, IL: Illinois State Historical Society, 1962.

Solzman, David M. *The Chicago River*. Chicago, 1998.

Steward, J. F. *Lost Maramech and Earliest Chicago*. Chicago, 1903.

Stover, John F. *American Railroads*. Chicago, 1961.

———. *The Life and Decline of the American Railroad*. New York, 1970.

———. *History of the Illinois Central Railroad*. New York, 1975.

Struever, Stuart, and Felicia Antonelli Holton. *Koster: Americans in Search of Their Prehistoric Past.* New York, 1979.

Surrey, N. M. Miller. *The Commerce of Louisiana during the French Regime, 1699–1763.* New York, 1916.

Taylor, James Rogers. *The Transportation Revolution, 1815–1860.* New York, 1951.

Thompson, Slason. *Short History of American Railways.* Chicago, 1925.

Turner, Frederick Jackson. *The Frontier in American History.* New York, 1920.

Vance, James E., Jr. *Capturing the Horizon: The Historical Geography of Transportation since the Sixteenth Century.* Baltimore, 1986.

Van Eyck, William O. "The Story of the Propeller *Phoenix.*" *Wisconsin Magazine of History* 7 (1924): 281–300.

———. *The North American Railroad: Its Origin, Evolution, and Geography.* Baltimore, 1995.

Wade, Richard C. *The Urban Frontier: The Rise of Western Cities, 1790–1830.* Cambridge, MA, 1959.

Walton, Clyde C. *An Illinois Reader.* DeKalb, IL, 1970.

Way, Frederick, Jr. *Way's Packet Directory, 1848–1994.* Rev. ed. Athens, OH, 1994.

White, John H., Jr. *The American Railroad Passenger Car.* Baltimore, MD, 1978.

———. *The American Railroad Freight Car.* Baltimore, MD, 1993.

Wood, Donald F., and James C. Johnson. *Contemporary Transportation.* 5th ed. Upper Saddle River, NJ, 1996.

Zimmermann, Karl. *Lake Michigan's Railroad Car Ferries.* Andover, NJ, 1993.

# Index